CARVING ELVES

Kelley Stadelman

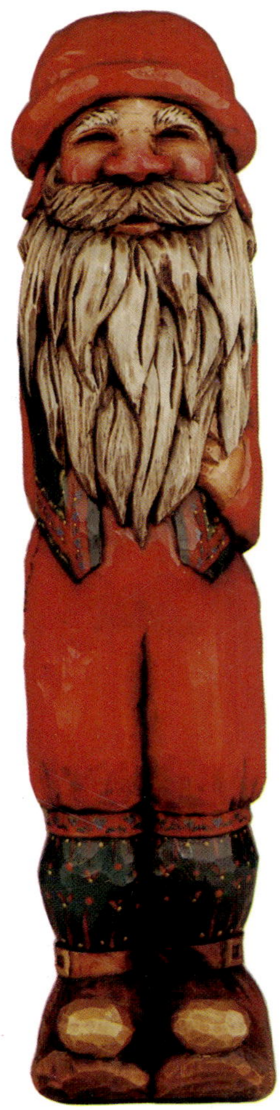

Text written with and
Photography by
Douglas Congdon-Martin

Schiffer Publishing Ltd
77 Lower Valley Road, Atglen, PA 19310

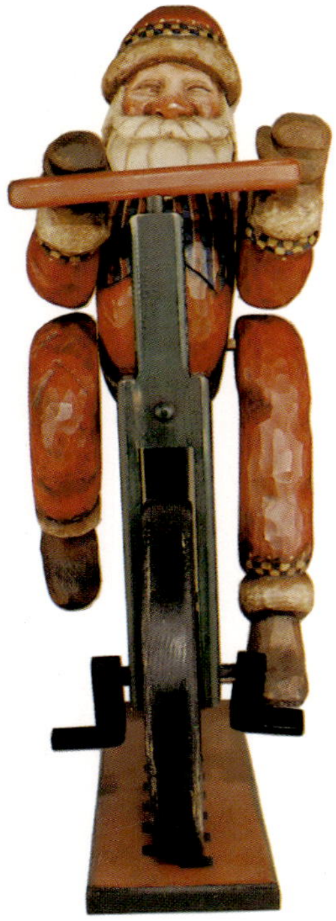

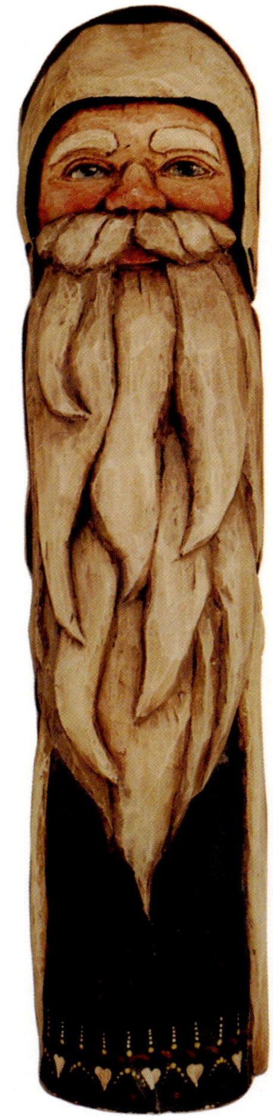

Published by Schiffer Publishing, Ltd.
77 Lower Valley Road
Atglen, PA 19310
Please write for a free catalog.
This book may be purchased from the publisher.
Please include $2.95 postage.
Try your bookstore first.

We are interested in hearing from authors
with book ideas on related subjects.

Library of Congress Cataloging-in-Publication Data

Stadelman, Kelley.
Carving elves / Kelley Stadelman.
p. cm.
ISBN 0-88740-709-9
1. Wood-carving. 2. Wood-carved figurines. 3. Elves in art.
I. Title.
TT199.7.S73 1995
731.4'62--dc20 94-32298
CIP

Printed in China.
ISBN: 0-88740-709-9

Contents

Introduction

Using no particular method to design a new project, I might begin with an idea and a chunk of wood or a sketch pad. The project will be large if the wood or paper is large. Somehow I am compelled to fill the whole given area. I have to make a conscious effort to stay within a certain size.

Being a serious Santa collector, a variety of shapes and sizes enhances my collection and its display. These larger pieces help create a theme and focal point in their display. They are quite striking all by themselves.

Working in large scale may seem more difficult to carvers. Actually I find it easier in many ways. The piece can be clamped into a vice so both hands are free to control the tools. Accidental chips and tears are no tragedy and will have little impact on the finished product because of the quantity of wood with which you started. The details are much larger and easier to carve. And, in a larger project the end result is much more spectacular regardless of its simplicity.

The Jolly Old Elf that we carve in this book is fun to carve. It is large, but no lamination is necessary. I start with a four inch thick piece of clear sugar pine, draw the side profile, and cut it out on the band saw. Then, before carving, I transfer the pattern on both sides and draw a midline along the length of the front and back.

The joy my students experience shines in their faces as they begin to discover the character hidden within the wood. The satisfaction they express grows with their skills. If you ask them what the one technique is which made the most difference in their carving they will most likely respond with one word: "Rounding."

If you were to observe the difference between their first project and their most recent, you would see how blocky and unrounded the first one is. Before you begin any detail on your Jolly Elf, be sure to carve off the corners dramatically. You might think of rounding as trying to eliminate corners and flat surfaces.

When your eyes are not sure your project is round enough, let your hands tell you. Run your hands over the length of your Elf. He should fill the curve of your palm. As you feel for corners roll him in your hand. If there is a corner you will find it.

This book follows the same steps that I have taught to the students in my classes. It takes the carver from the laying out of the pattern to the final antiquing of the painted piece. While only one elf can be carved completely, with step-by-step illustrations, there are patterns and photographs in the gallery to help you apply these skills to other projects.

Because I love painting, these large projects are particularly enjoyable. There are large surfaces just begging for decorative work. I have tried to give the reader several ideas about how to apply some of the techniques of decorative tole painting to these carvings.

Enjoy.

Carving Tools and Terms

Chisel: A tool with a flat cutting edge. It may have a single or double bevel.

Skew Chisel: This chisel has a double bevel and is slanted obliquely along the chisel edge.

Gouge: A tool with a single bevel and a cutting edge that is curved or shaped in a compound configuration.

Bench Knife: A carving tool with the cutting edge parallel to the handle.

Disposable blades: These blades fit into a special handle. They are made of thin metal and are extremely sharp. Generally they are not resharpened.

Care of Tools

After investing in quality tools, care should be taken to maintain their sharpness. Contact between your tools and surfaces other than wood may chip and dull them. Most towns have fine cutlery stores which provide sharpening services. However, I am of the opinion that the art of sharpening should be learned by carvers. There are several books that will give you instructions in the techniques of sharpening.

Carving Safety

Remember you are using a sharp tool. You may become comfortable with carving tools in your hand, but they are obviously more dangerous than a pen or a paint brush. I have held a paint brush in my mouth, scratched my head with one and even used one as a pointer. Doing these common gestures with a carving tool could cause harm to you or someone else. Protect yourself and your carving companions. Avoid pointing or talking with your hands with a carving tool in hand. Avoid placing tools on the table top so that they might roll off the table and onto (or into) someone's foot.

Whenever possible carve on the table top, not in your lap. Build up your chair with a pillow or two so you are well above your carving. Place your wood in a clamp or on some type of device to hold it in place. I like to use the non-skid grid that is used under throw rugs.

I have cut myself. I do not cut myself very often anymore. I have a good sense for what my tools and wood will do. Carving when you are tired or tense will increase the chance of being cut. Take many little breaks. Know your limits. Be careful and have a good time!

The Elf Pattern

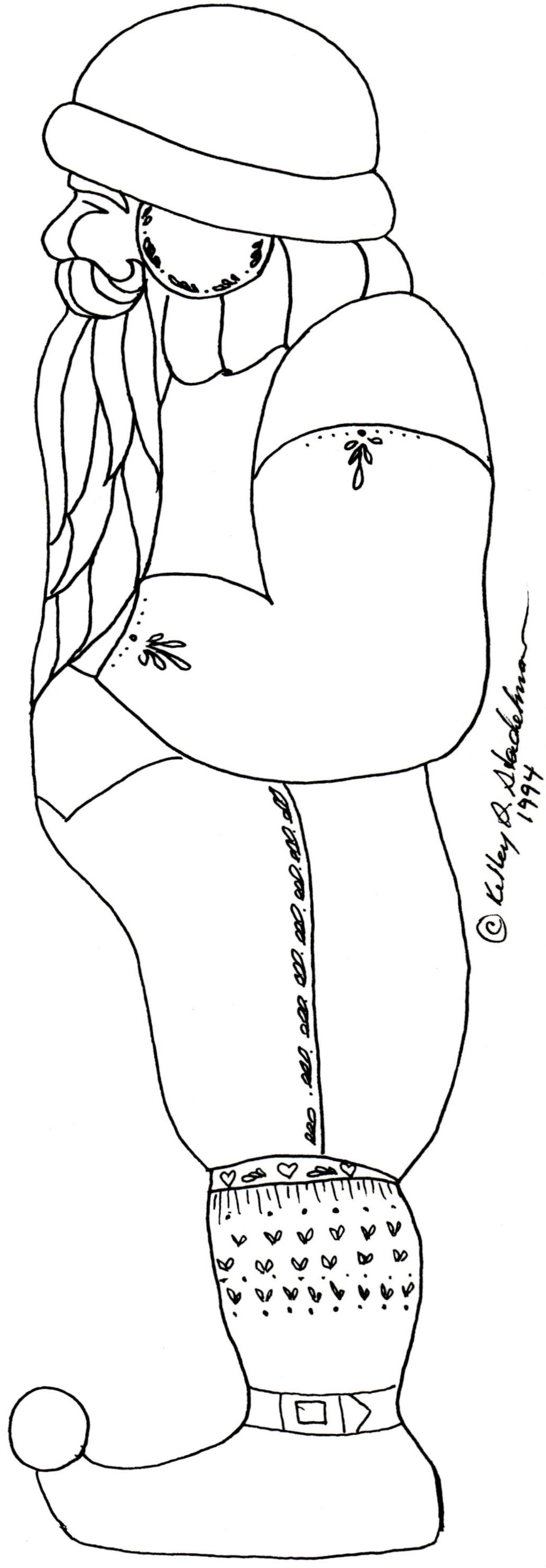

You can use this pattern any size, but the original carving was 17 1/4" tall. To get to this size, enlarge this pattern 170%.

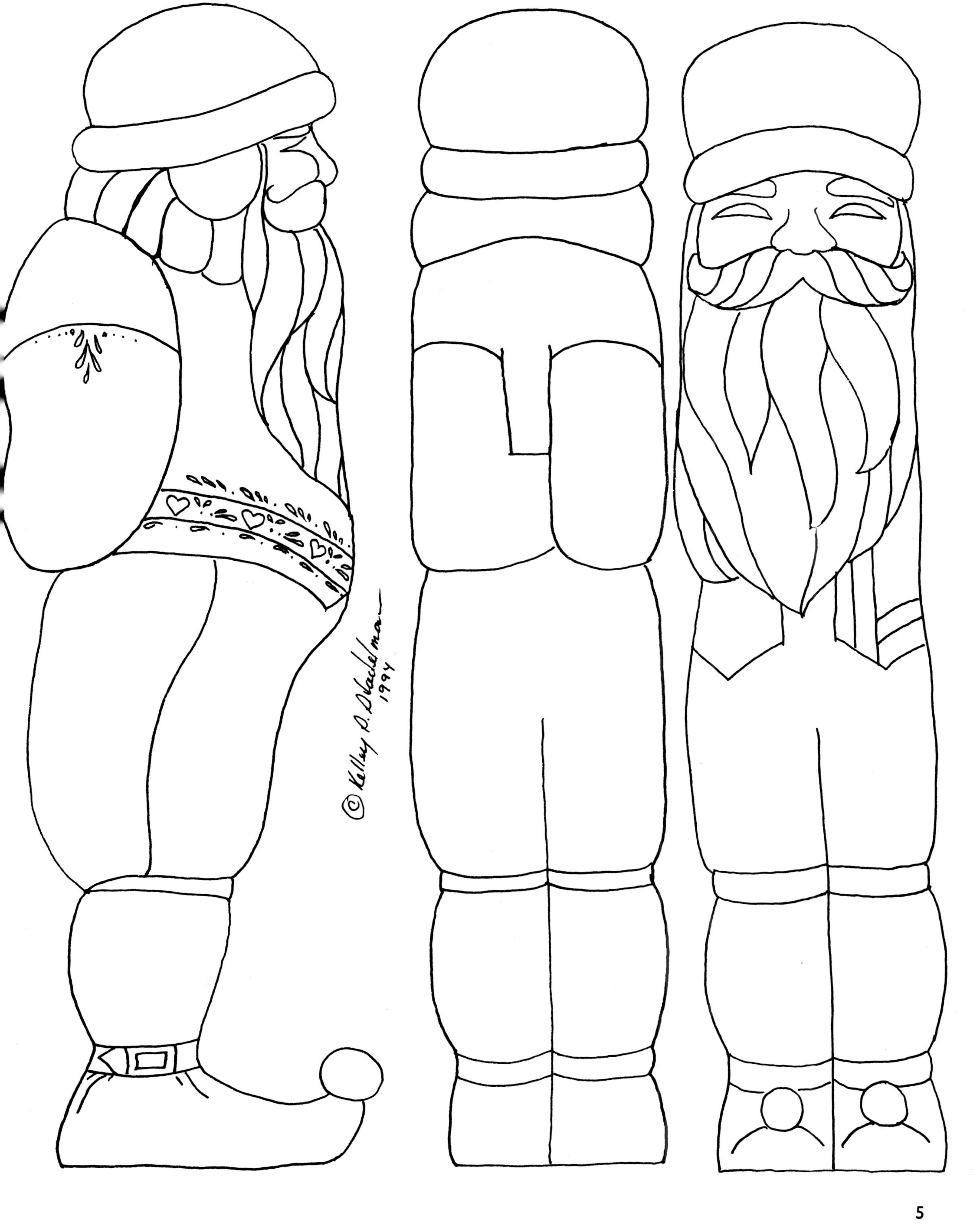
© Kelley D. Stadelman
1994

Carving the Elf

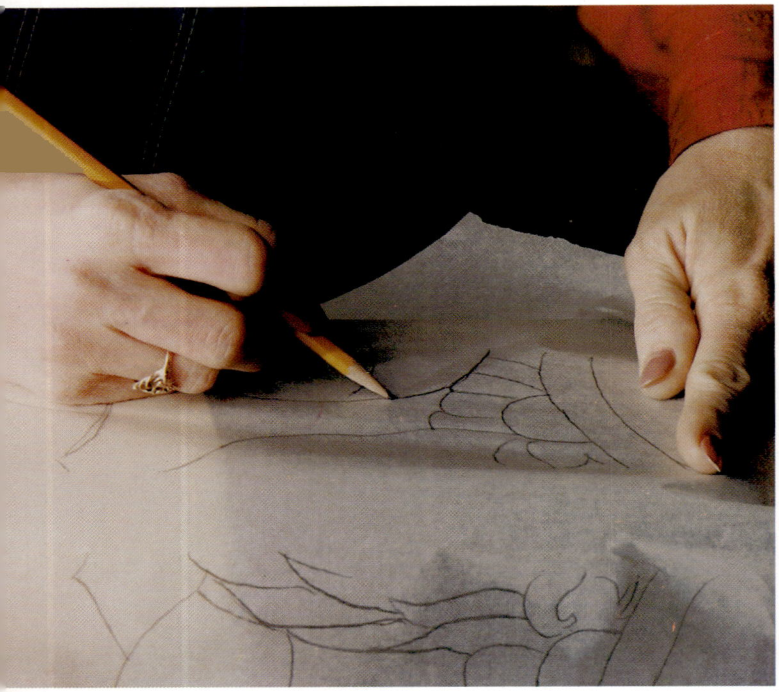

For this carving I use a 4" thick piece of sugar pine. I cut the general outline on a bandsaw, then transfer the pattern to the sawn blank.

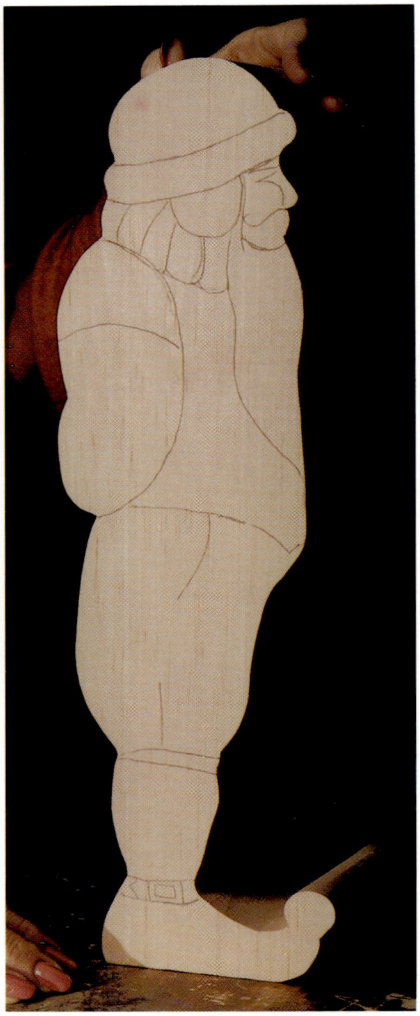

The details drawn. Repeat on each side.

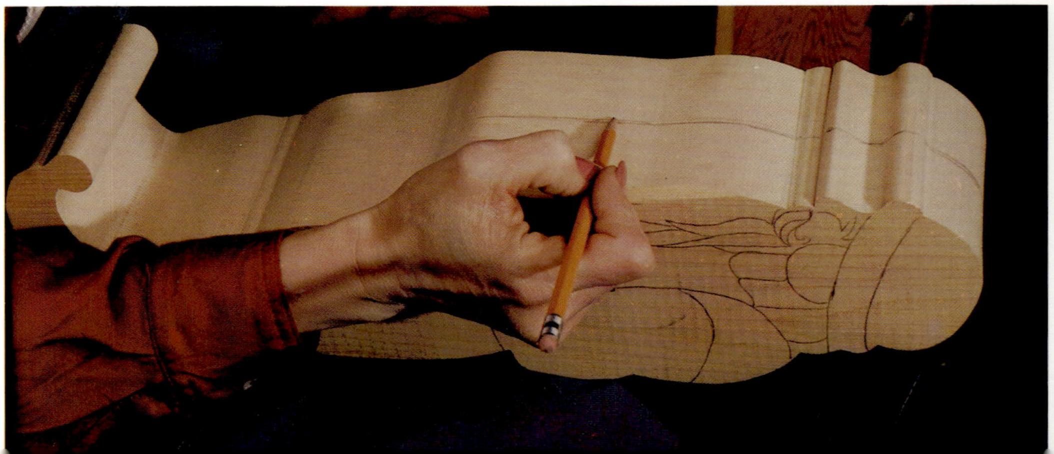

Draw a midline all around the figure.

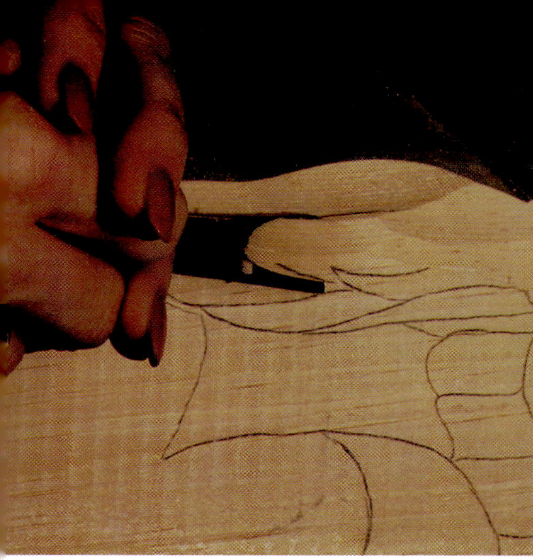

Knock off the four corners.

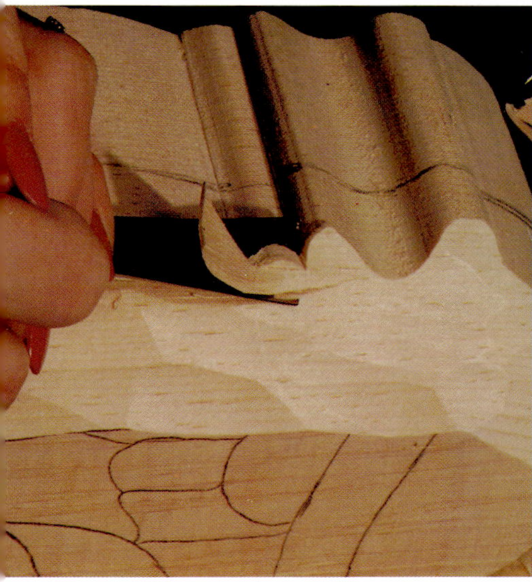

Carry the cut right through the ridges and shapes of the blank. If you stop at the ridges you create lines you don't want.

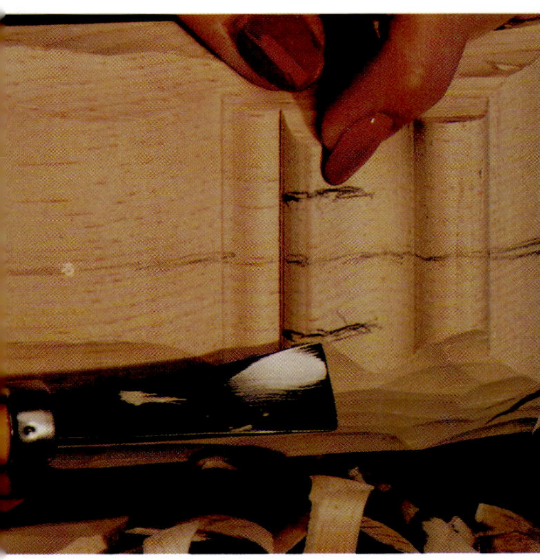

I've marked the nose to make sure I leave plenty of width for later.

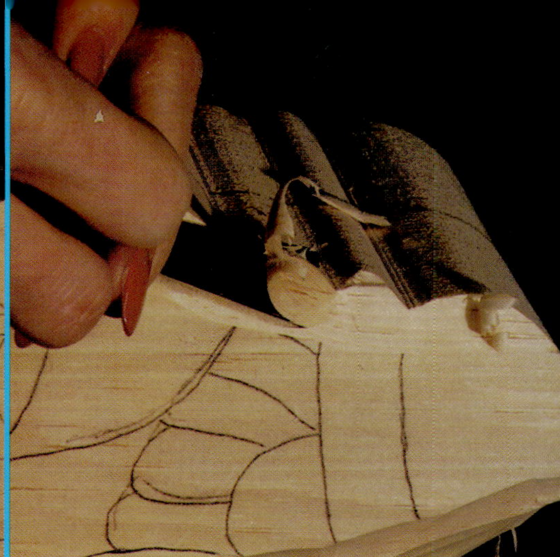

Continue on the back corners...

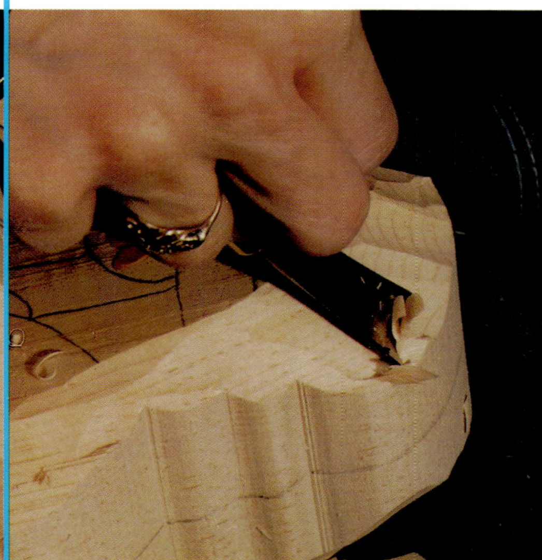

and over the top of the head. This cut is across the end grain and will take a little more effort.

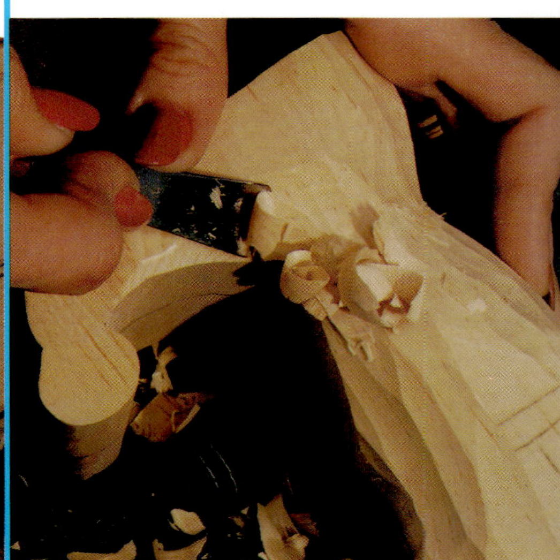

The feet need a curved cut along the upper edge.

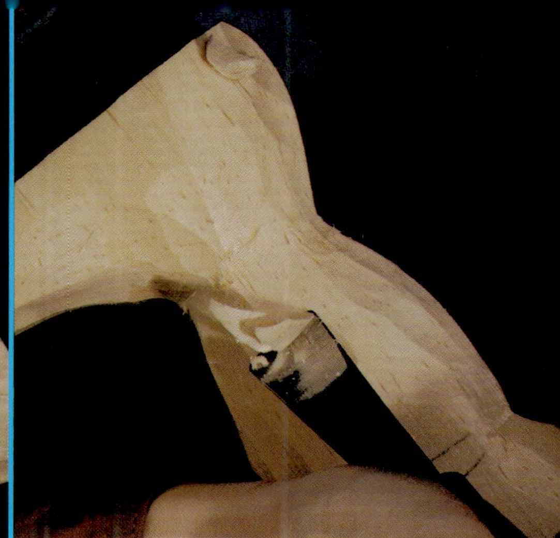

Bring in the side of the lower leg toward the ankle.

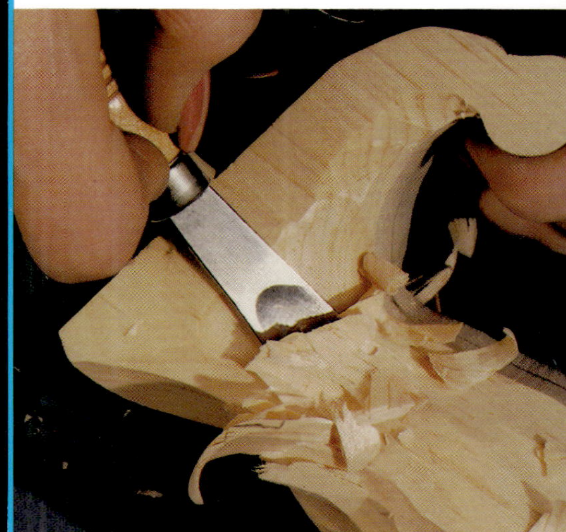

Come up to the ankle from the foot.

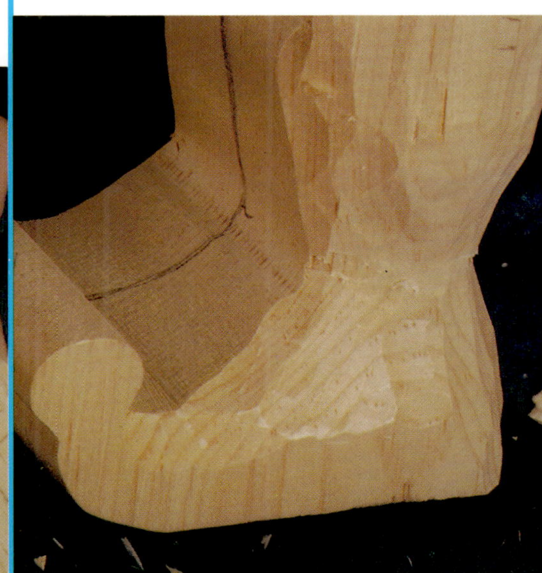

Take the feet to about this point. I leave the toes untouched for now.

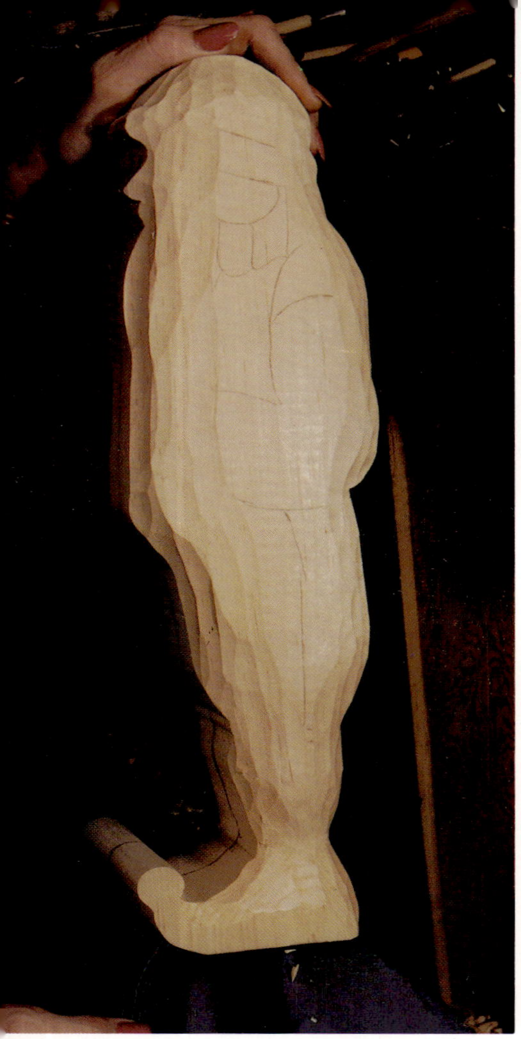

The corners roughed out.

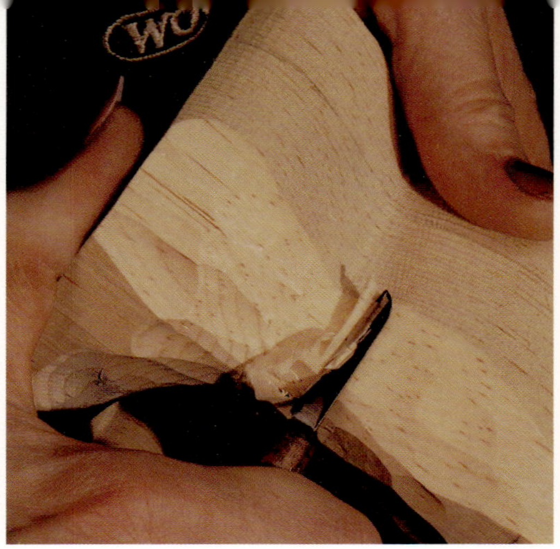

Here at the ankle I don't want a line, so I switch to a knife and use a curl cut to make the smooth transition from leg to foot.

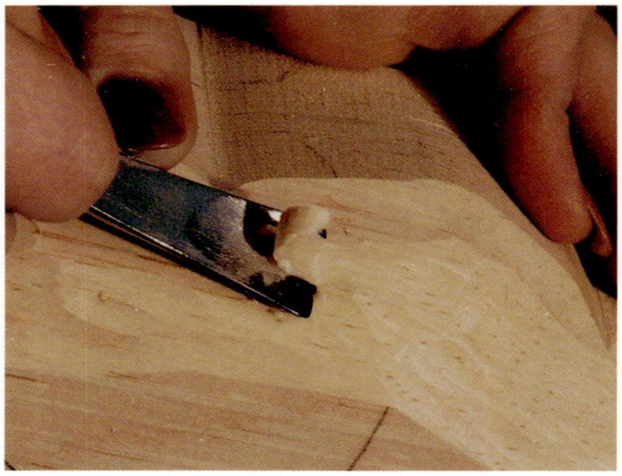

Part of the refining process is smoothing the ridges left by the rough cutting.

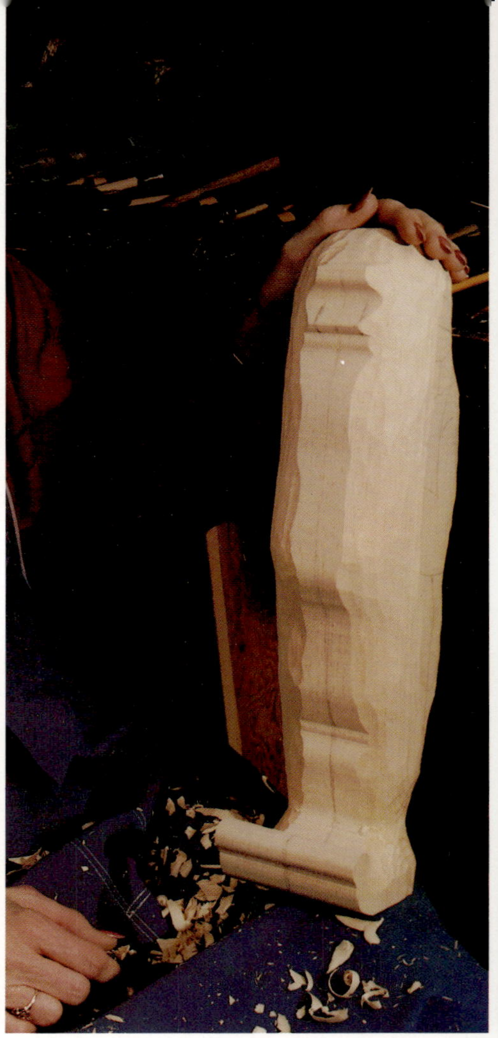

At this point it is good to check the overall body shape and look for places that need further refinement.

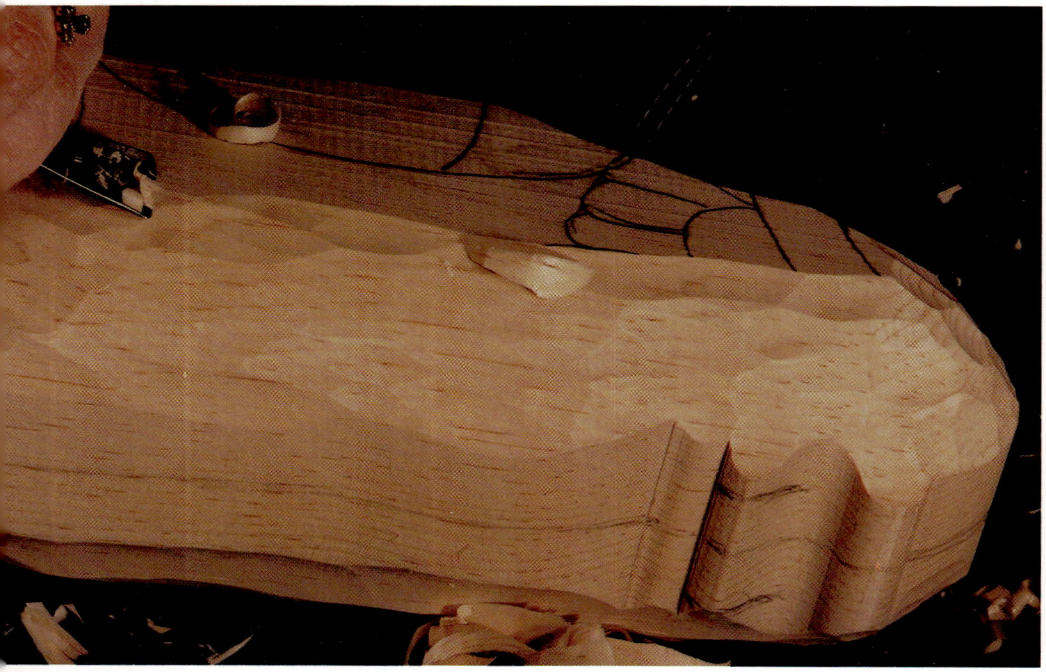

Go back and refine.

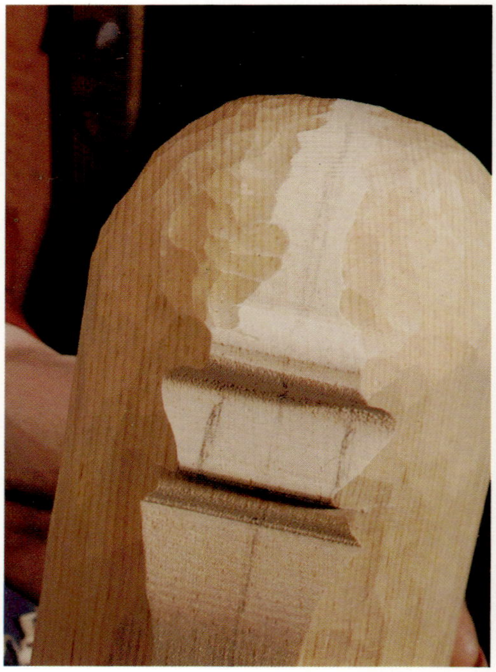

The top of the head is rounded.

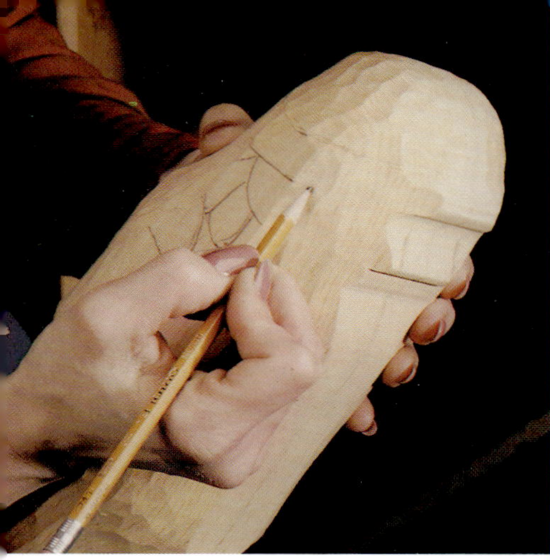

Redraw the lines of the pattern. From drawing the pattern earlier you are left with some remains that act as guidelines for the redrawing.

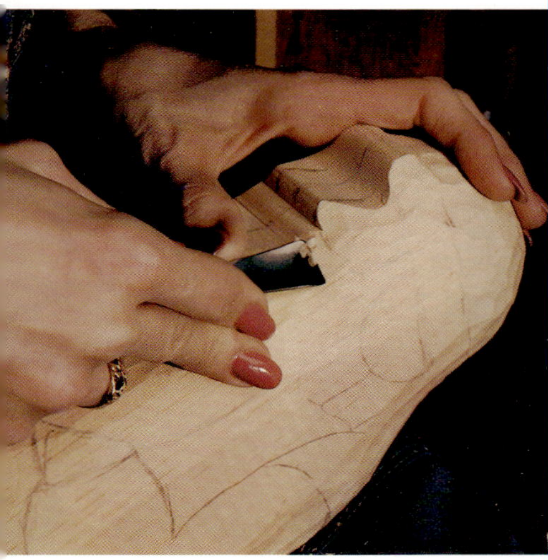

As you redraw it will be easy to tell where you haven't rounded enough. Stop and fix those spots before continuing with the drawing.

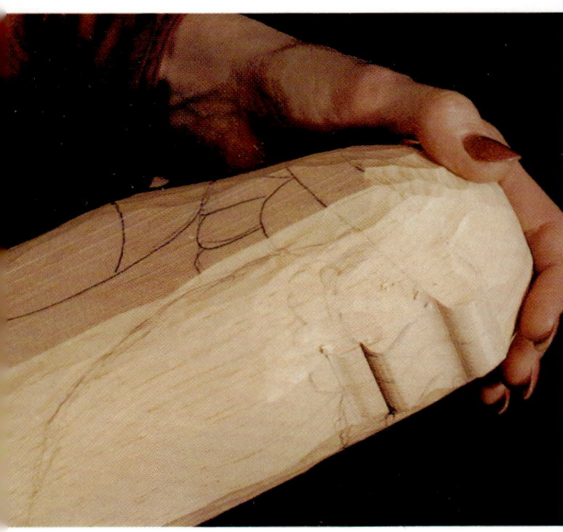

What I'm worried about now are the major features like arms, beard and hair. Clothing will wait until I am nearer the end.

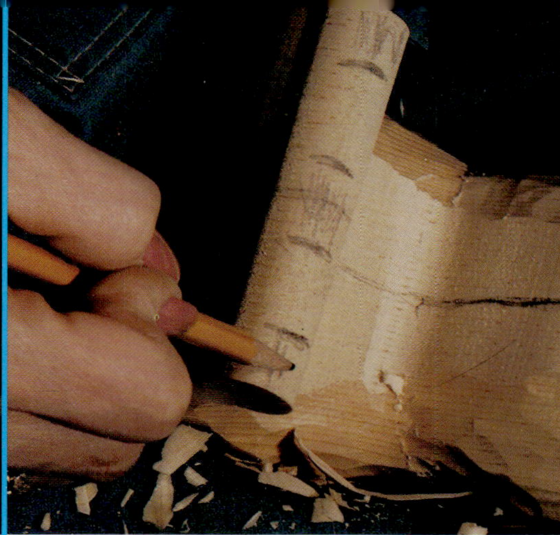

The pom-poms are drawn now, with the areas to be removed darkened. I will not shape them until later, though, because they are easily broken.

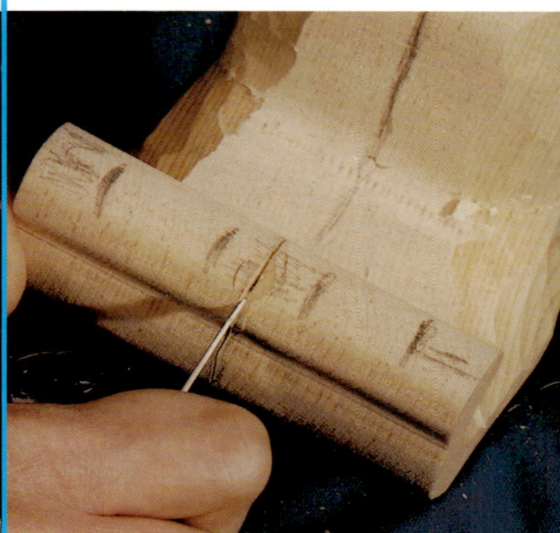

Score the center line between the pom-poms...

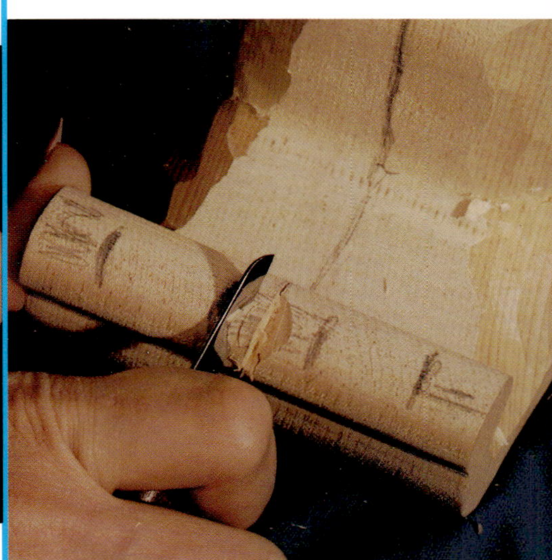

and cut back to it from both sides to wedge it out.

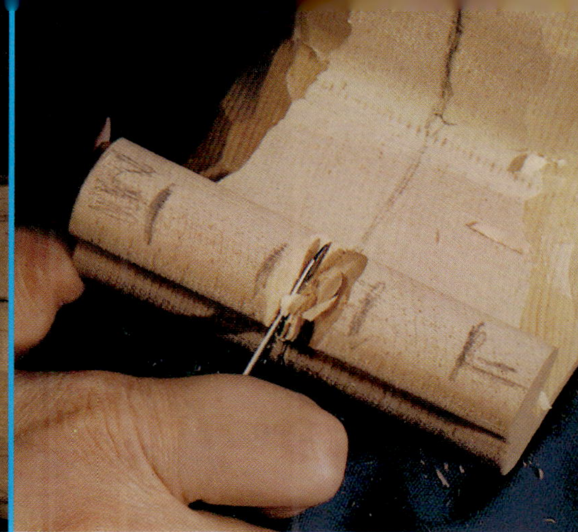

Deepen the wedge.

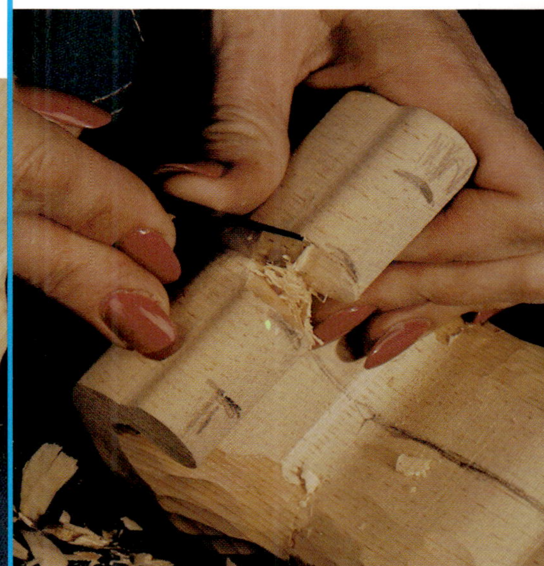

After you get a good start with the knife you can switch to a chisel or gouge.

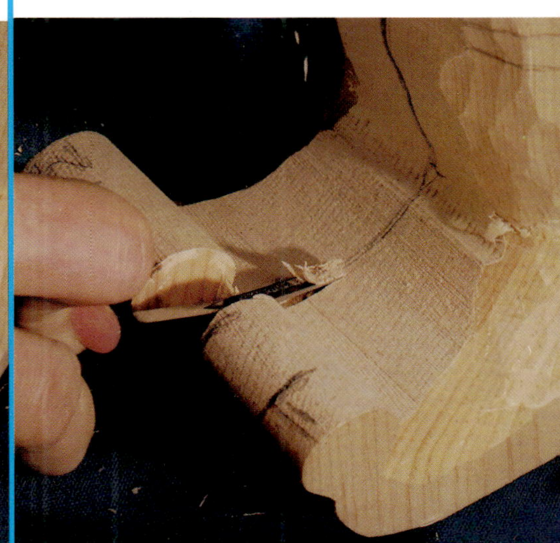

Follow the line between the feet with a v-tool. This bent v-tool makes it easier.

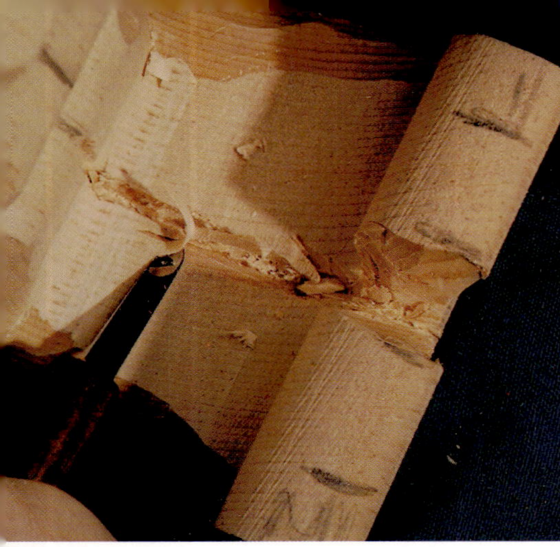

Continue shaping between the feet with a knife or other tool. There is no perfect tool for this, so use what works for you.

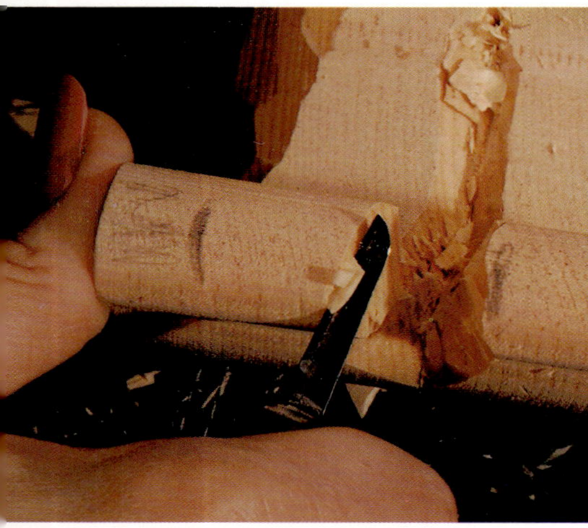

Round off the inside of the pom-pom, making the space you need to get at the shoe.

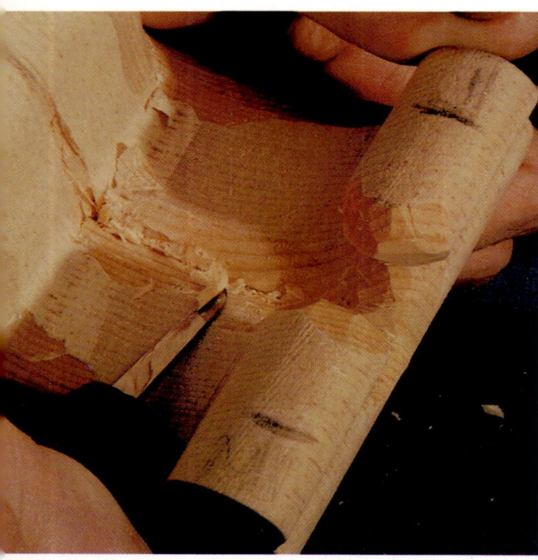

The tops of the shoes are probably the hardest spots to get at in this carving. Not only that, they are also end grain and curved. The best you can do is pick at them until you get it right. Good luck!

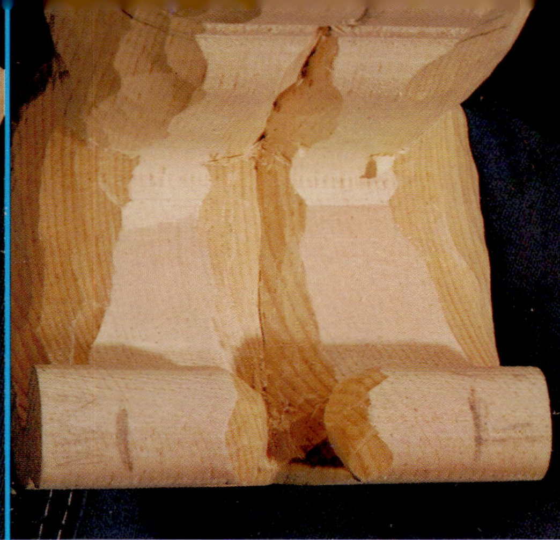

The top of the feet for now. I'll come back to it when I finish the toes.

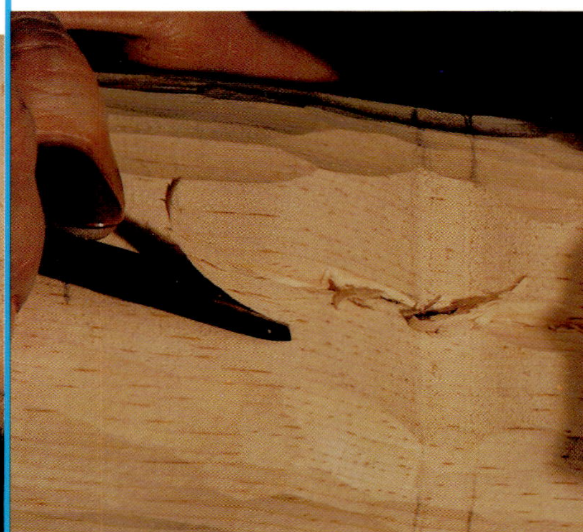

Cut a wedge between the legs using a chisel. Do the front first.

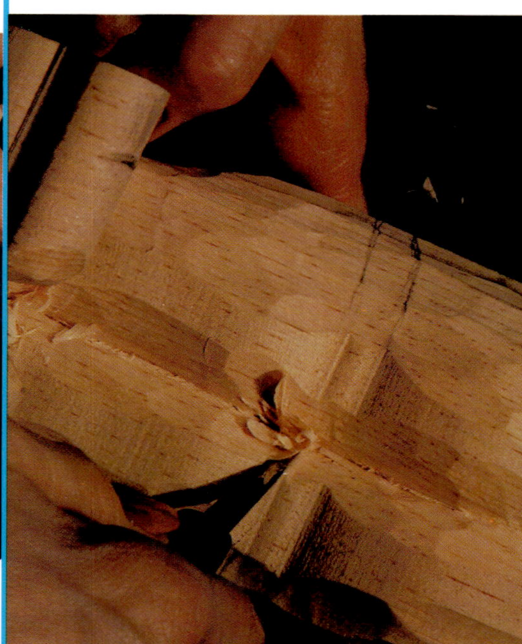

Refine the groove with a knife.

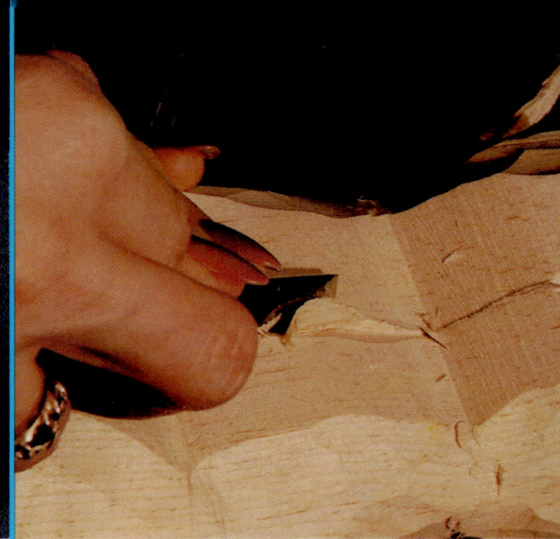

Repeat on the back.

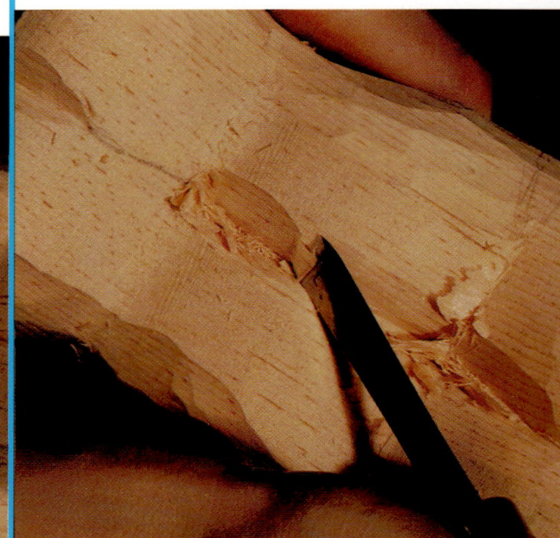

Begin to shape the calves, bringing out the muscle pattern.

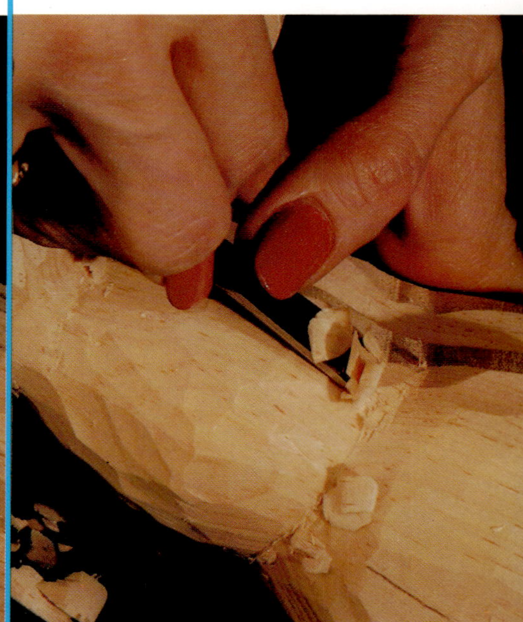

Continue shaping the calf to the sock line.

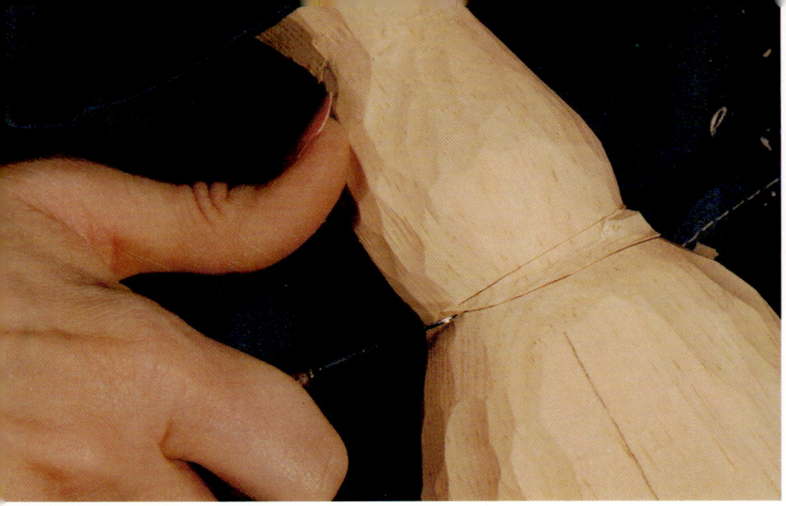

Establish the leg band with a score line on the upper and lower edges.

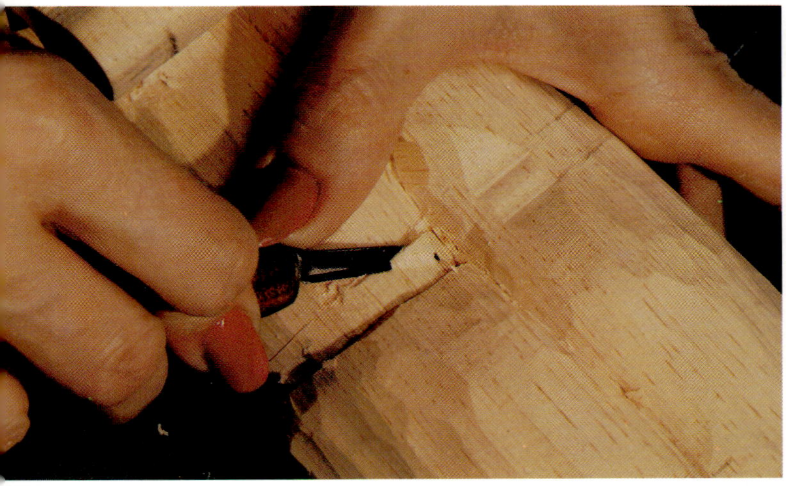

Shape the leg band. You want the pants above to blouse over the leg band. In the back of the leg they almost obscure it completely.

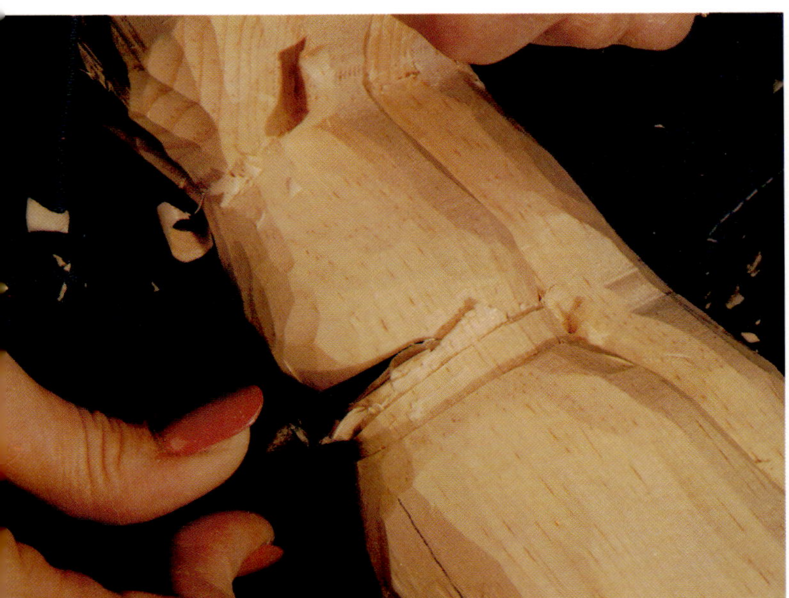

Cut from the sock up to the band. The sock will go under the band.

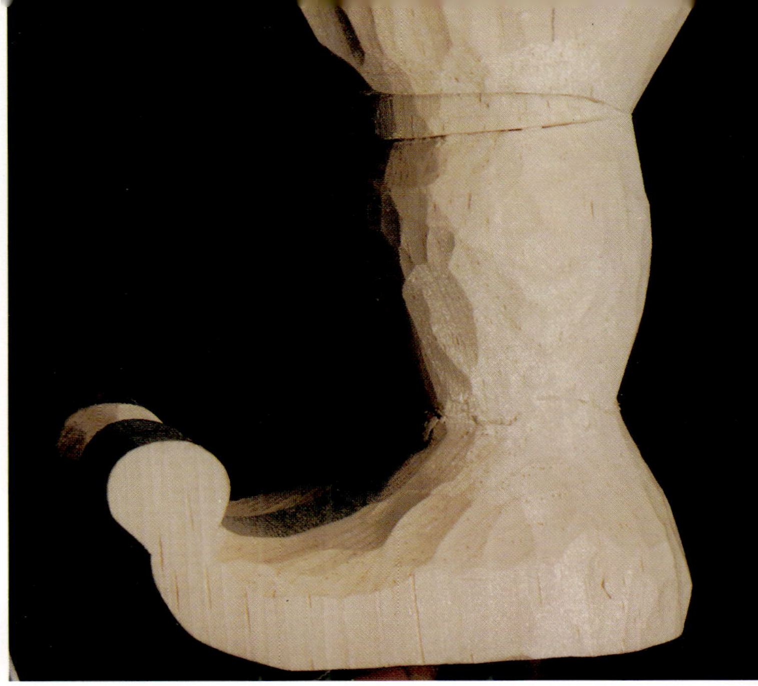

Progress.

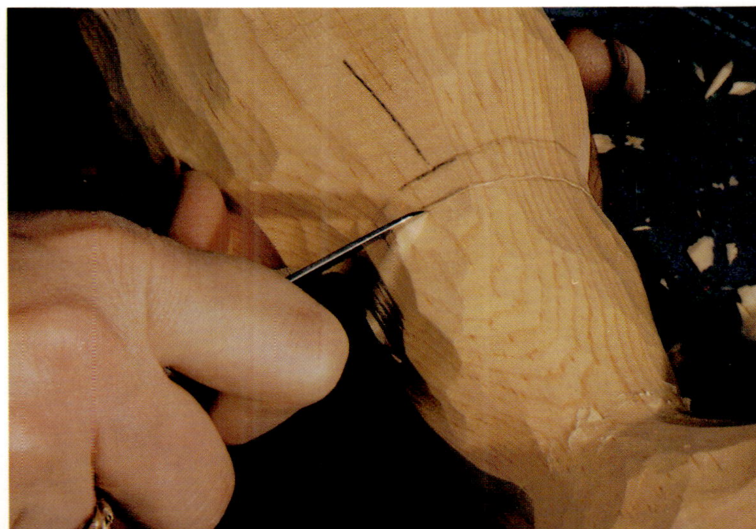

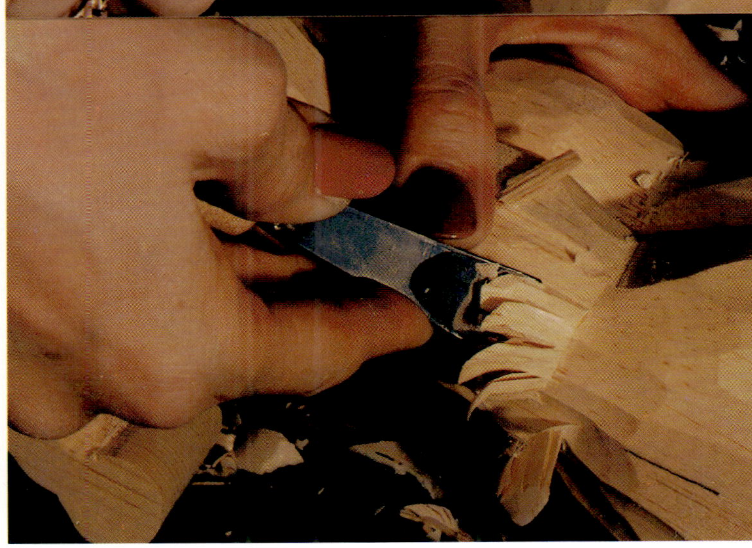

Repeat on the other side.

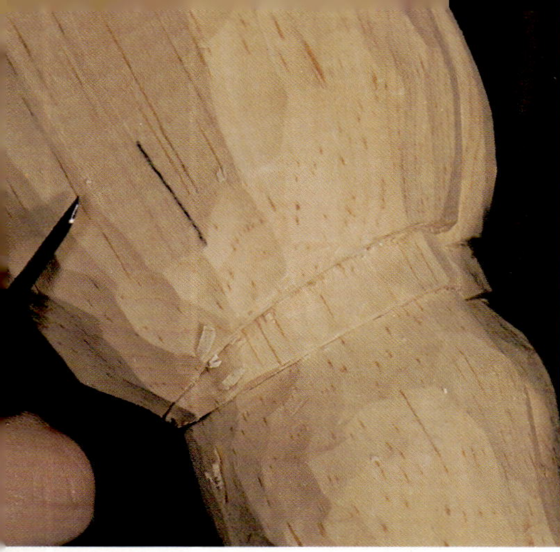

The leg band is just a thin piece of fabric, so fight the tendency to make it too deep.

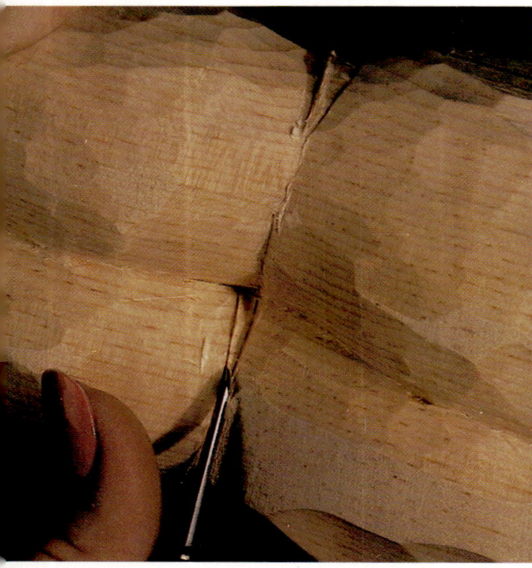

We don't want to completely lose the band in the back, so score a line for it...

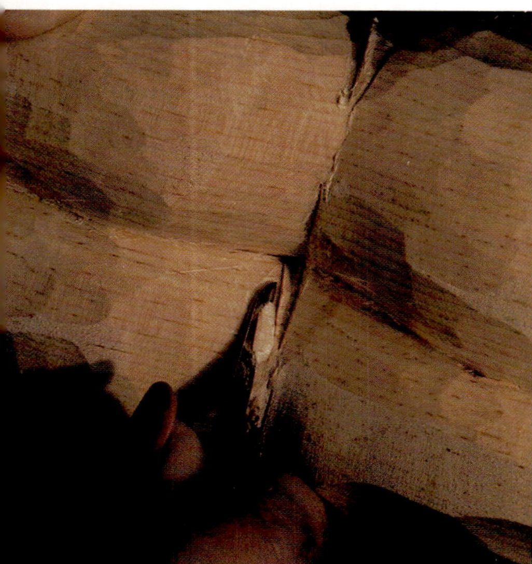

and trim back to it from the sock.

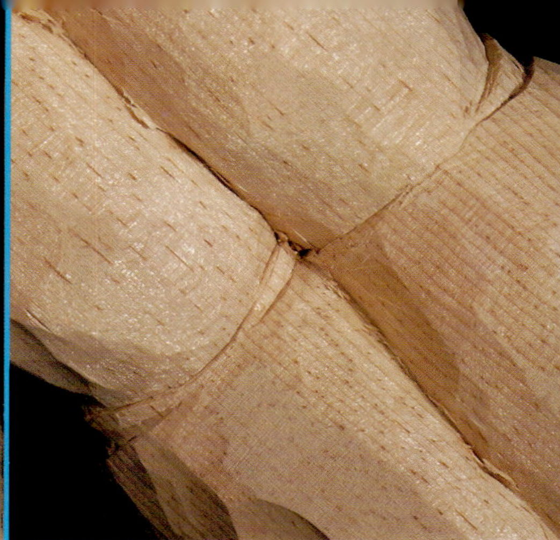

The result is just a hint of leg band between the sock and the pants. Repeat on the other side.

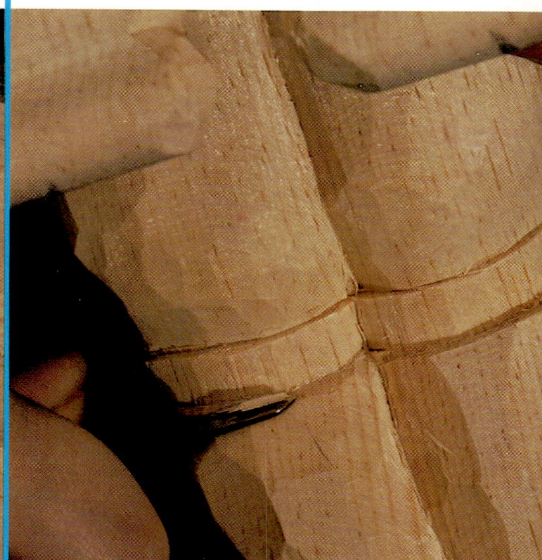

Round the pants down the band in the back.

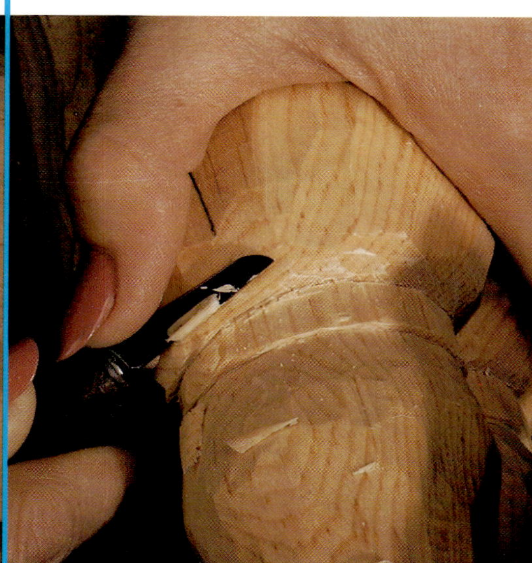

and around the sides.

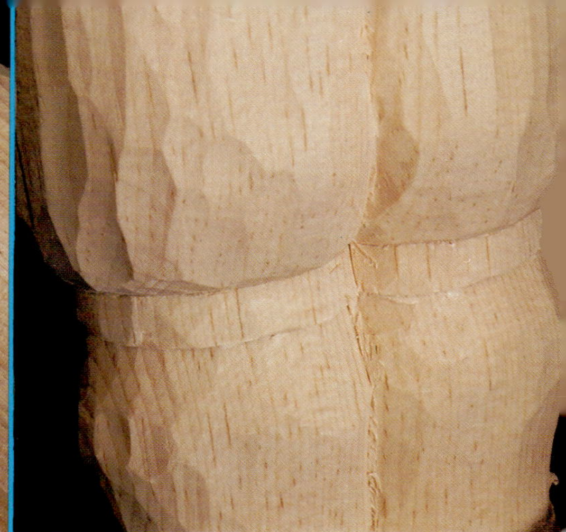

Progress.

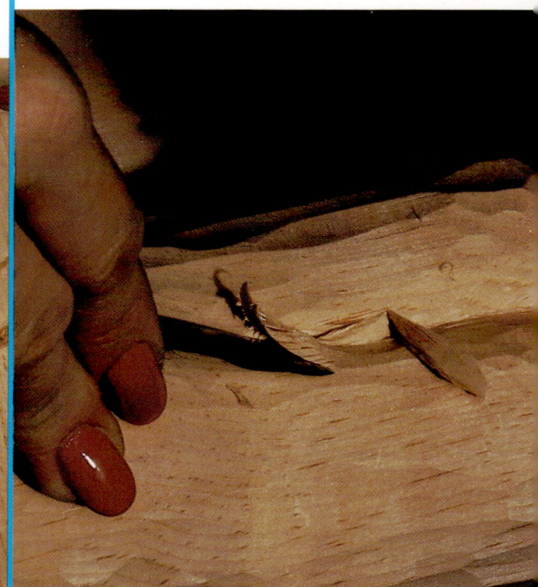

Moving up the elf, deepen the line between the legs.

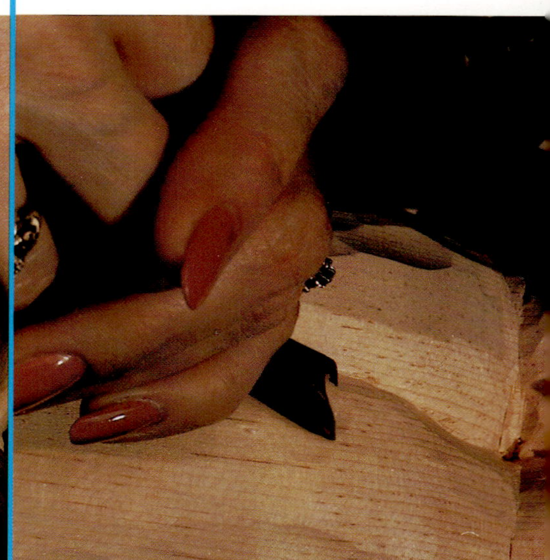

Shape the pants.

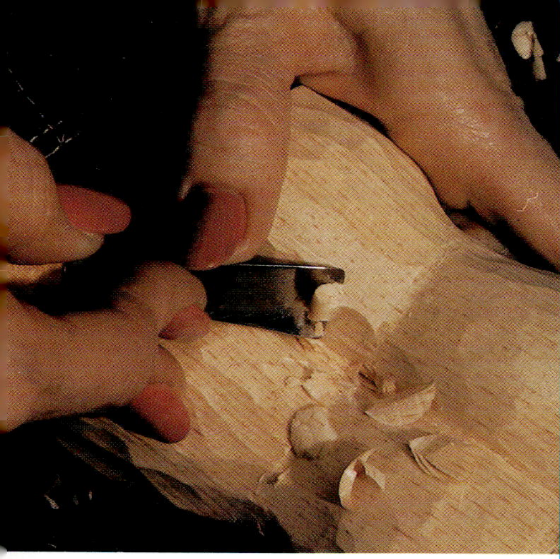

As you go you might see some places that need work, like shaping the heels.

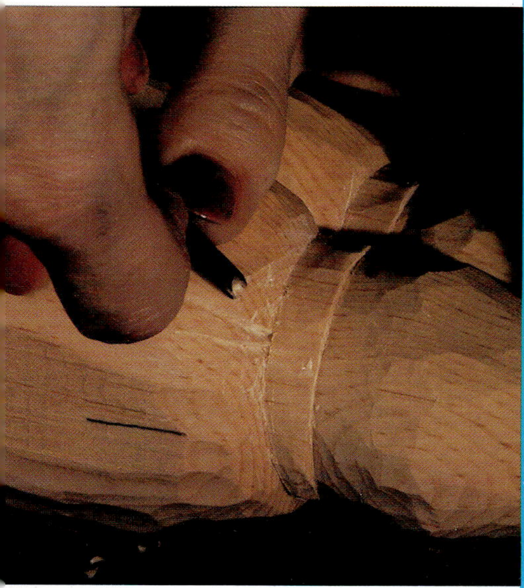

Use a v-tool to put three tucks in the outside corner of the pants, above the leg band.

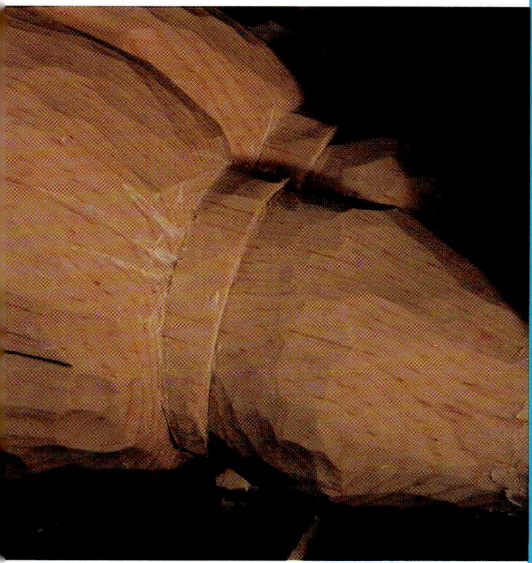

The result.

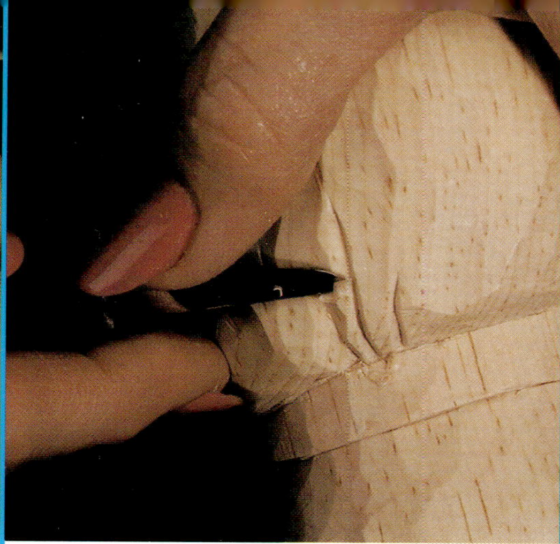

Soften the edges of the tucks.

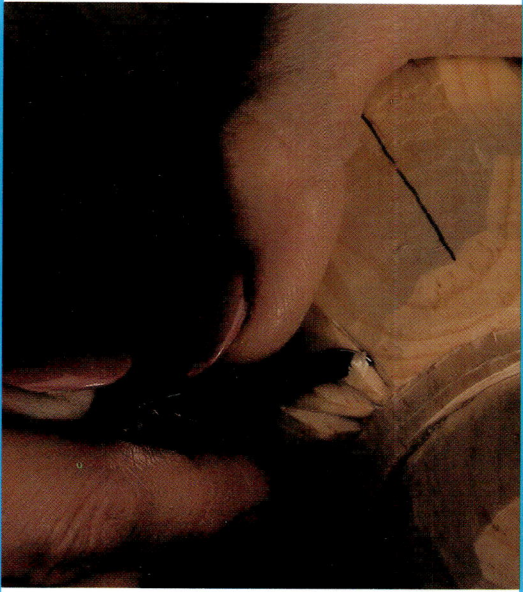

Repeat at the back corner and on other leg.

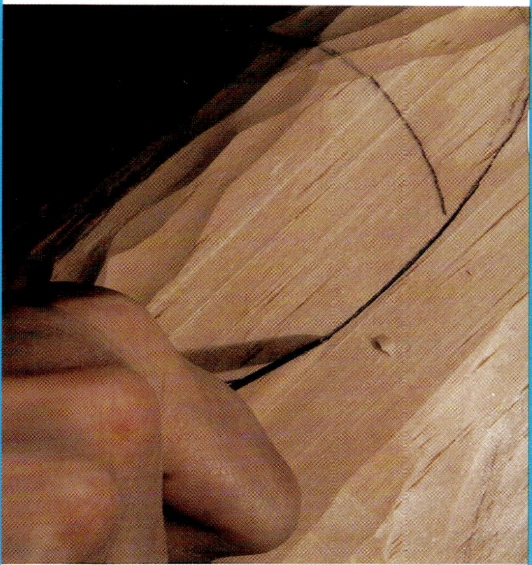

Score the line of the arm.

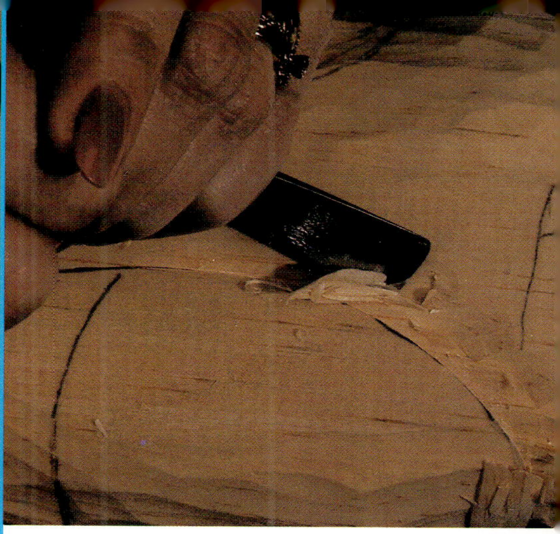

Slice along the score line with a gouge.

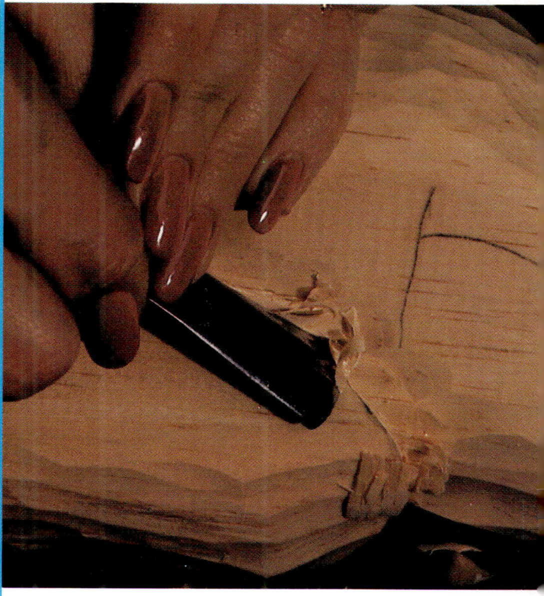

Turning the gouge, run it along the edge of the arm to clean the previous cut.

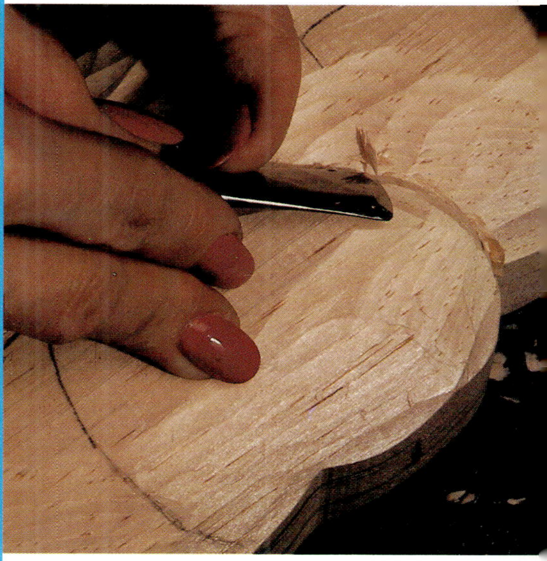

Round the arm down into the line.

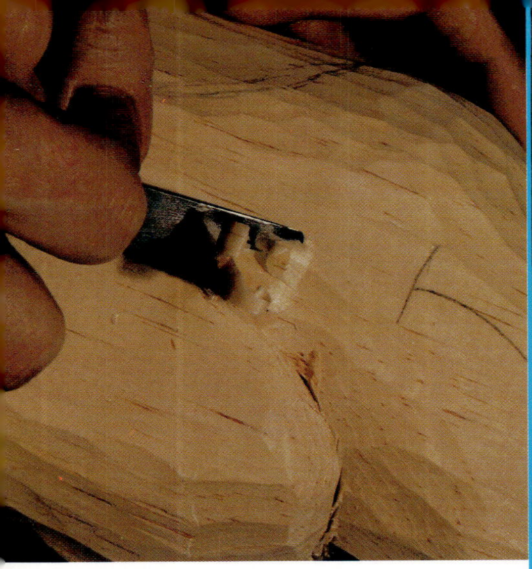

Shape the torso to get rid of the bump.

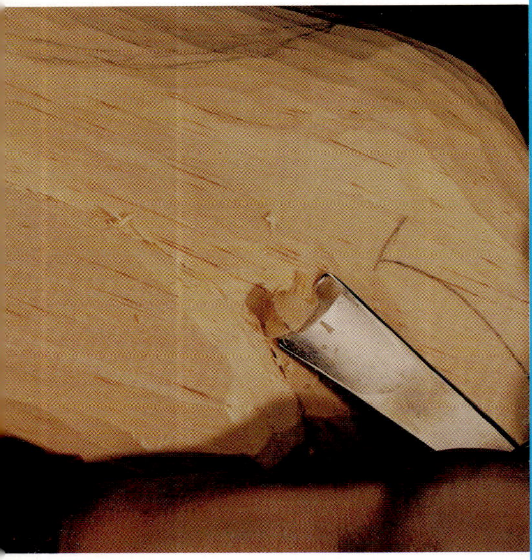

As the grain changes you will need to change the direction of your cut.

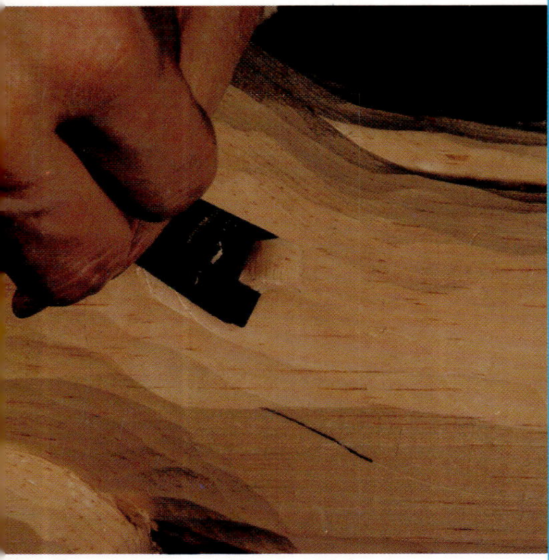

Shape the front of the hip to bring out the belly.

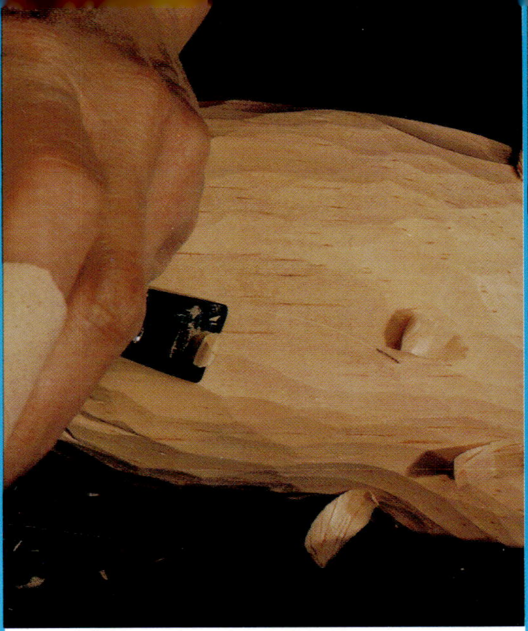

Continue shaping around the sides of the legs.

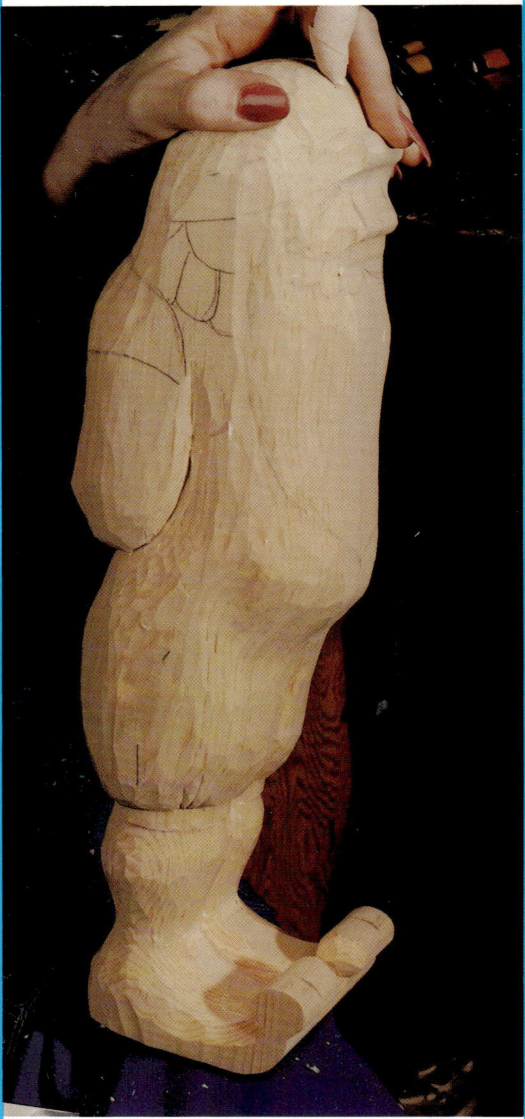

Progress on one side.

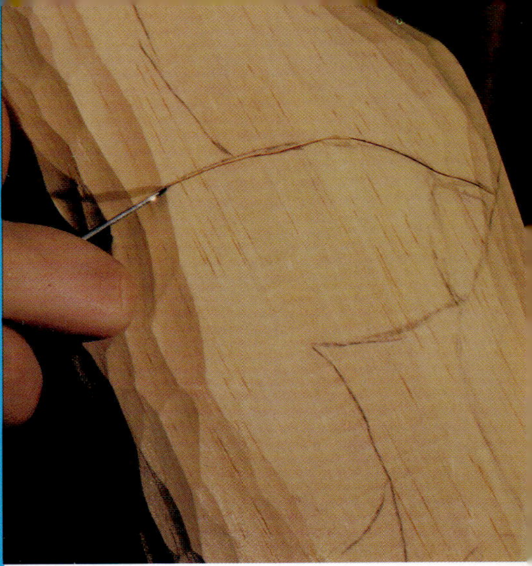

Score the line of the other arm. There are two sides, the bottom...

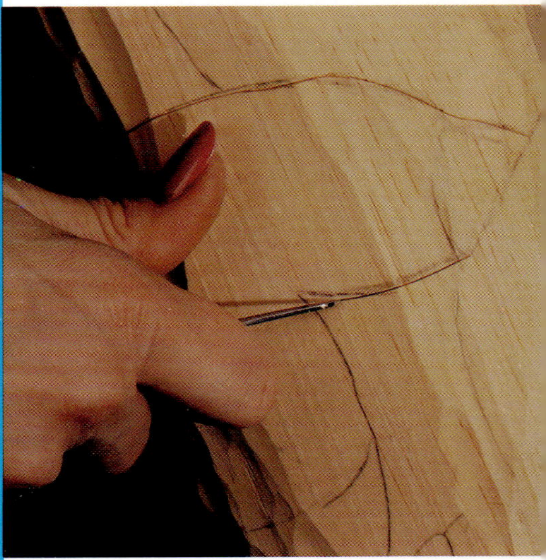

and the top.

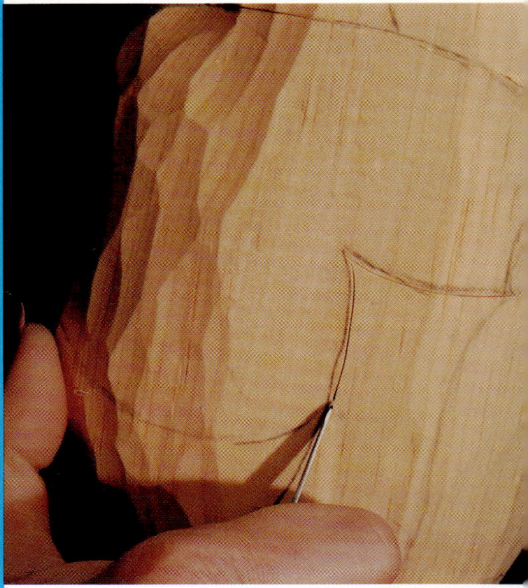

Continue up the front.

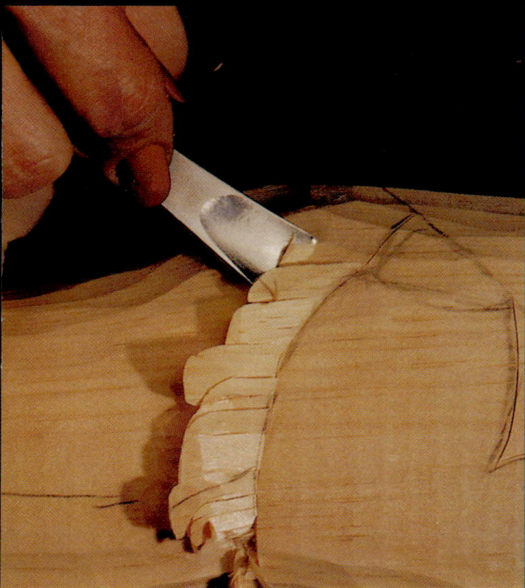

Under the arm cut back to the score line with the chisel.

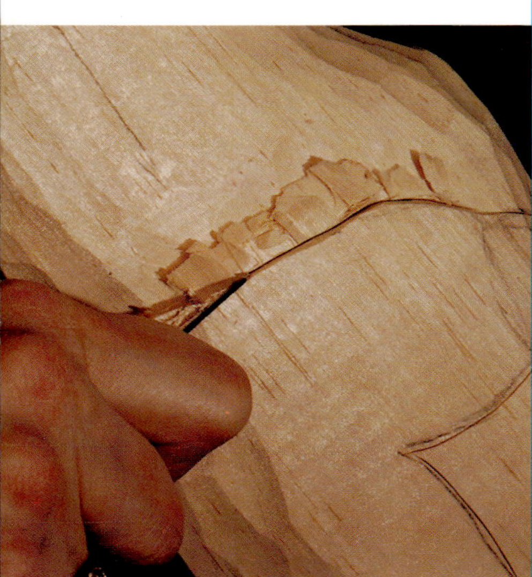

Slice off the chips with a knife.

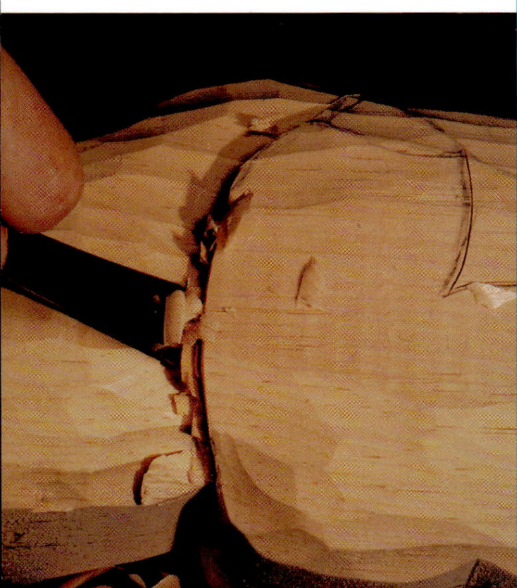

Repeat the process to deepen the line.

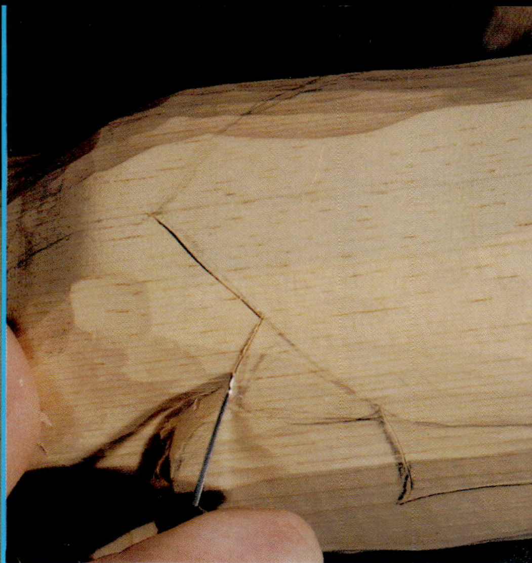

Score under the beard and in front of the glove.

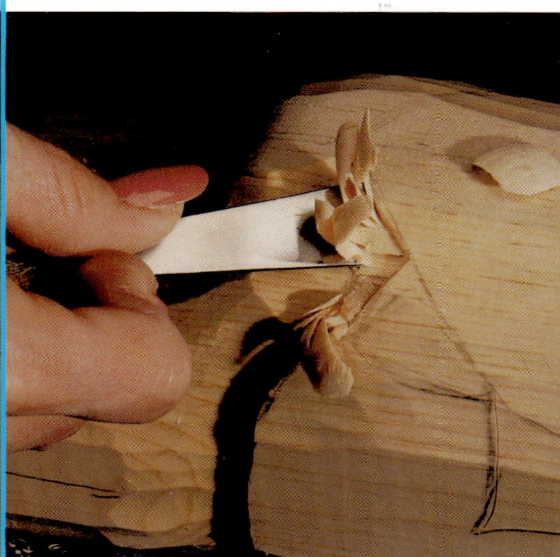

Come back to these lines from below.

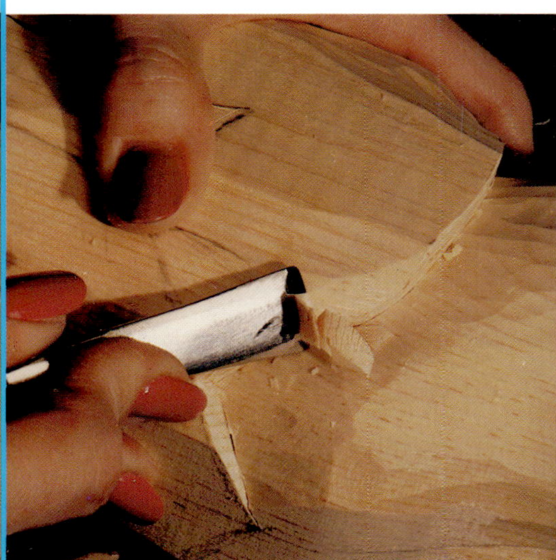

With the cup side of the gouge against the piece, round the lower edge of the arm.

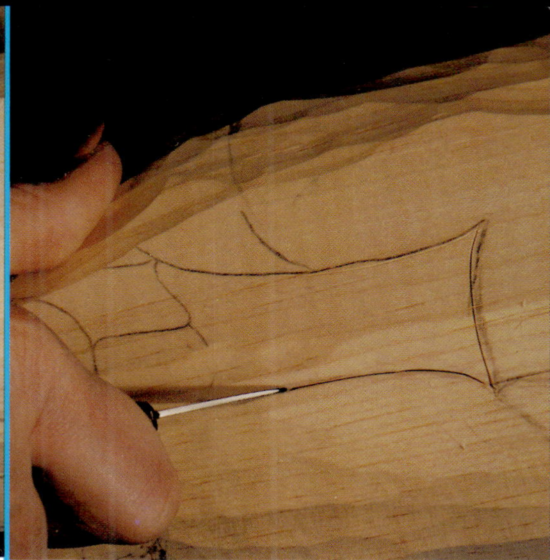

Before cleaning out the upper edge of the arm, score the beard line.

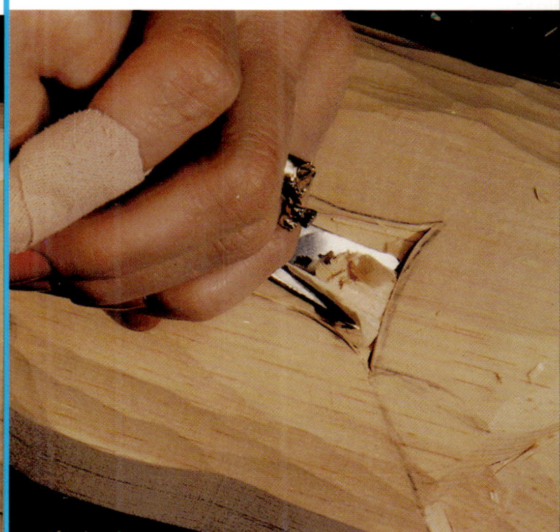

That prevents tearing as you cut back to the arm with the chisel.

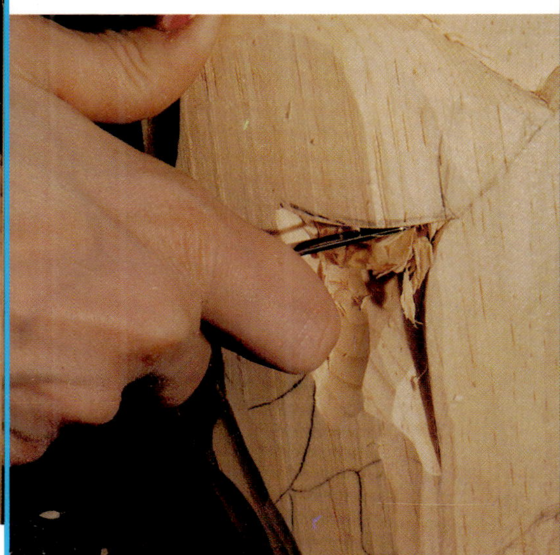

Cut off the waste with the knife.

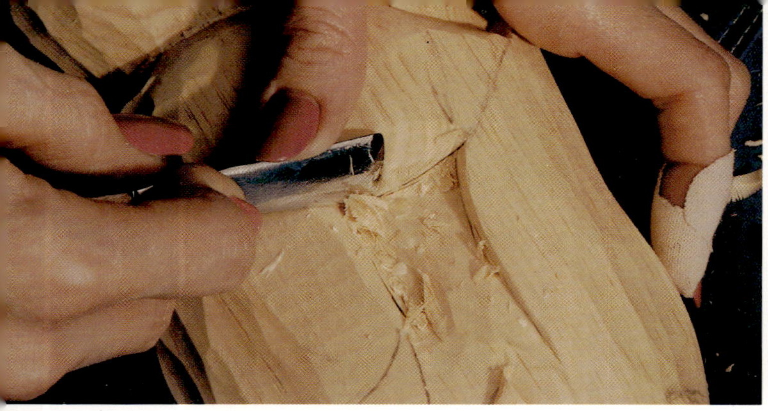

Round off the arm.

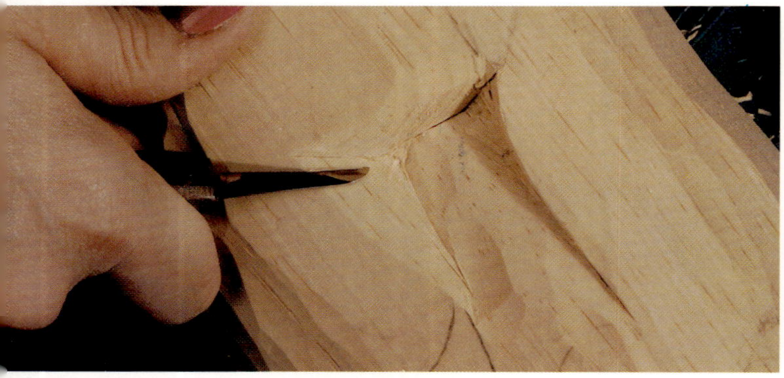

In the crook of the arm, where the two surfaces meet, clean up the carving with a knife.

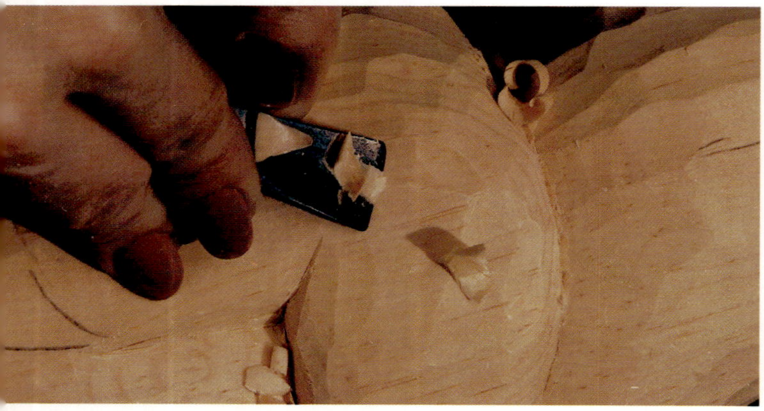

Shape the whole arm.

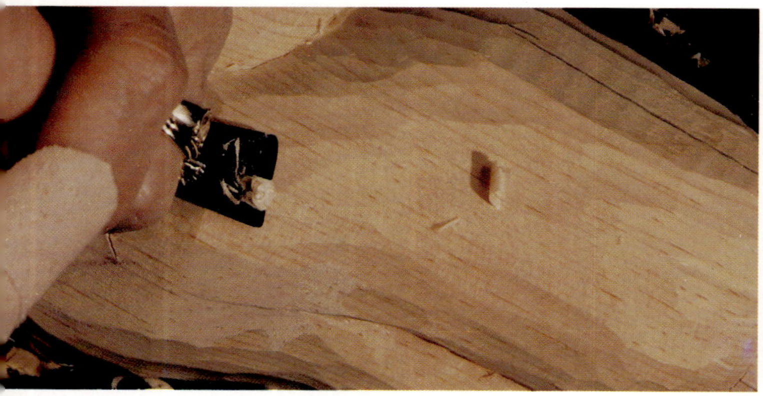

Shape the stomach and hips.

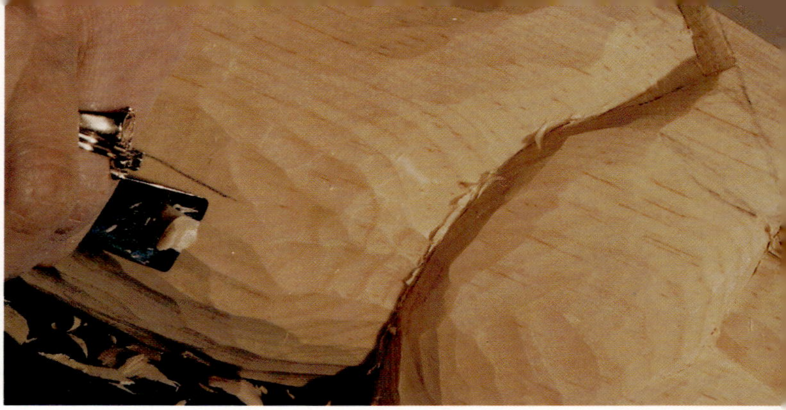

You want to remove all the flat places left from the blank.

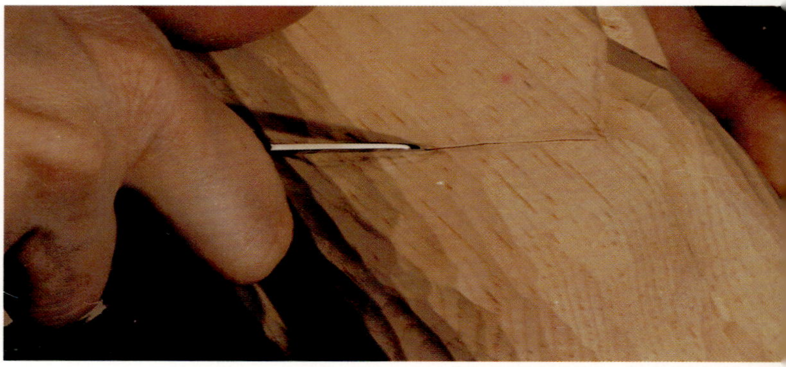

Score the other side of the beard.

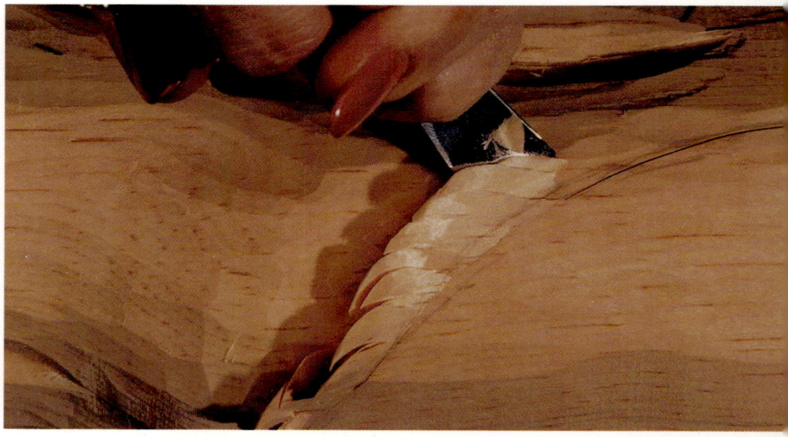

And cut back to it from the belly.

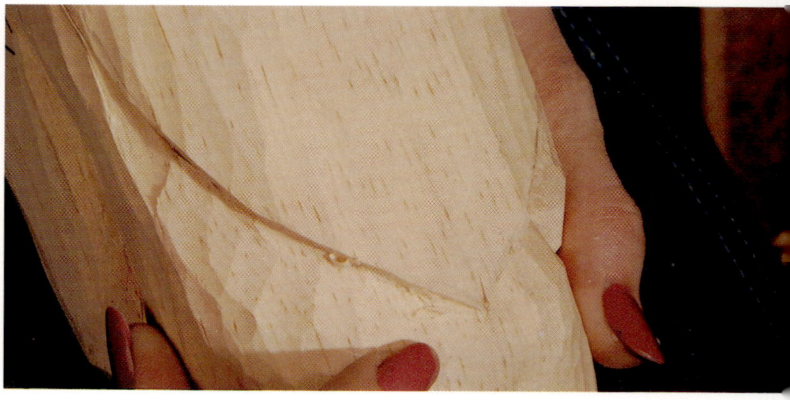

The beard will naturally be thinner at its tip...

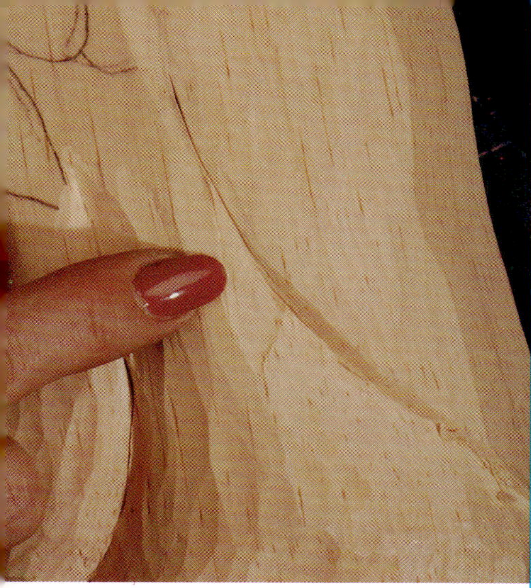

than along the sides.

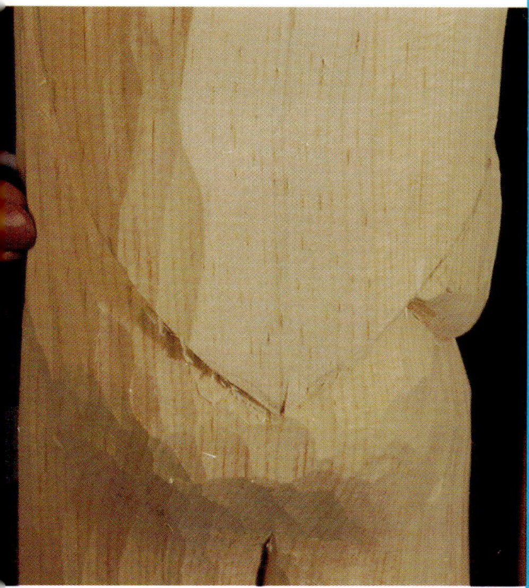

To get the torso on this side to match the other...

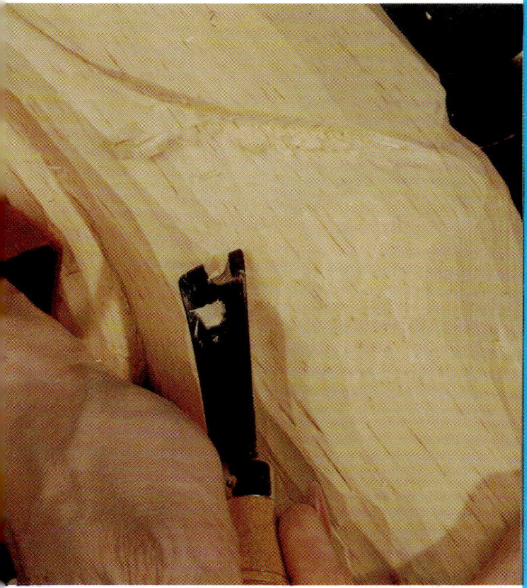

you need to trim it down.

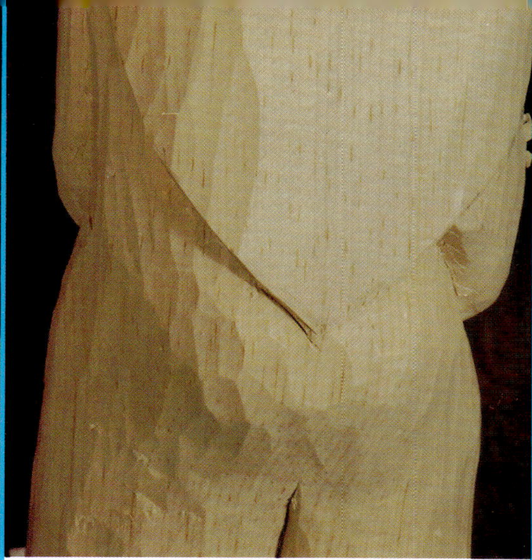

The results of the diet.

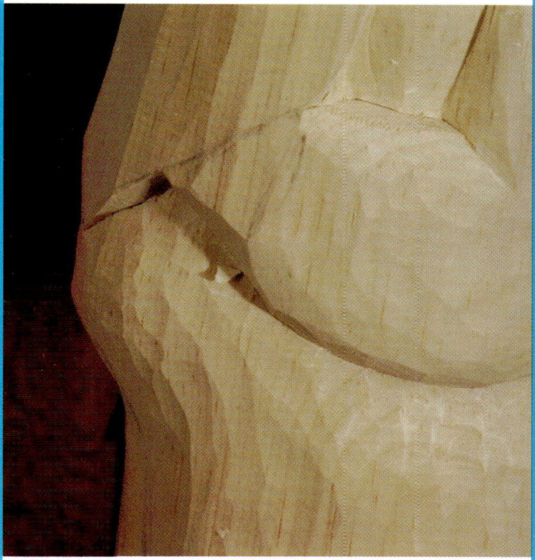

This is a great tummy!

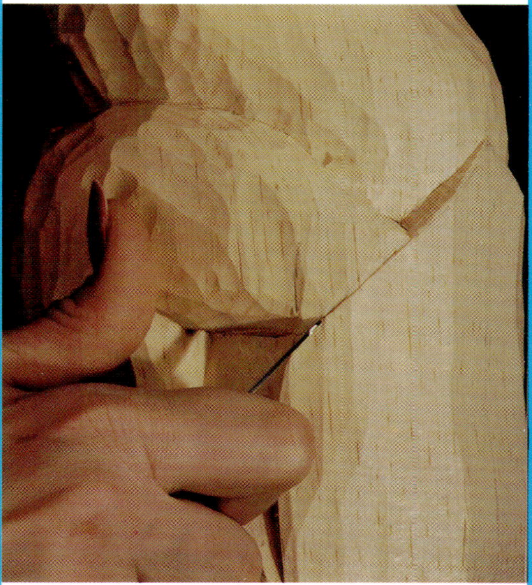

Score the hand at the beard...

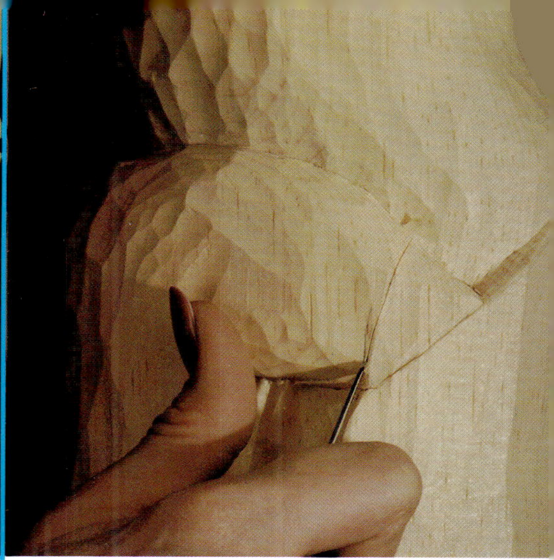

and the wrist.

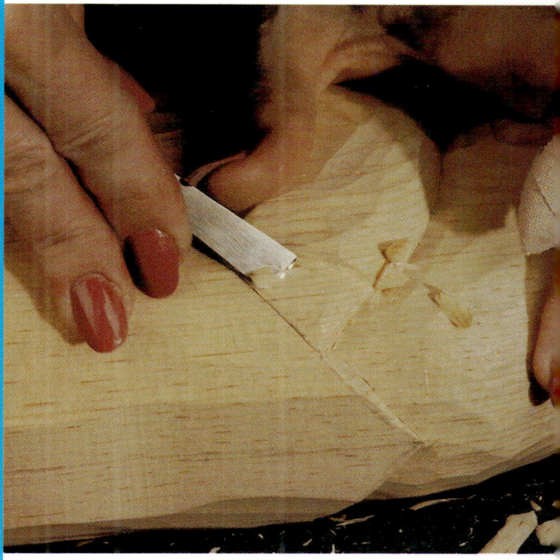

With a chisel, slice along the score lines to relieve the hand area.

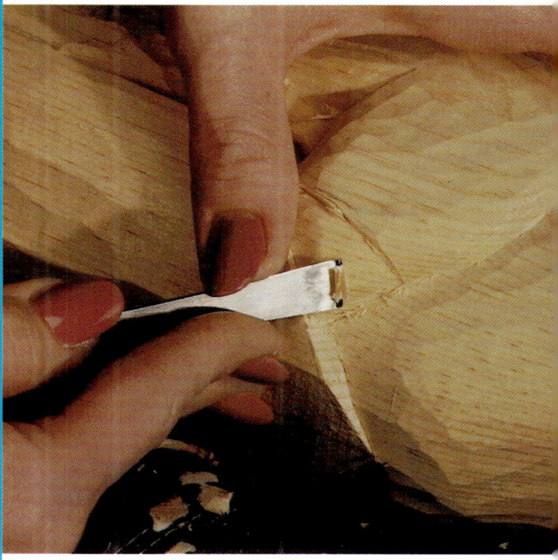

Round off the hand.

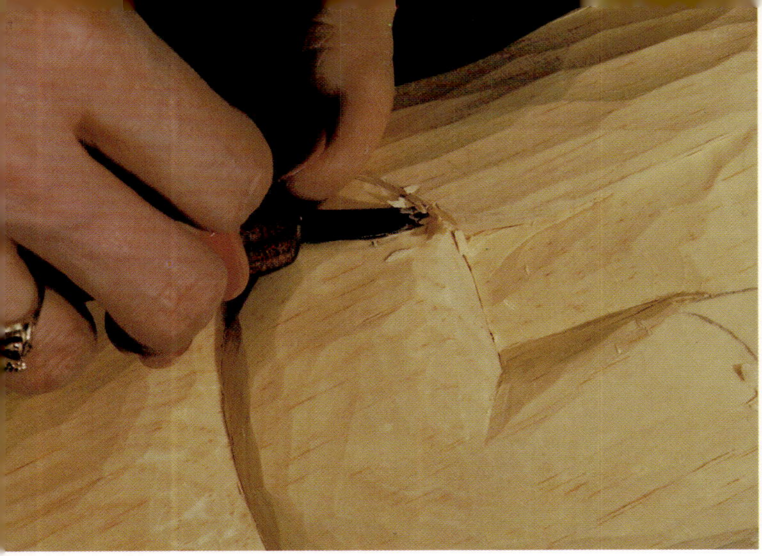

A knife is useful for getting into the corner.

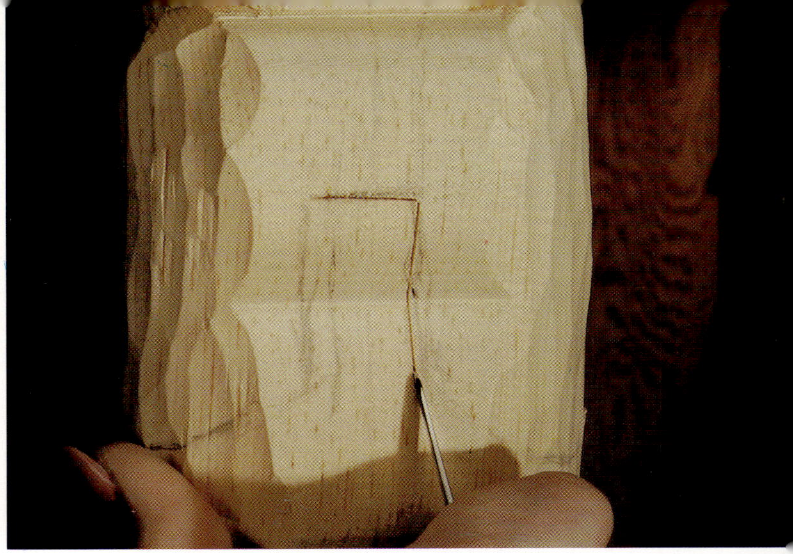

and down one inside edge...

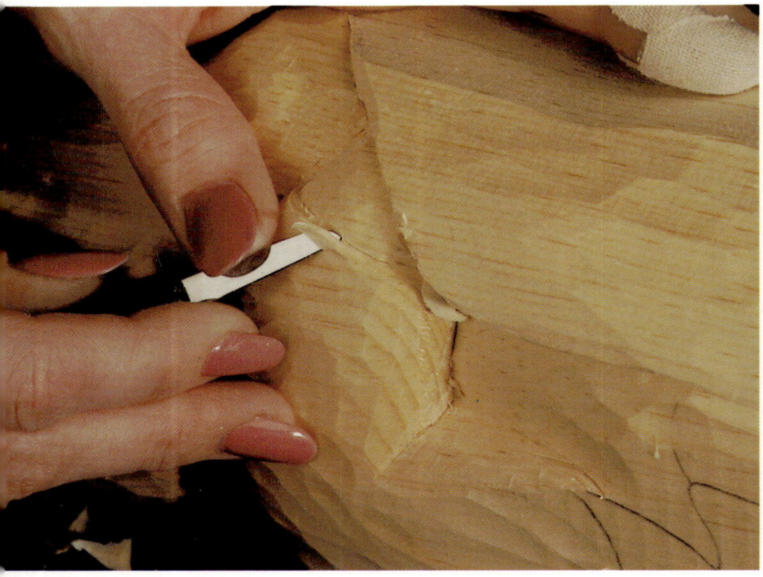

Round the sleeve to the hand.

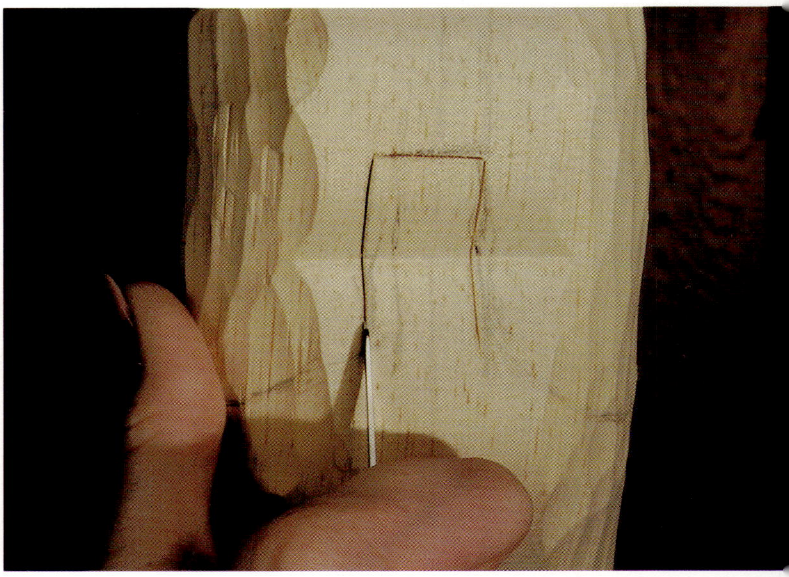

and the other.

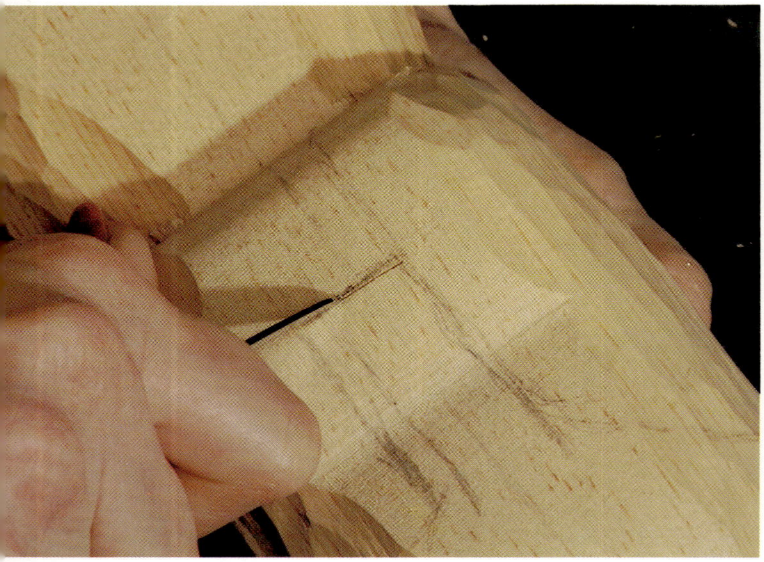

On the back, score a line across the top of the arms...

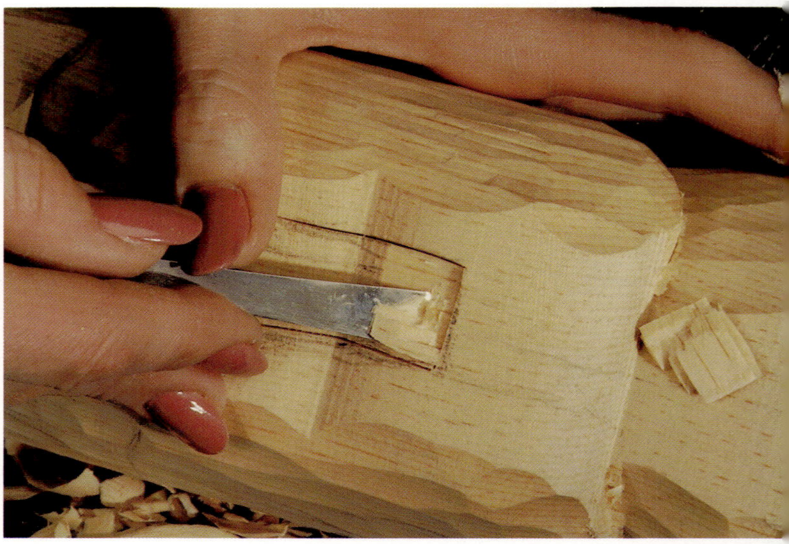

Chisel out the area between the arms. It will be much deeper here at the bottom...

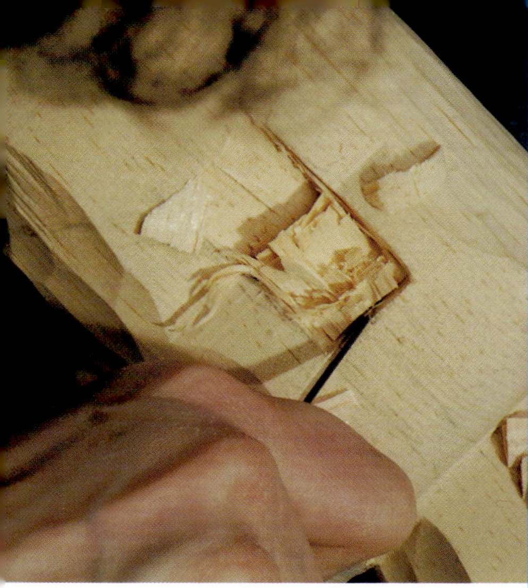

so go back and deepen the cut...

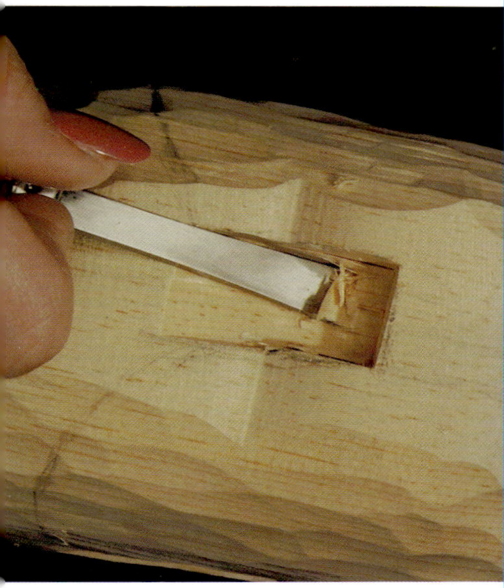

until it reaches the depth you wish. There should be a slope between the arms running from the shoulders to the waist.

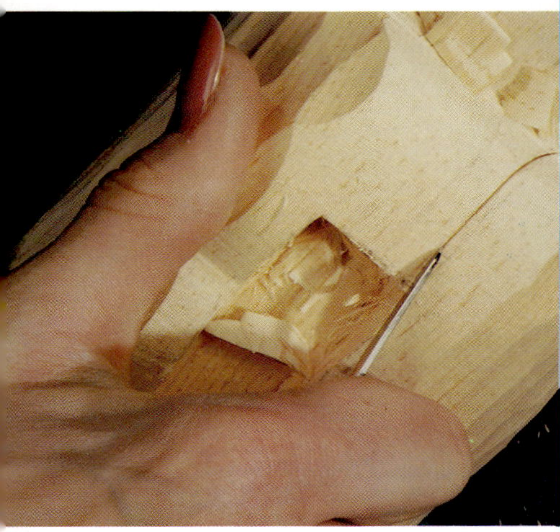

The elf's right arm goes under the left. Score the inside line of the left arm...

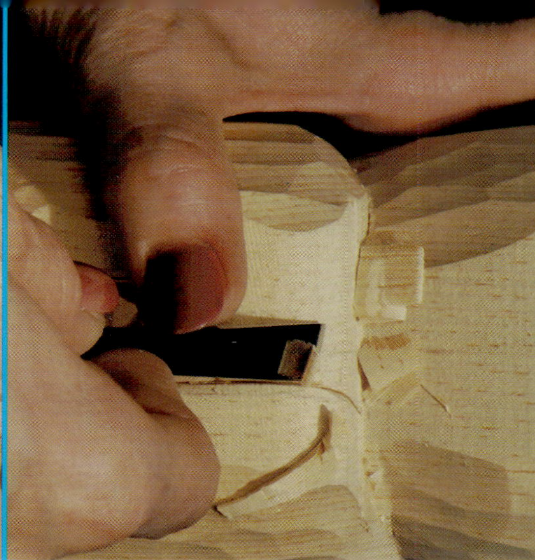

and slice the right against that line so it appears to go under.

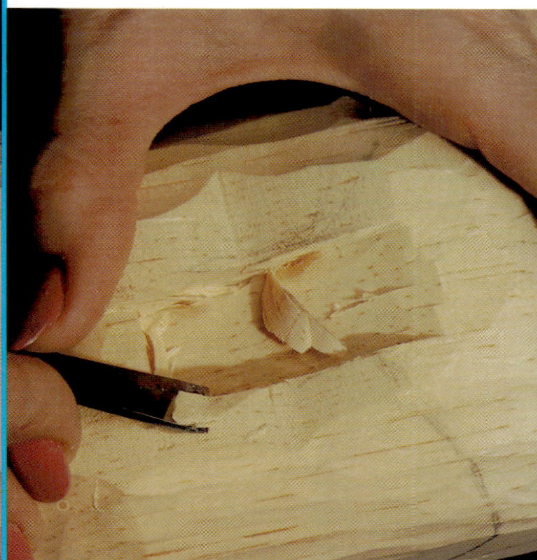

Round the edge of the right arm.

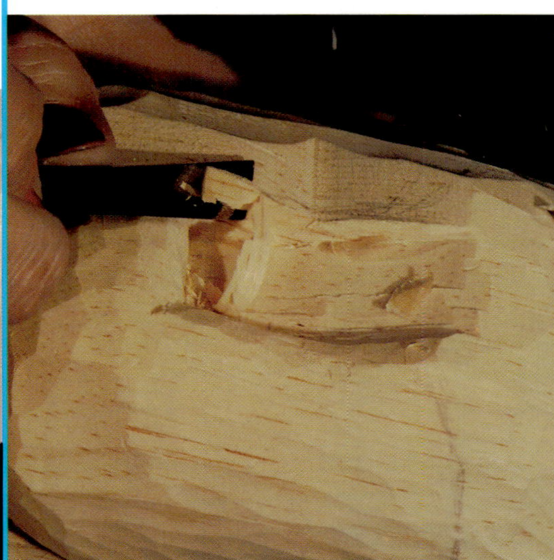

With the right arm rounded, round the edge of the left.

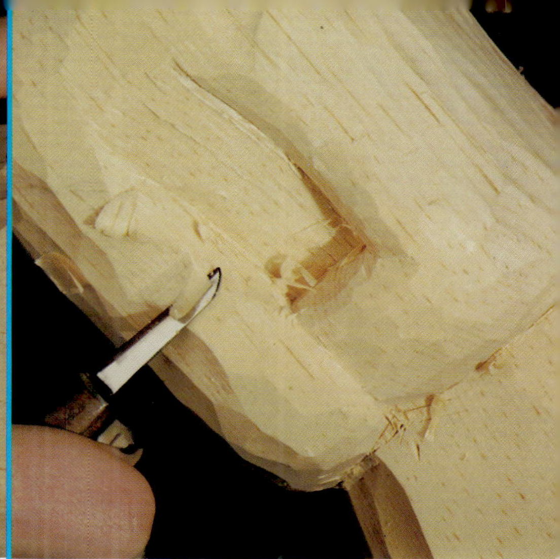

Shape the arms.

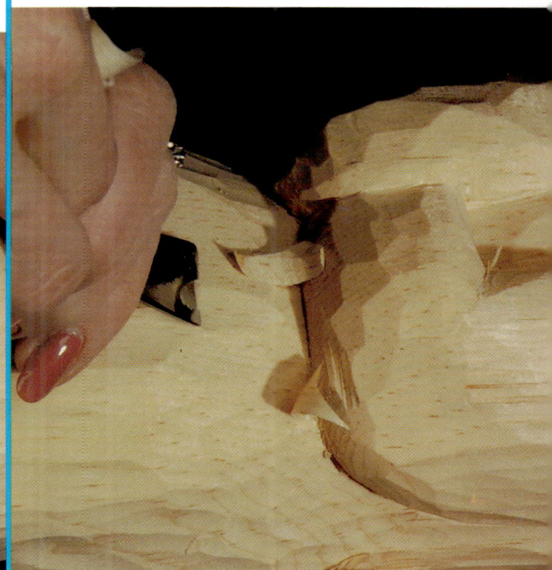

While in the back clean up the flat areas left from the blank.

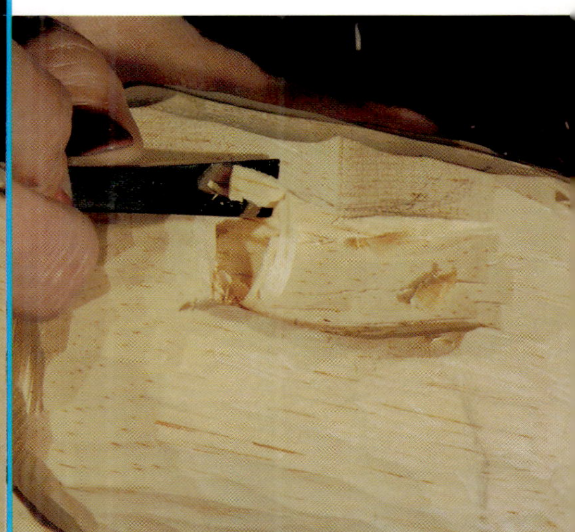

Continue shaping until you are satisfied with the arms.

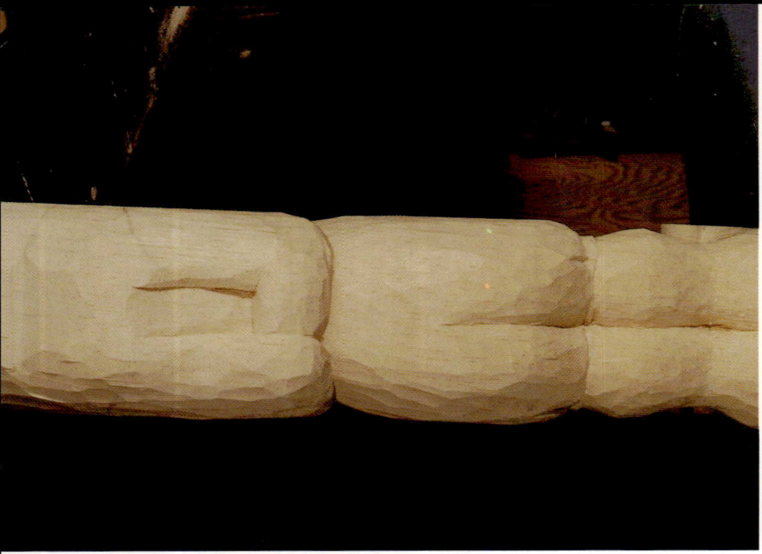

Progress on the back.

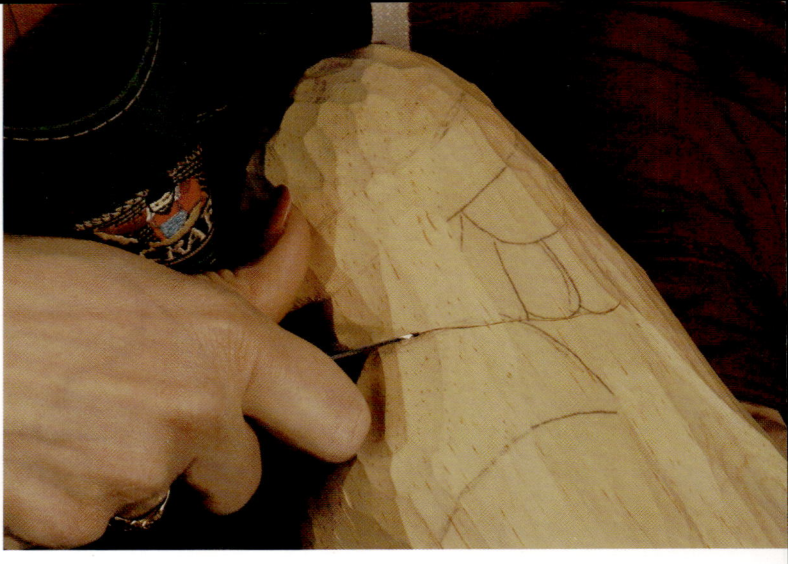

on both sides.

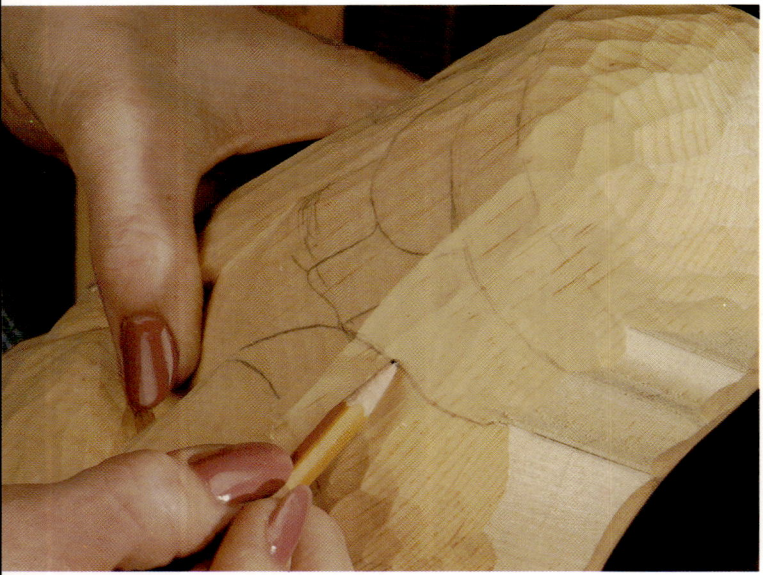

Redraw the line of the bottom of the hair.

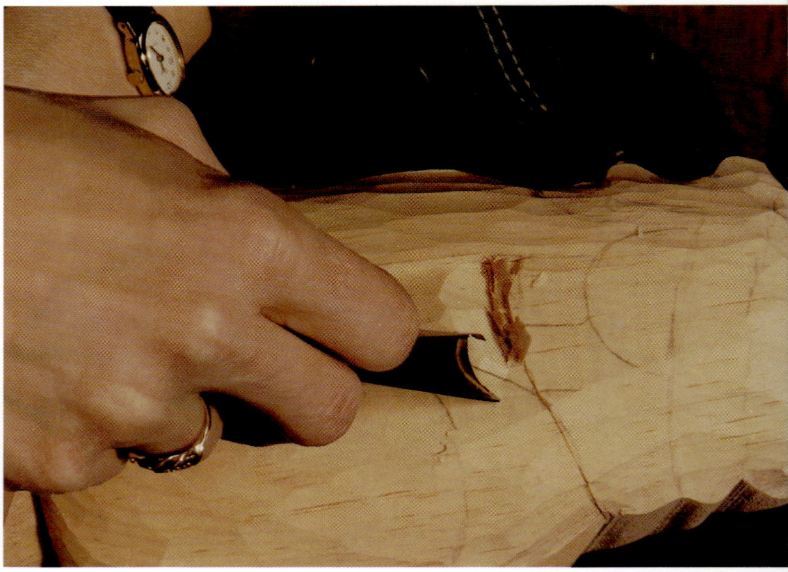

Cut back to it from the body.

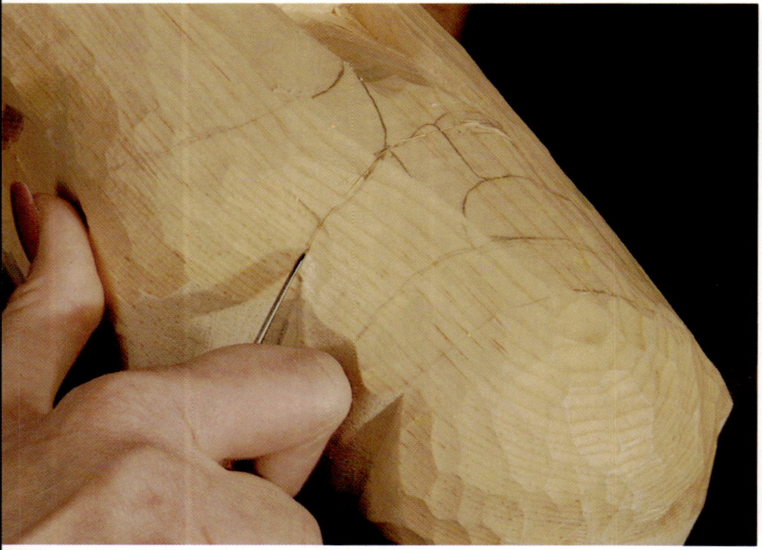

Score the line...

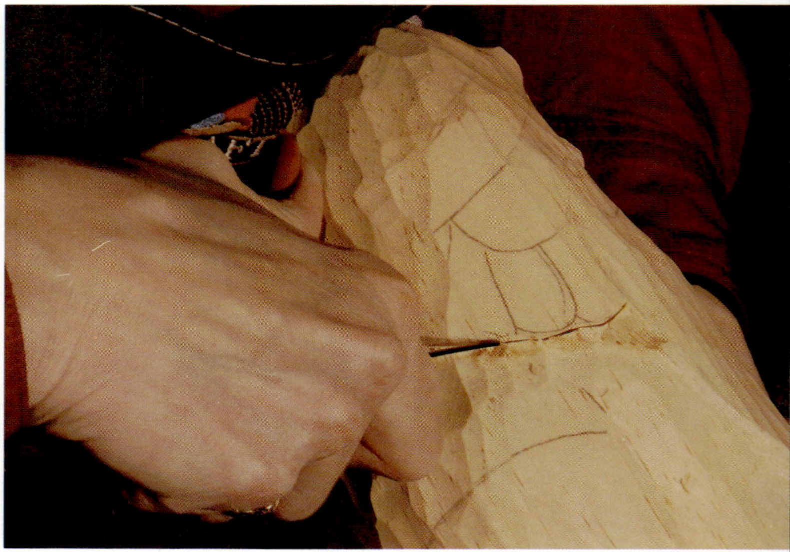

To deepen, rescore the line...

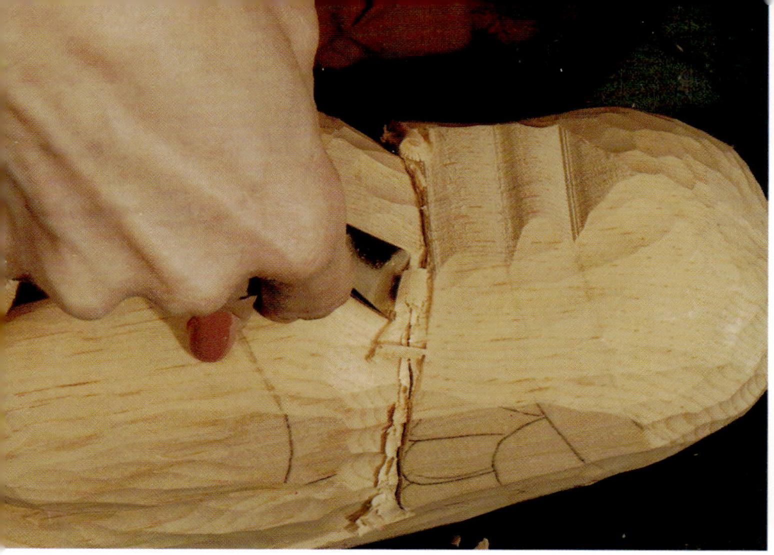

and trim again.

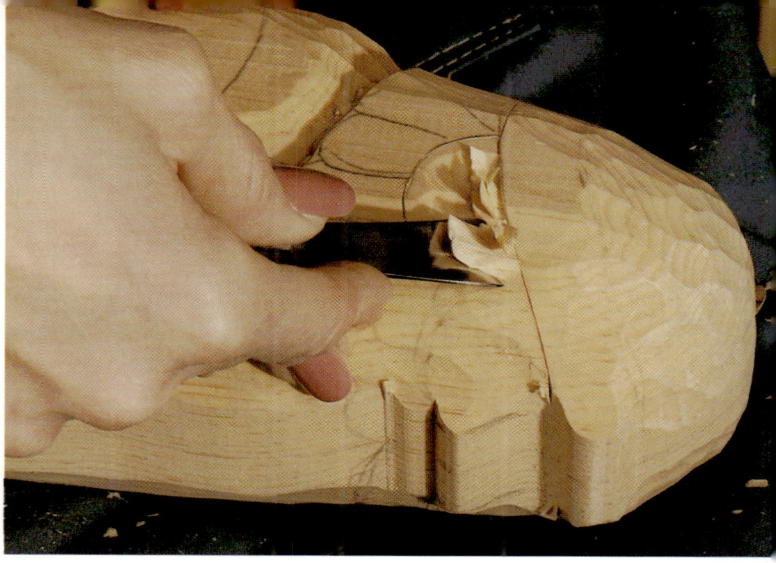

Trim back to the line of he hat from beneath.

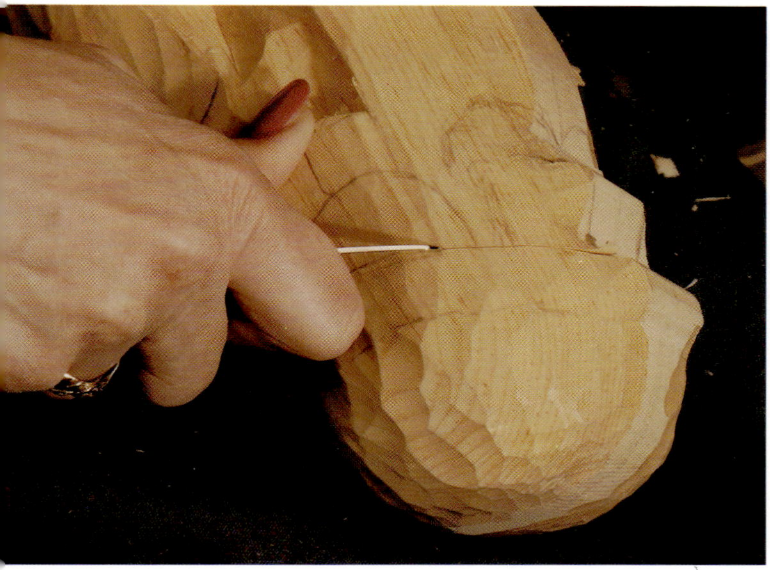

Score the bottom of the cap all around.

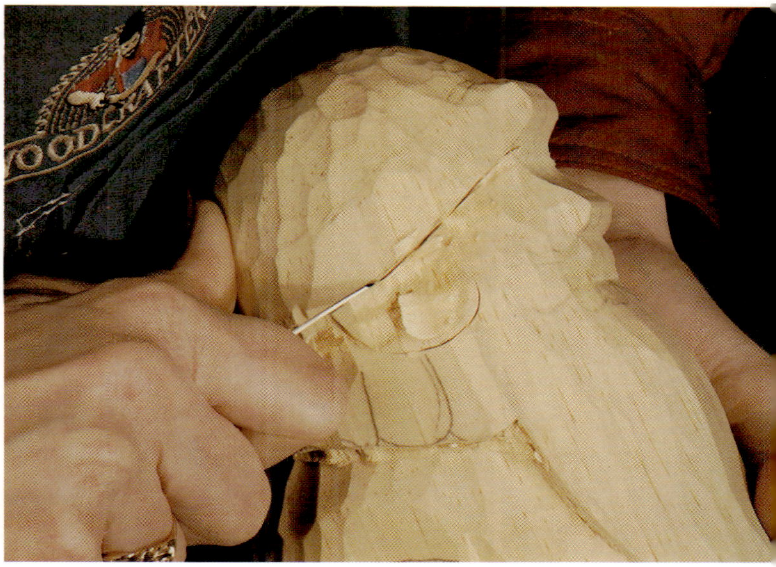

Score again...

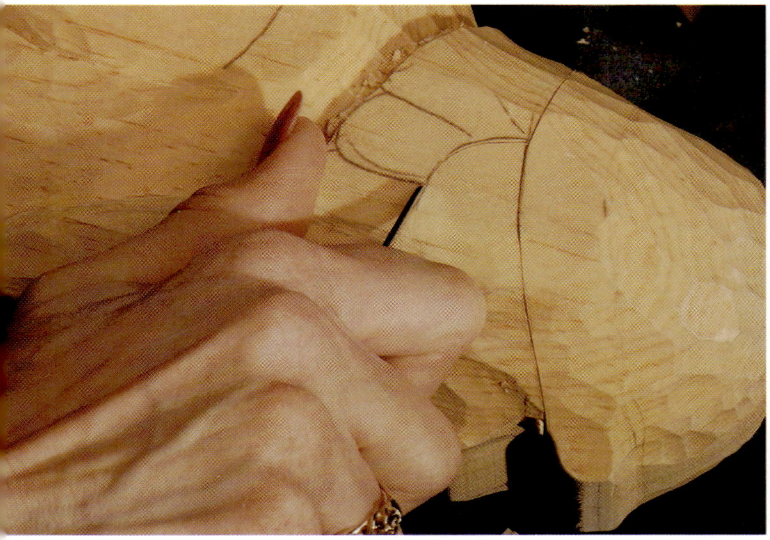

Score the ear flaps. You will be carving them off, but the scoring will leave a line underneath.

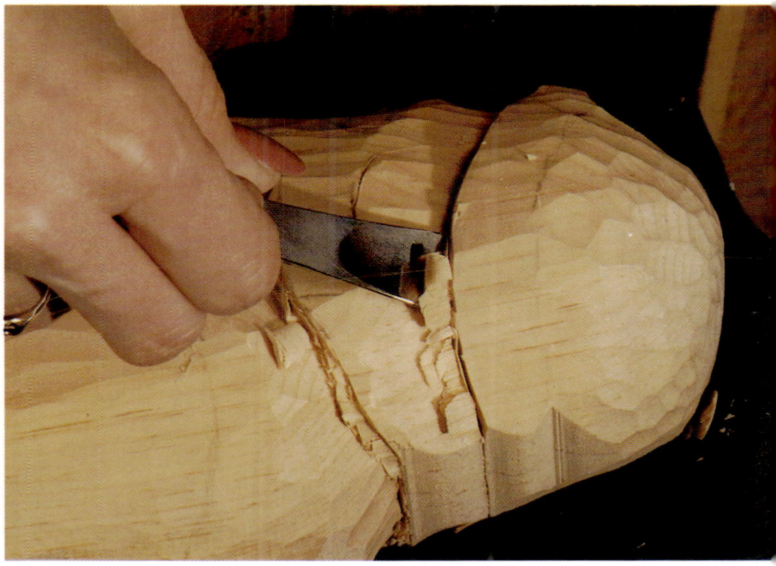

and deepen the cut.

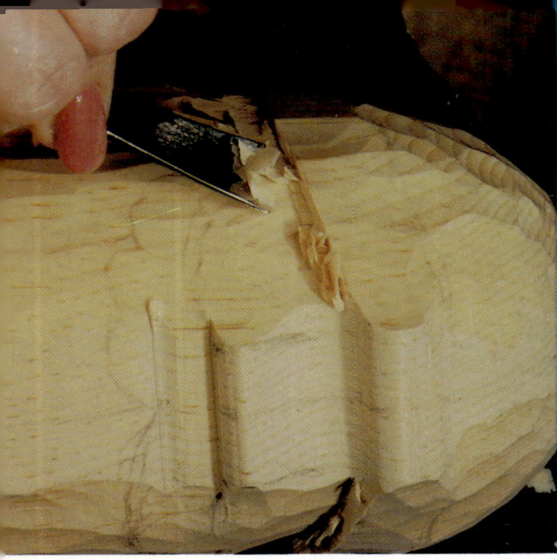

At the front and back of the hat the shape was basically established in the blank.

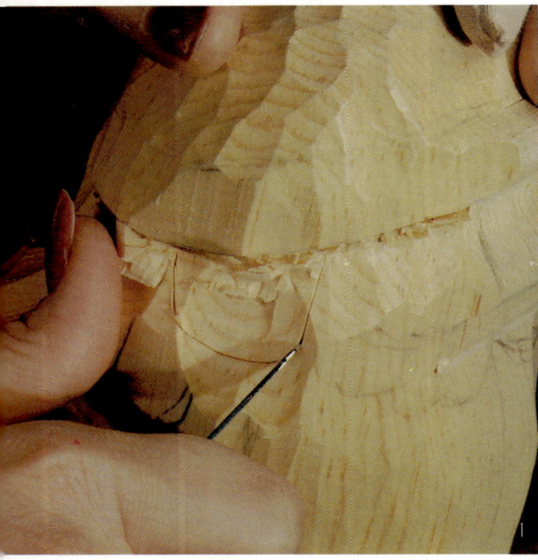

I was getting below the score line of the earflap, so I need to redo it.

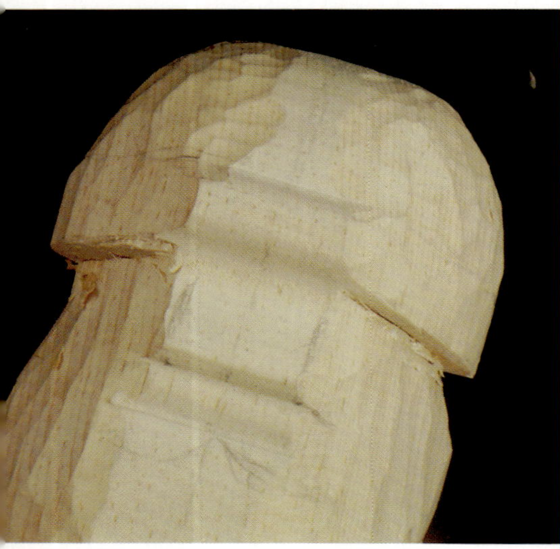

Shape the hair so it comes under the hat like this.

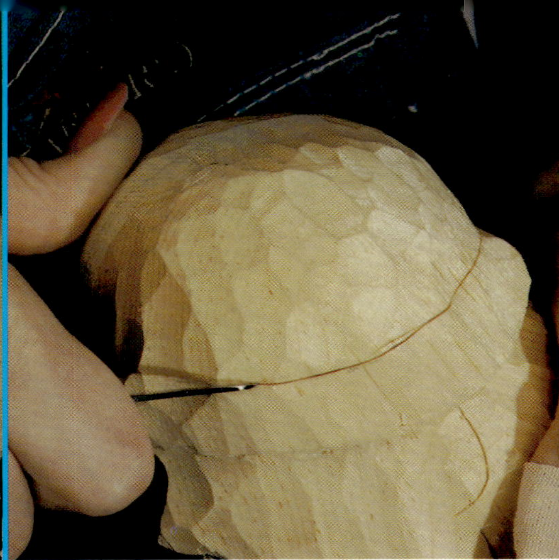

Score a line around the upper edge of the hat brim.

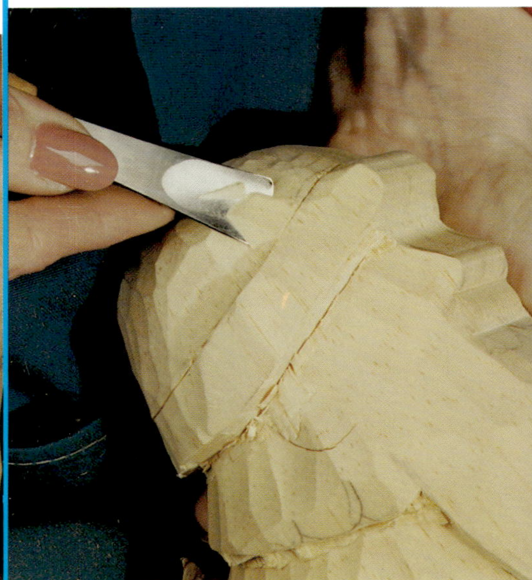

Trim back to the line from the crown.

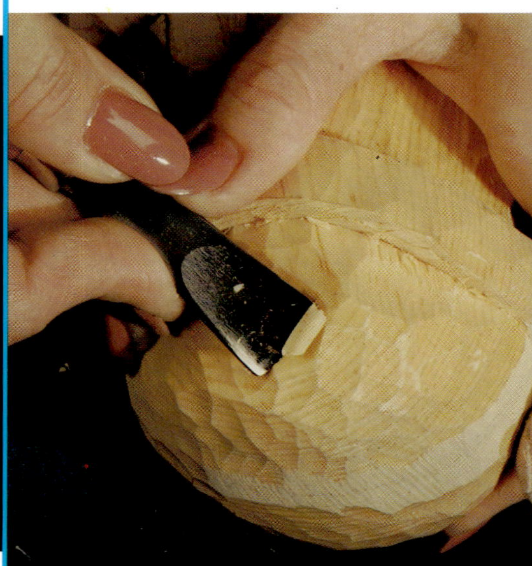

Reshape the hat to fit the head.

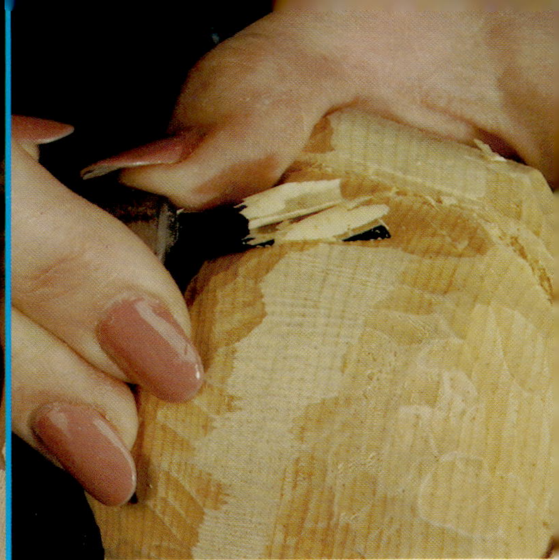

At the front and over the middle of the top I just need to skim away the saw marks. I switch to a knife to get more control.

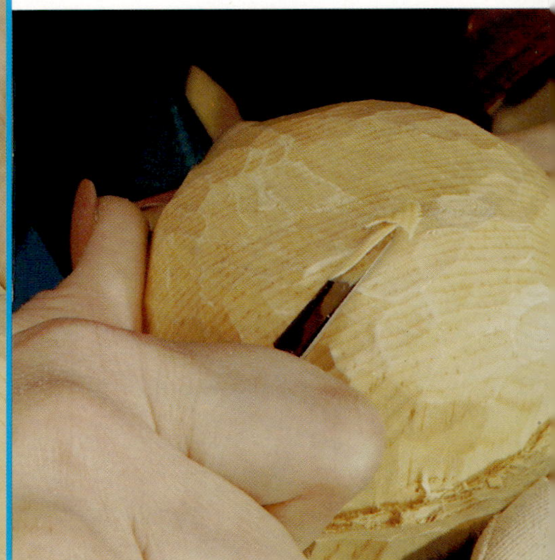

Continue to clean up the hat.

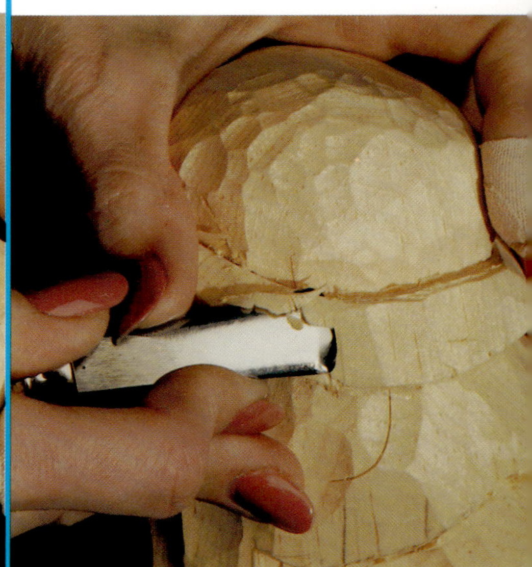

Shape the roll of the hat.

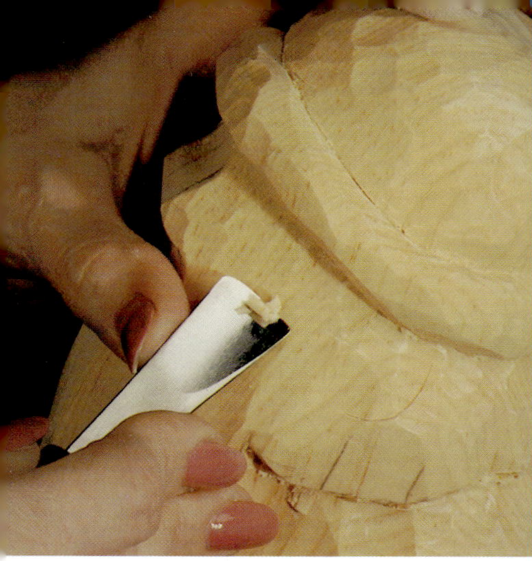

I like to get the hat done before the face. It helps establish the size of the face, and keeps me from slipping later and putting a knife into a beautifully carved face while I'm carving the hat. Shape the hair back to the cap.

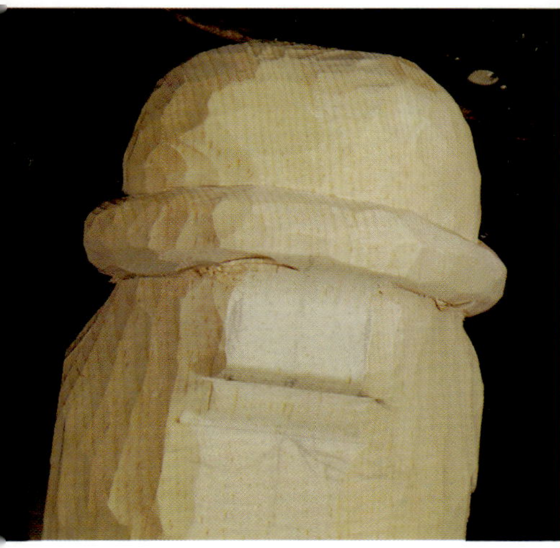

Take a look for balance. The hair is longer on one side than the other.

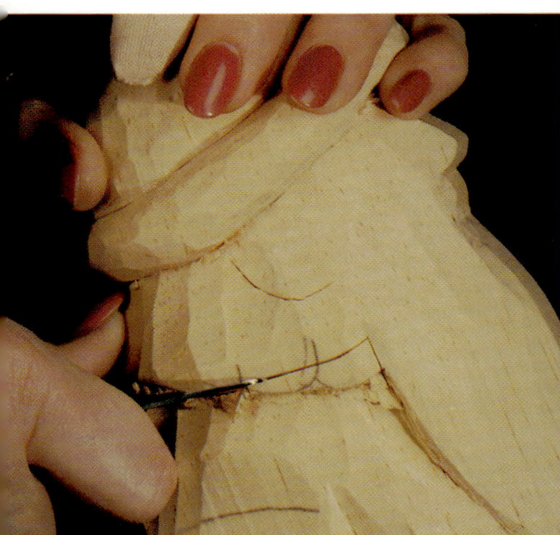

Cut a score along the beard line and across the hair where it needs to be shortened.

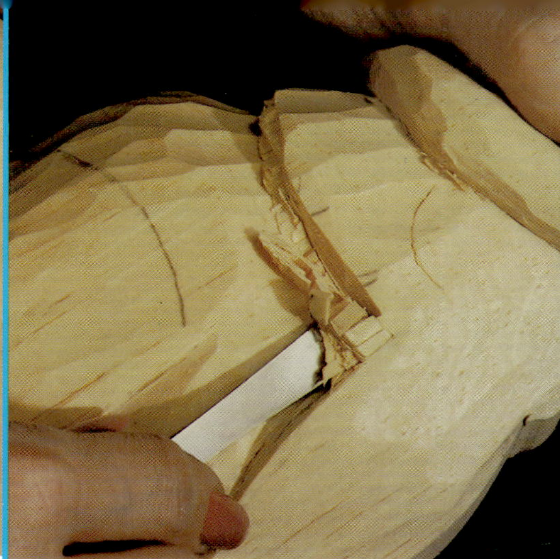

Trim back to it.

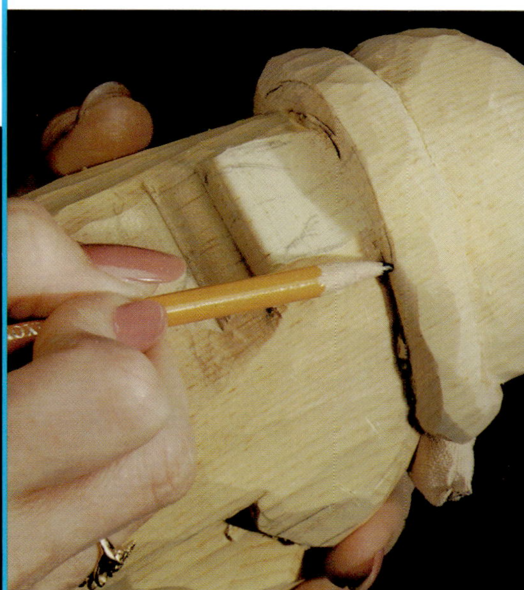

I need to raise the front of the hat roll to give me more room for the eyes.

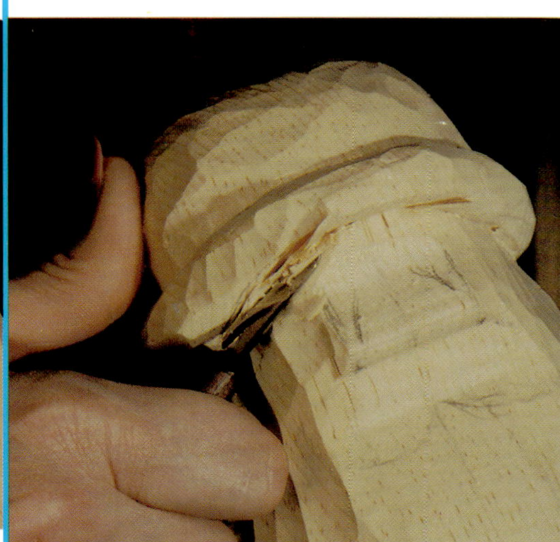

Trim along the line and cut back to it from the face.

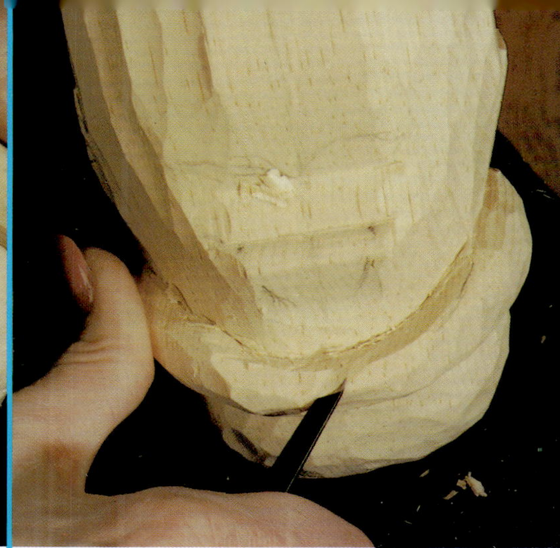

Round the underside of the hat roll.

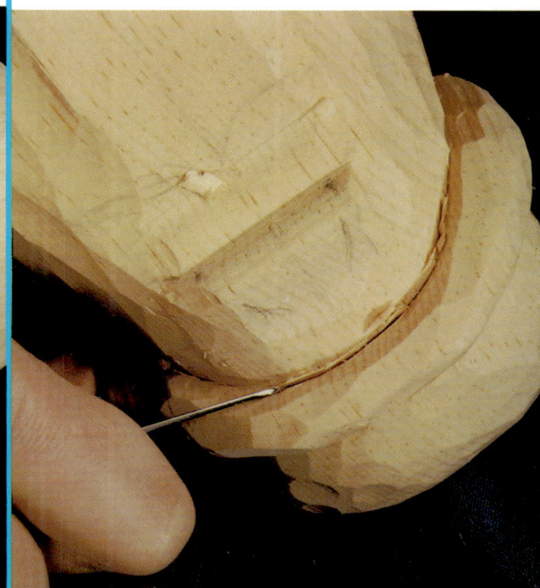

Undercut the hat band to make it separate from the head. Cut a score line...

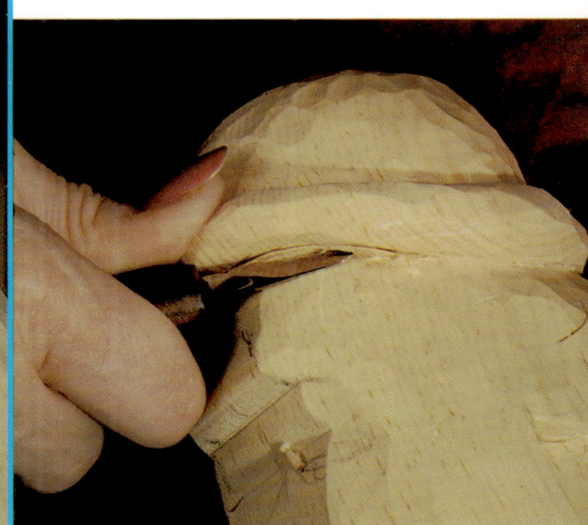

and come back to it from the face and hair.

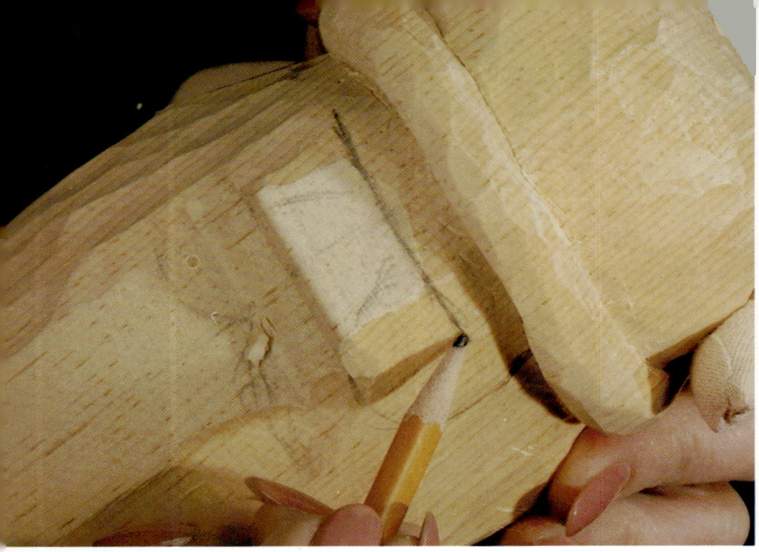

Draw in the line of the eyes...

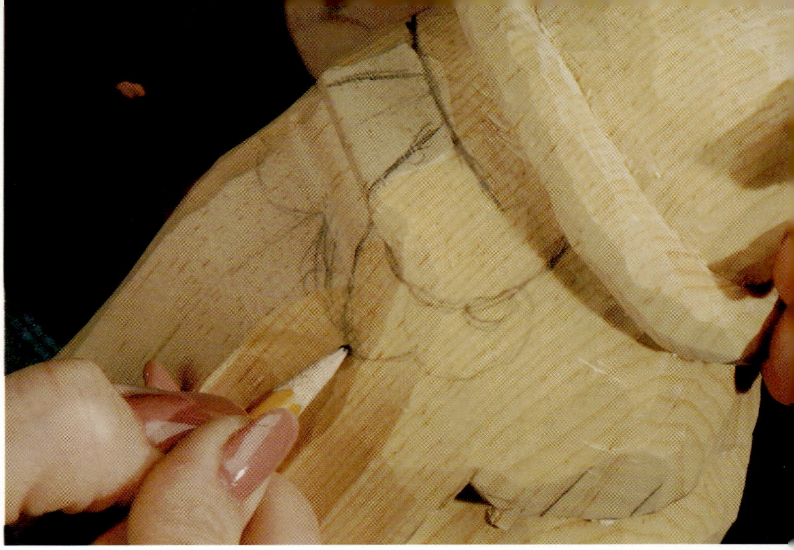

and the segments of the moustache.

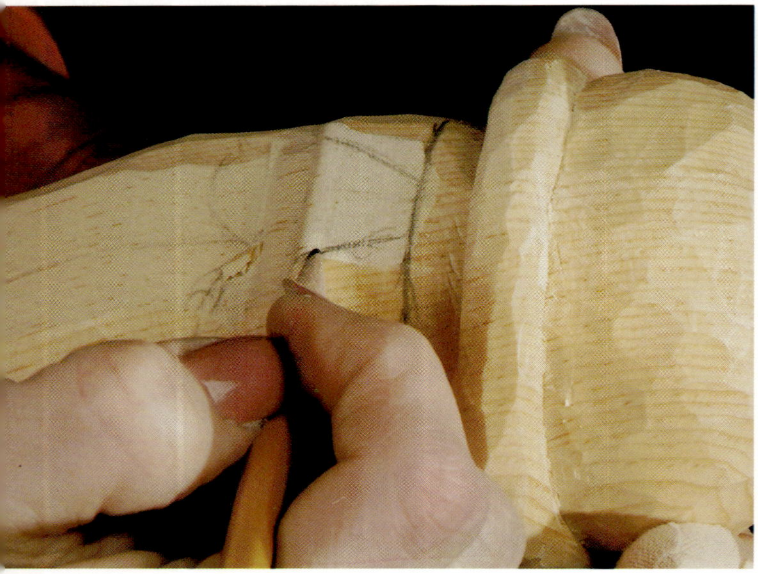

the outline of the nose...

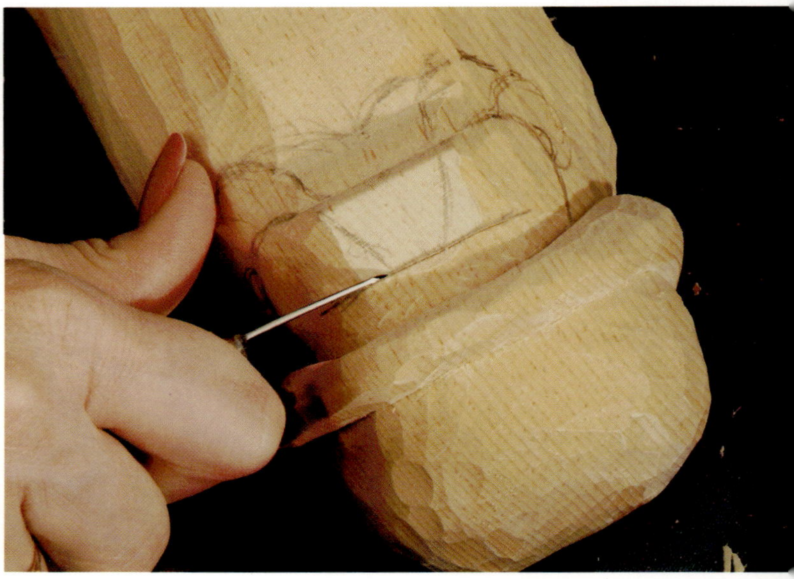

Score on the eye line.

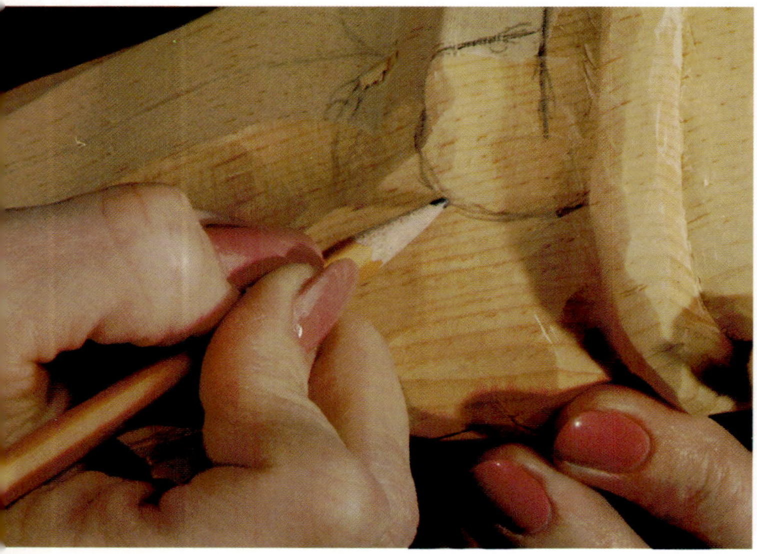

the cheek line...

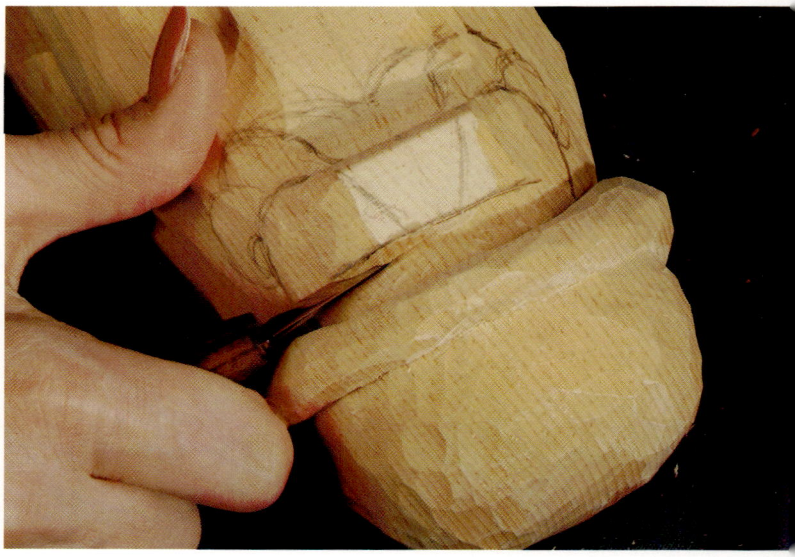

Make a wedge cut back to the eye line from the top...

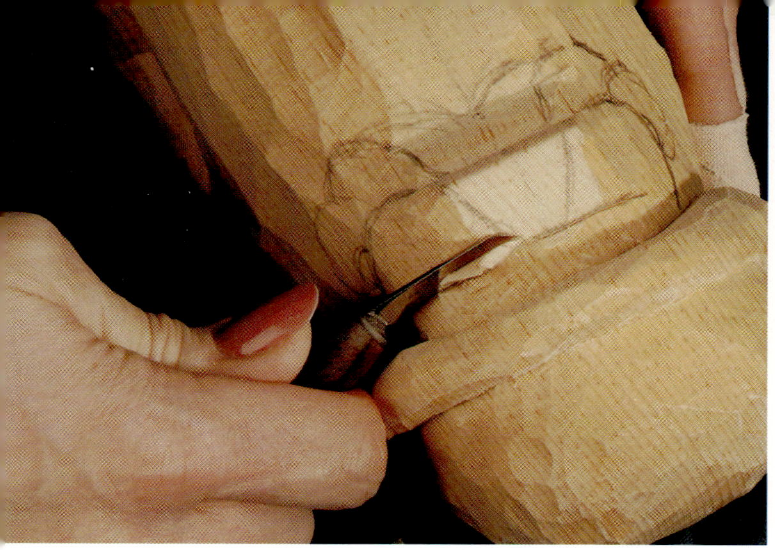

and the bottom.

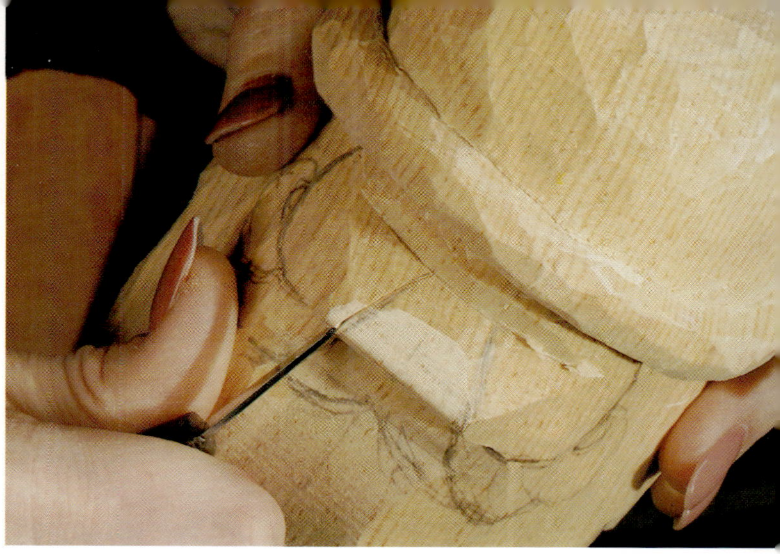

and make score cuts in them. Be careful not to underscore the nose line.

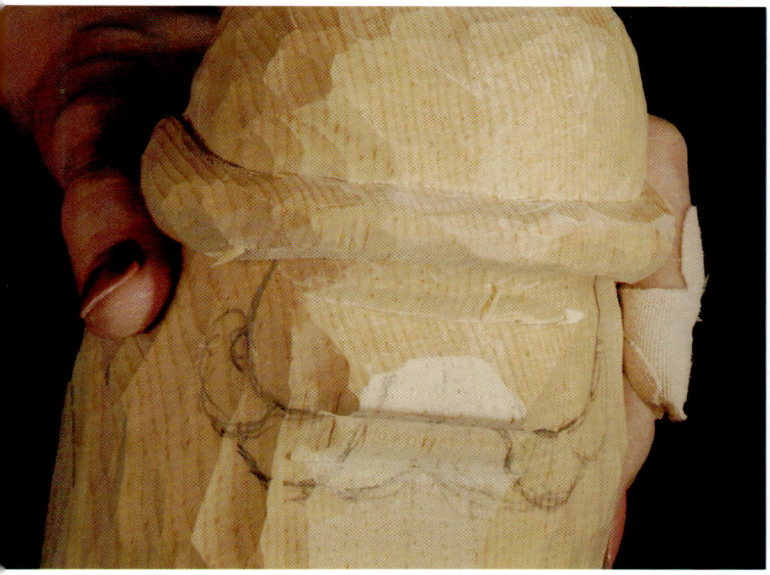

The bottom slope from the eye line is fairly long, following the slope of the nose.

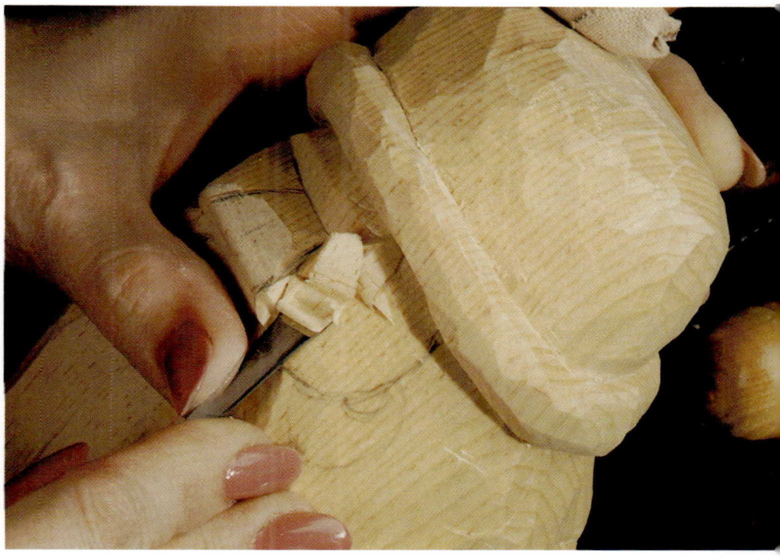

Come along the nose line and drop the cheek back to the eye line.

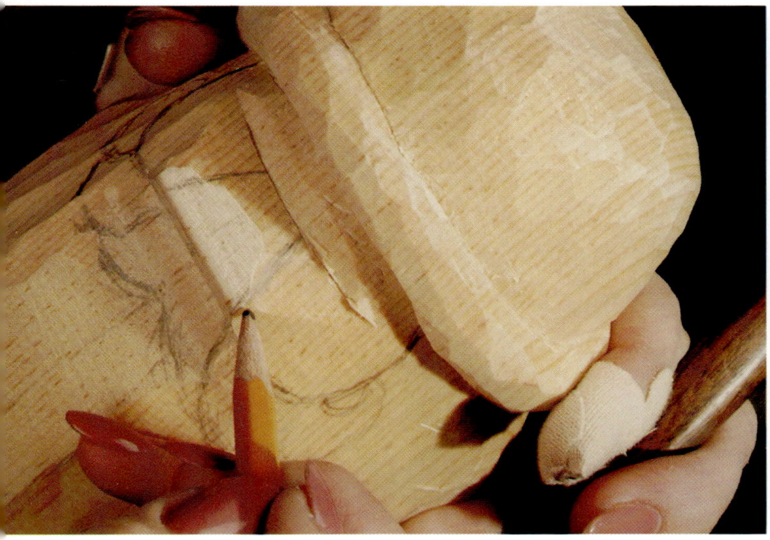

Redraw the nose line...

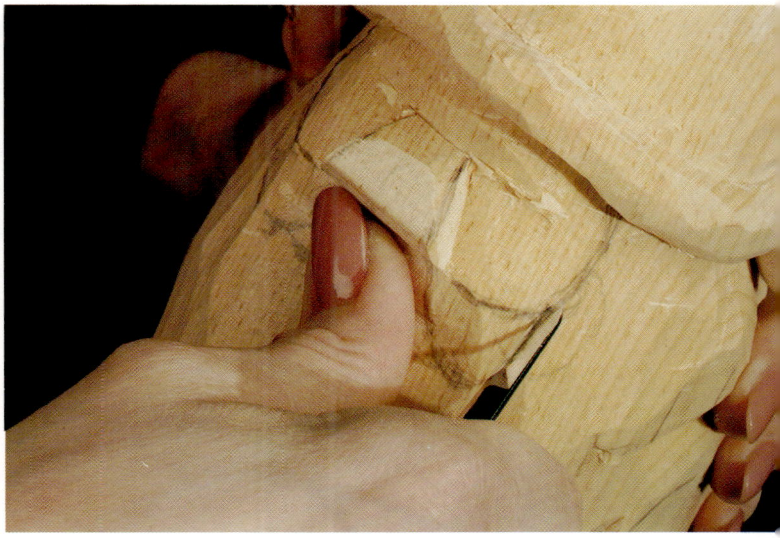

Score the cheek line to the nose.

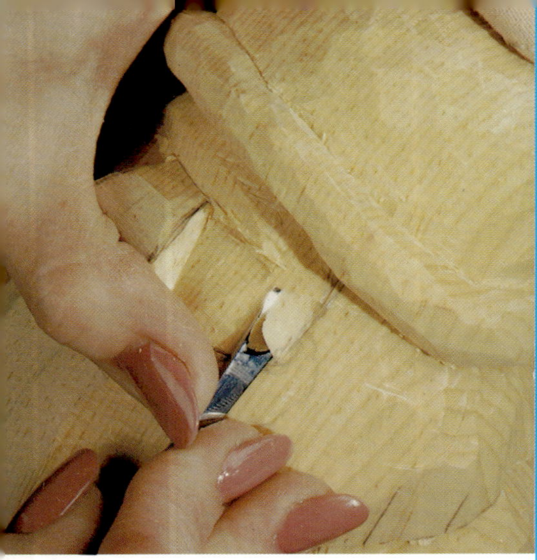

Go along the hairline to bring the cheek down.

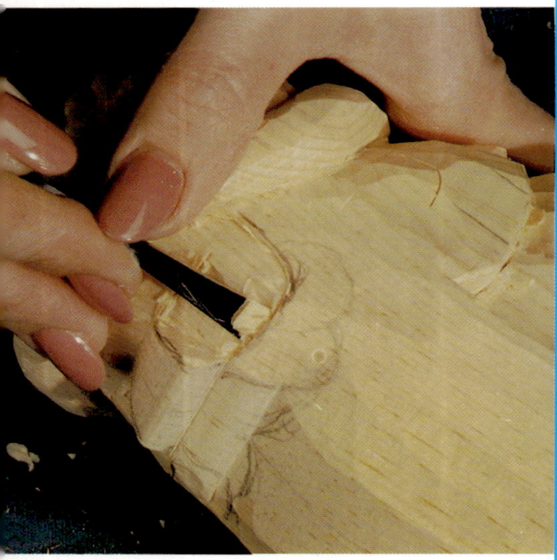

Come down the cheek to the moustache.

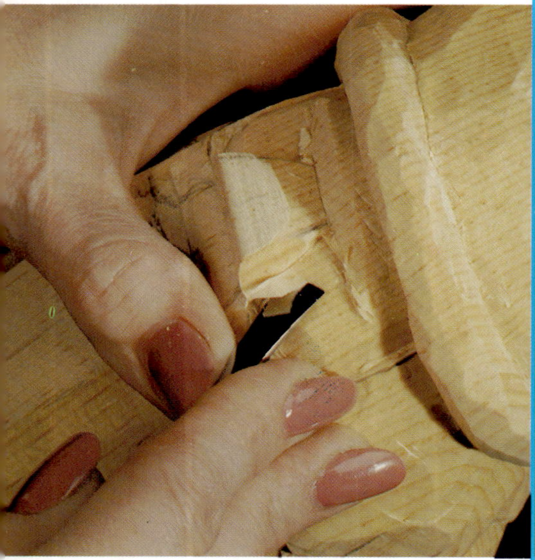

Go back and deepen the cheeks until the nose protrudes the way you want it.

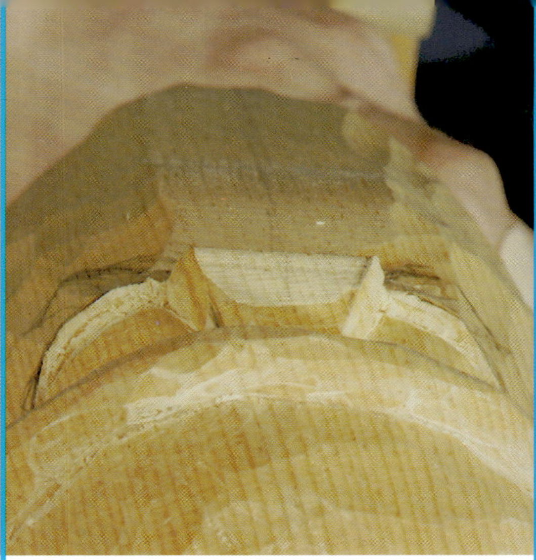

Looking from the top will help you see if the cheeks are even and of the same depth.

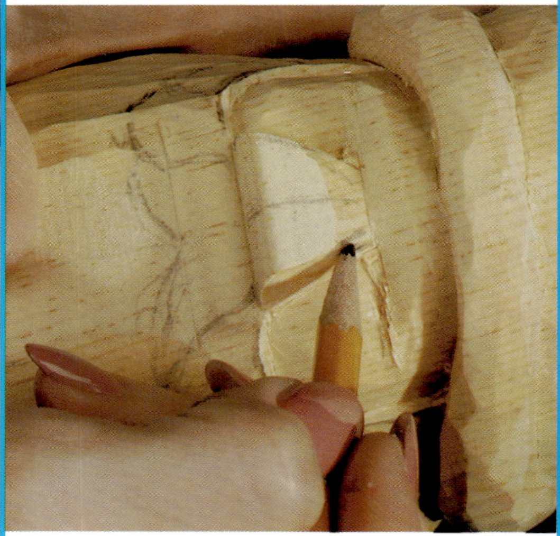

Redraw the midline of the nose. The narrowest point is at the bridge.

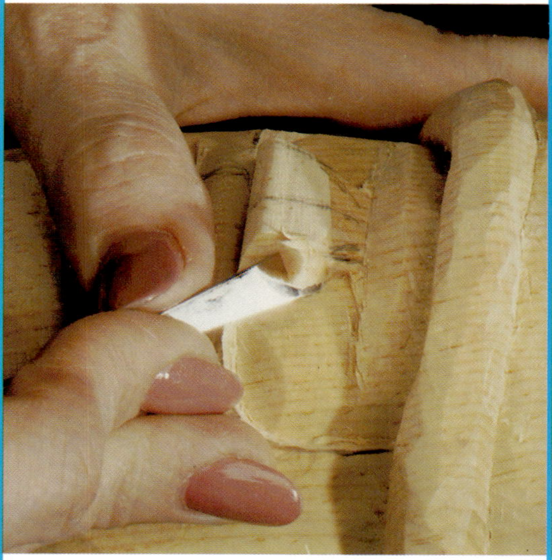

Work your way from the bottom edge of the nose to the bridge.

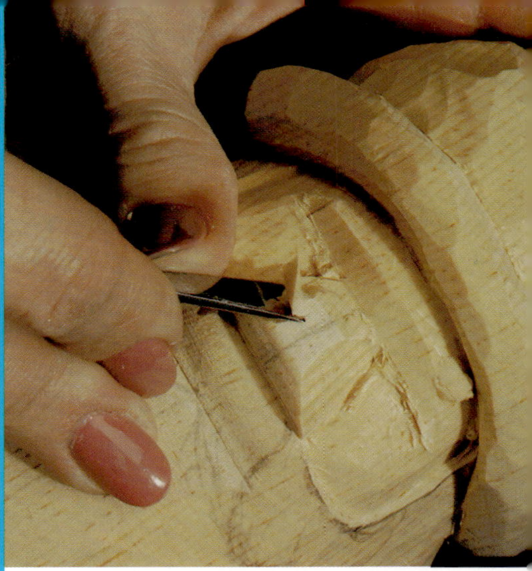

The chisel should follow the surface of the side of the nose.

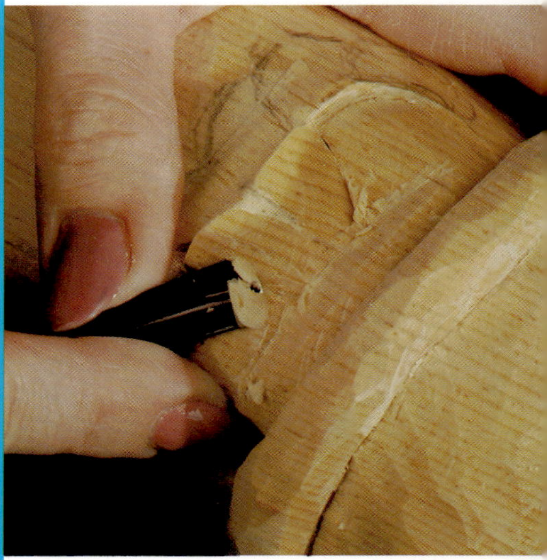

With a gouge, scoop along the line between the nose and cheek to erase the score line and soften the transition.

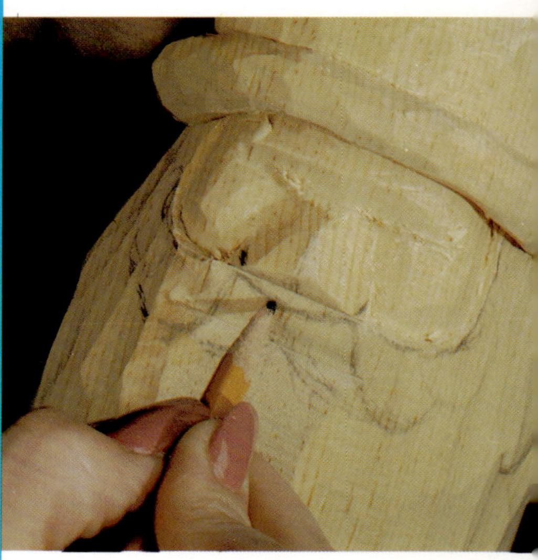

Mark the back of the nostrils and an arc under the bottom of the nose.

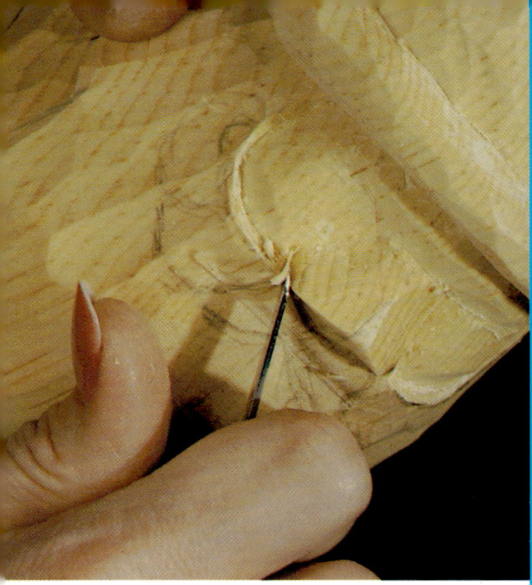

Clip off the corners of the nose...

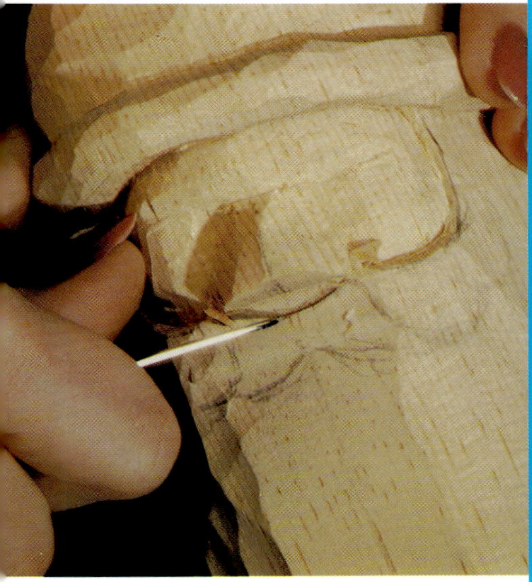

and score the line underneath.

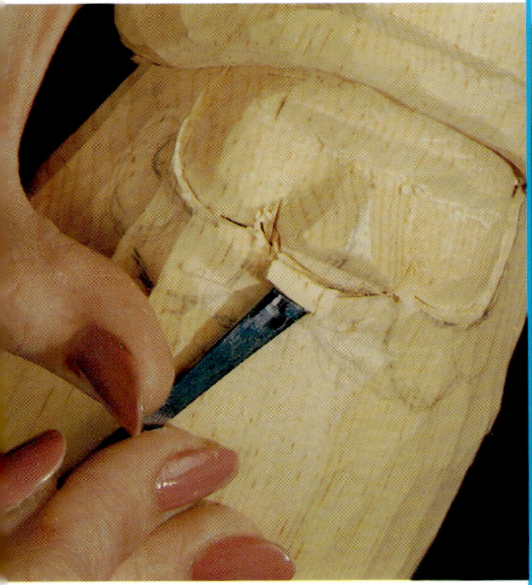

Come back to the line from the moustache, using a chisel.

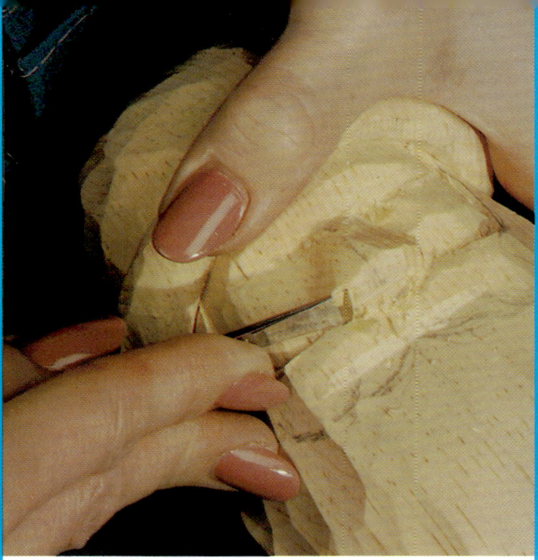

Shape the bottom of the nose, making it rounder and taking away the bandsaw marks.

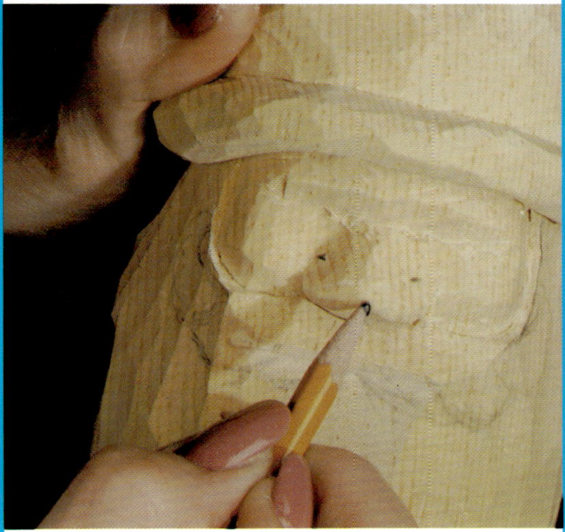

Mark the top corners of the flange of the nostril and the tip of the nose.

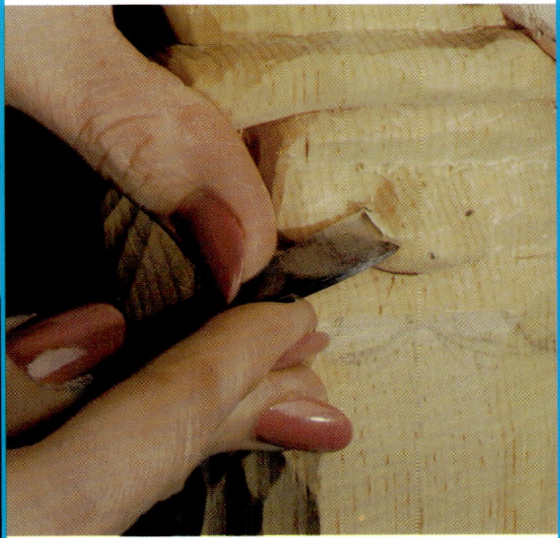

Put one corner of the chisel at the top of the flange and align the blade with the end of the nose. Push in...

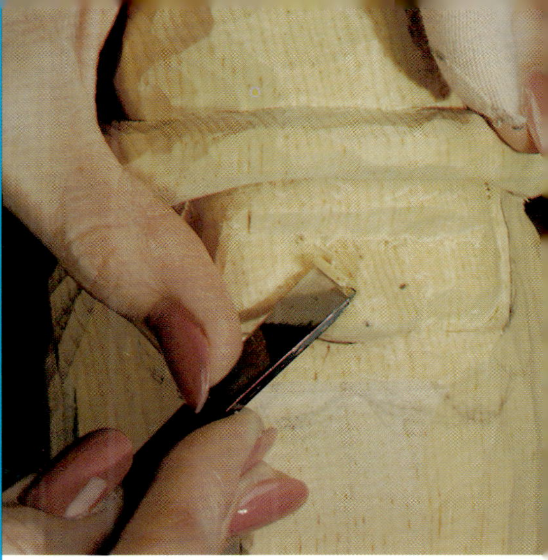

and curl up the side of the nose. Repeat on the other side.

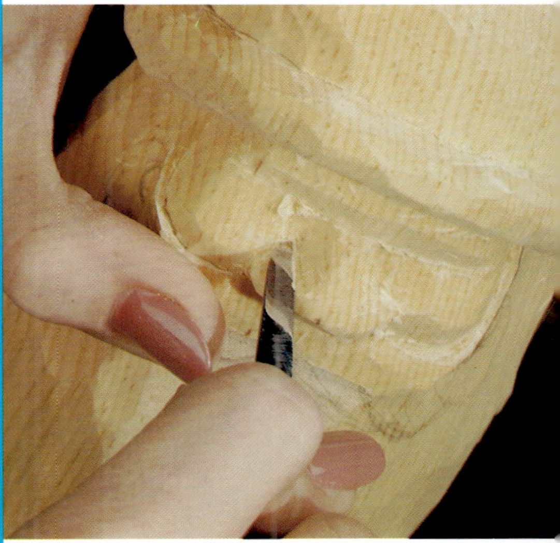

Make the nostril crease more predominate with a curl cut using the knife.

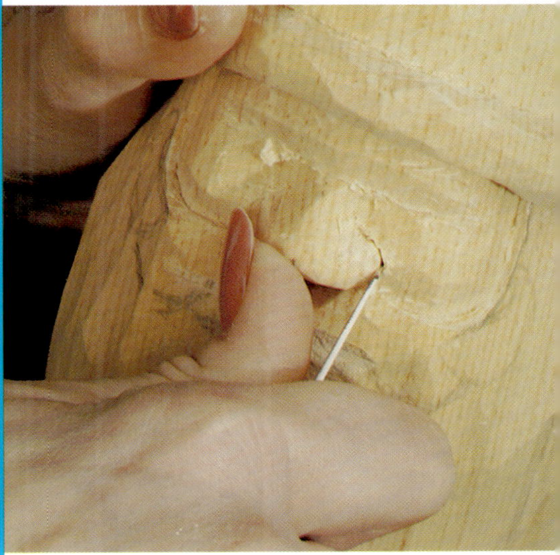

Start at the top of the nostril flange, and score around it on the cheek.

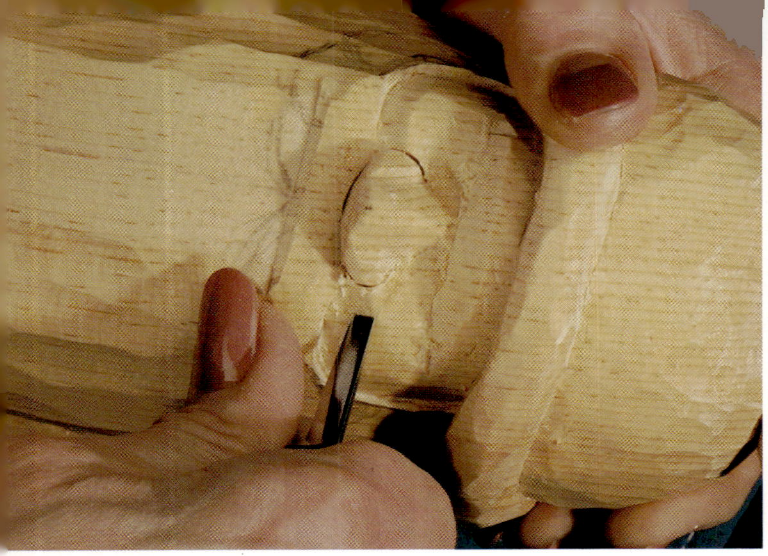

Coming from the cheek, reach back to the top of the flange and slice down the cheek.

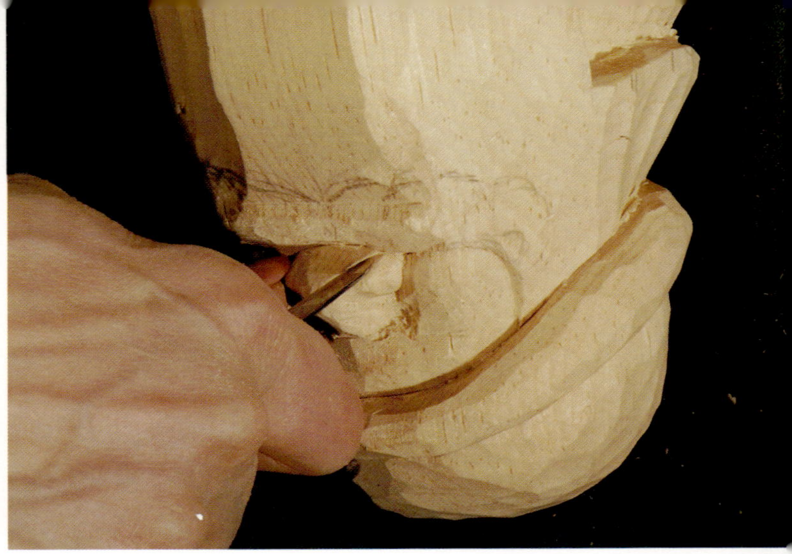

Scoop out the nostril.

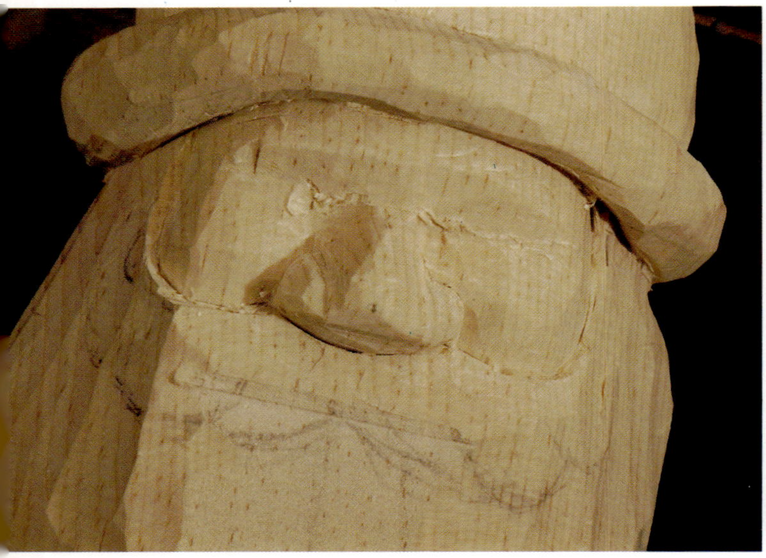

This raises the cheek and creates a smile.

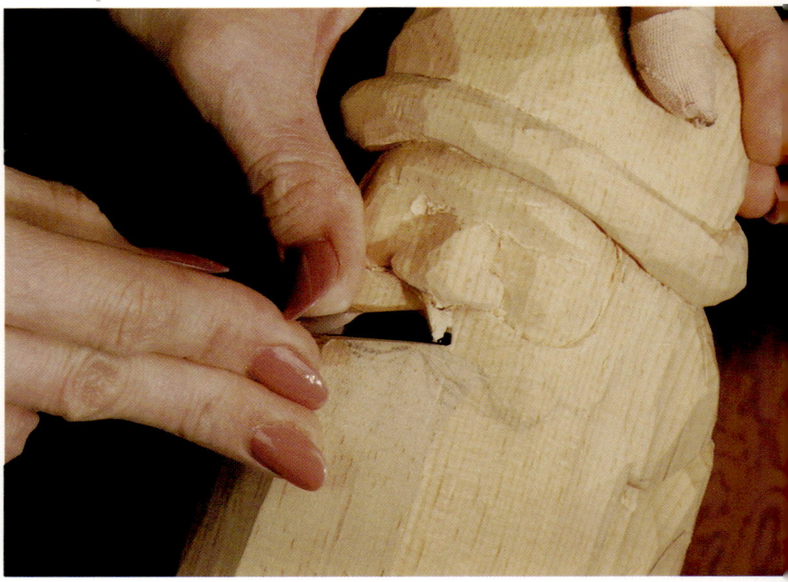

Clean up the moustache under the nose.

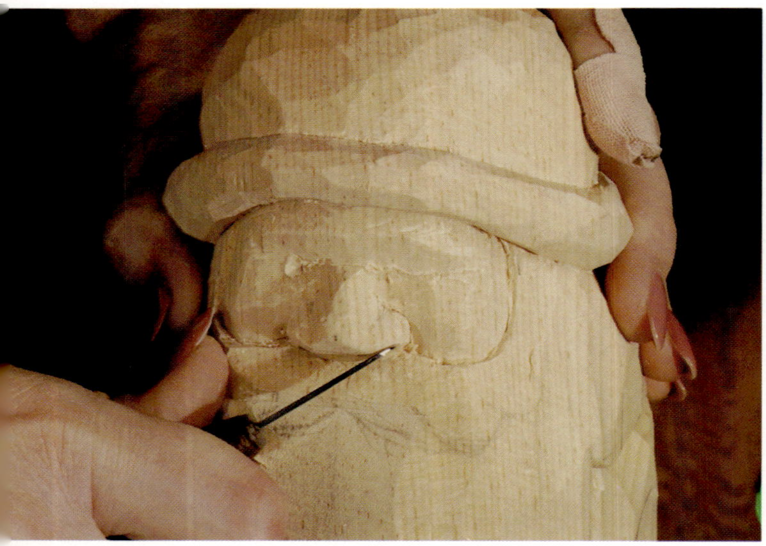

Trim the underside of the nostrils so they come up higher than the center of the nose.

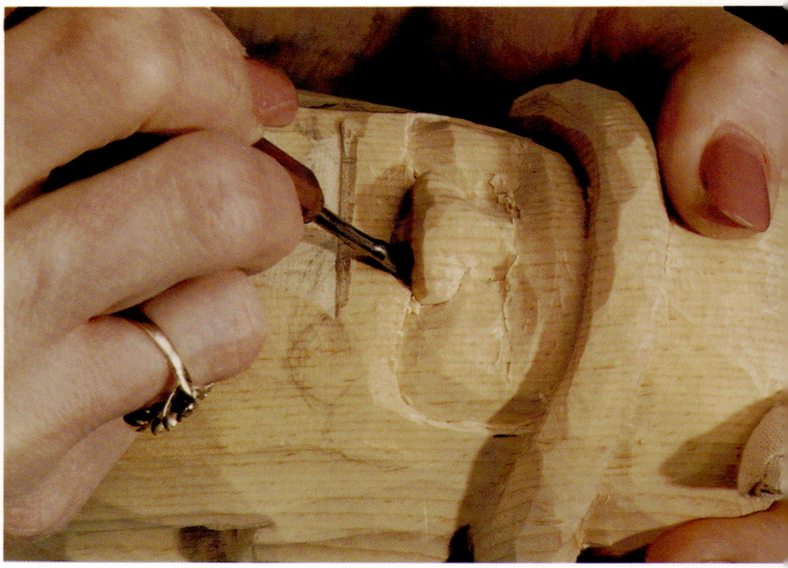

A micro gouge will deepen the nostril and accentuate it.

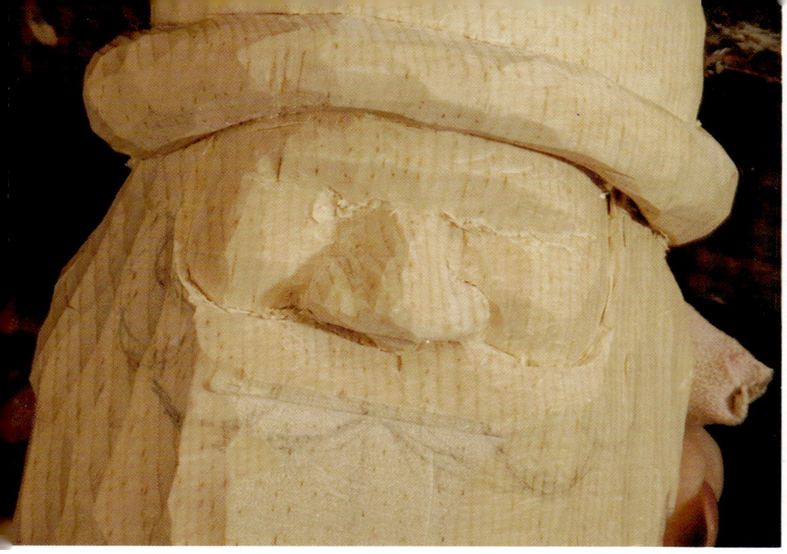

Progress on the face.

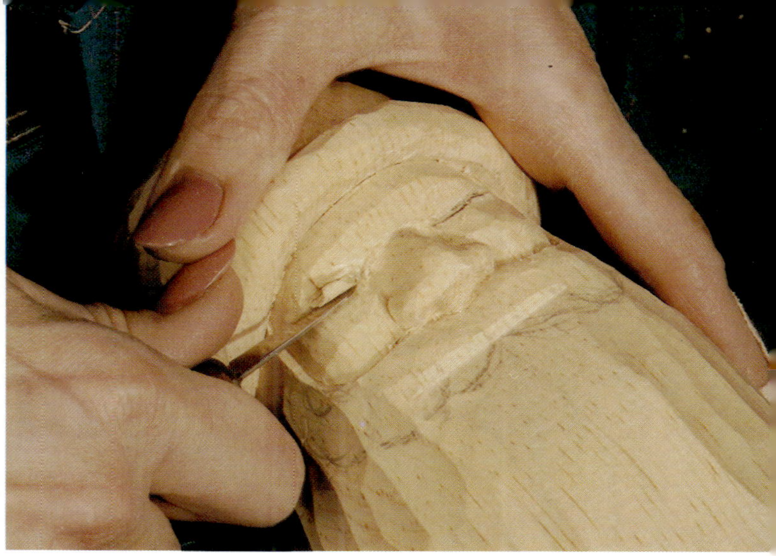

then up from the cheek.

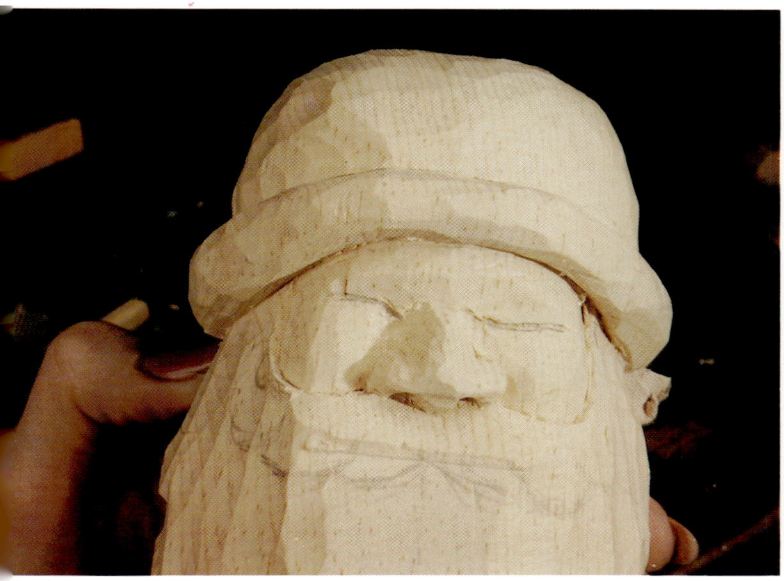

By drawing in the eye lines you can easily see that one of them needs to be straightened.

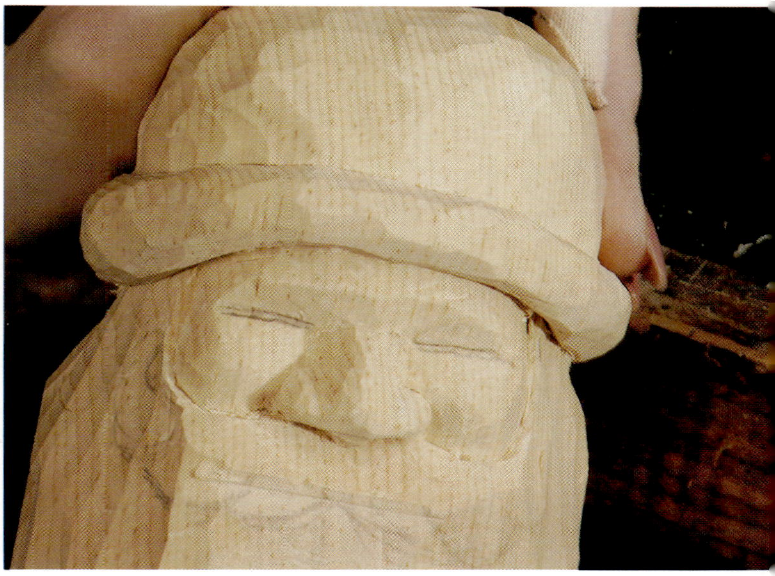

That's much better.

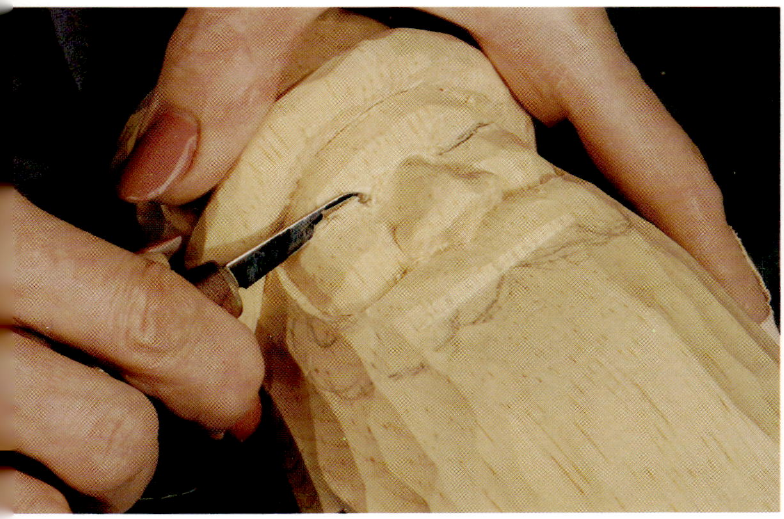

I'll fix the problem by lowering the right side. First I cut down from the brow...

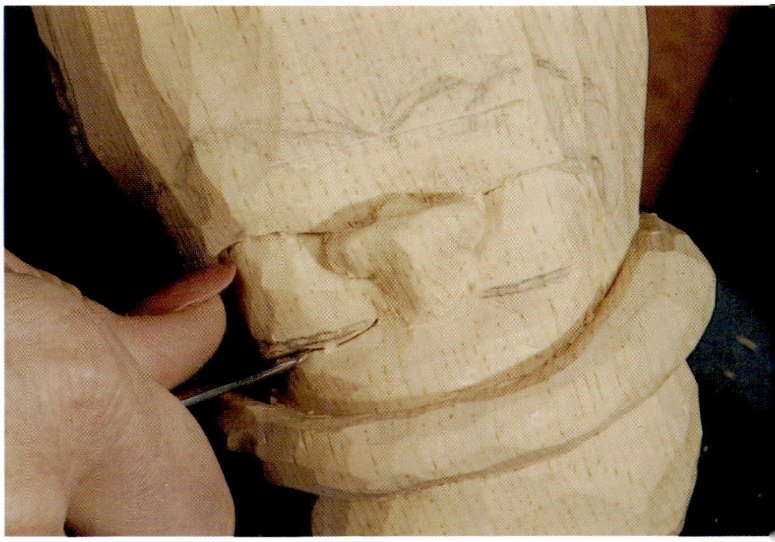

Start at the inside corner and score a crescent above the line of the eye to the outside corner.

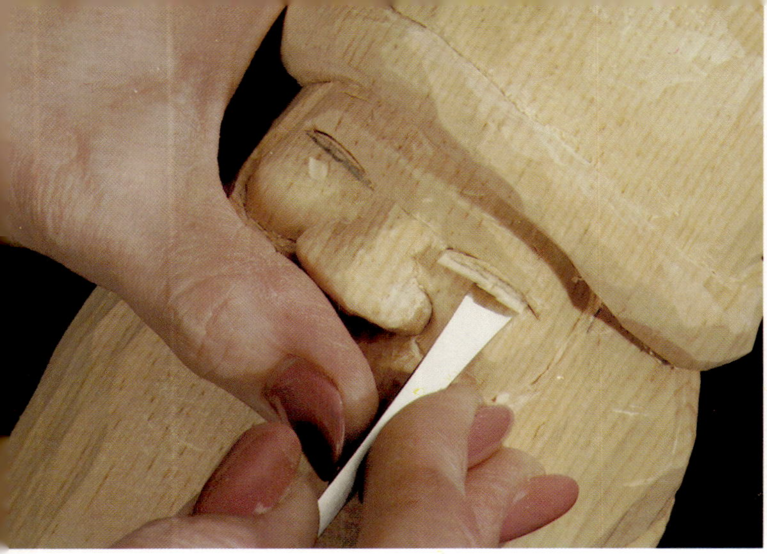

Chisel up to the line from the cheek.

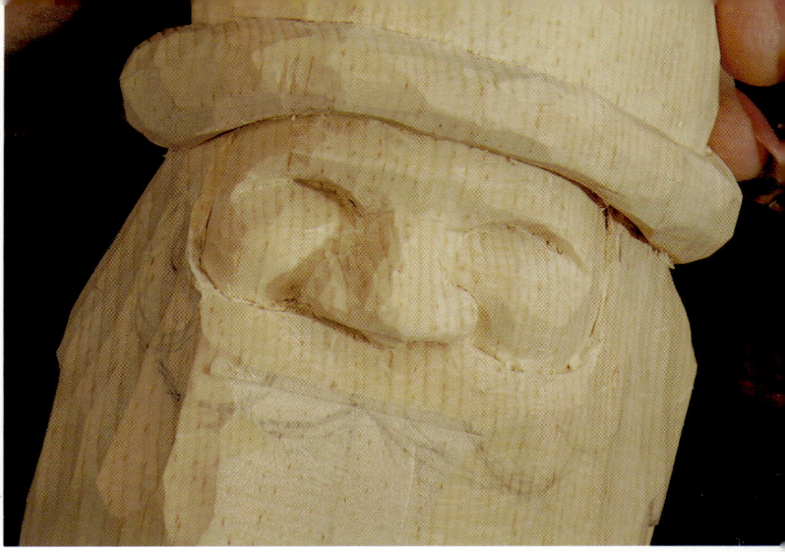

Do the other side to match. Soften all the ridges and knife marks.

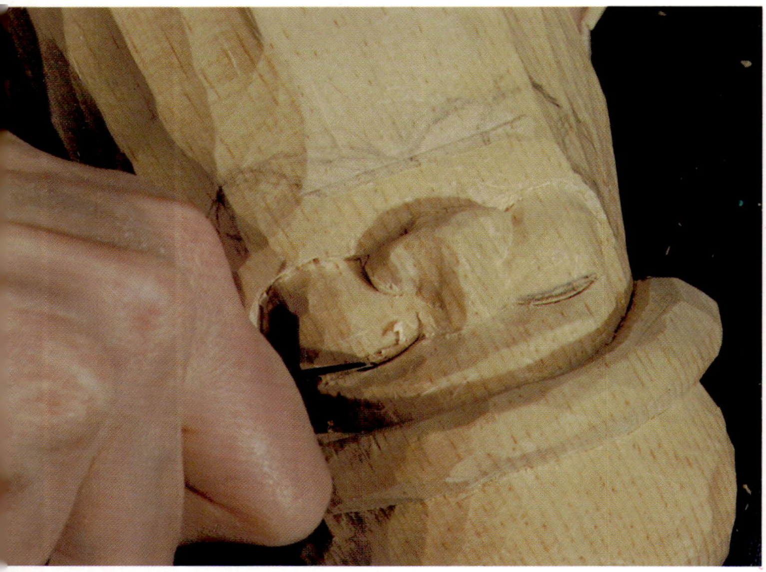

Repeat the process, arc...

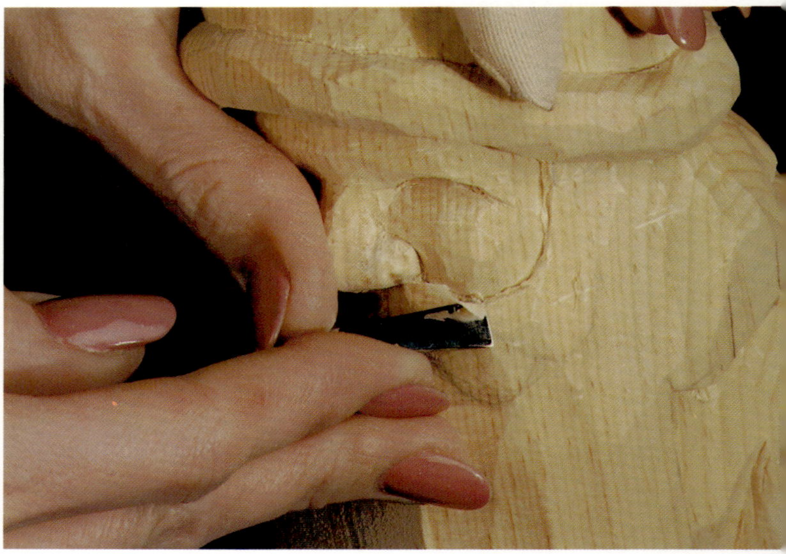

Round the moustache...

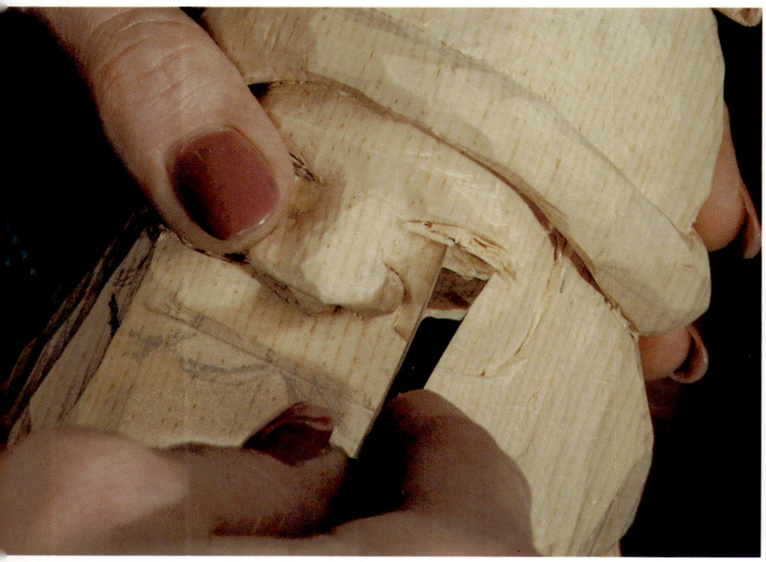

and trim.

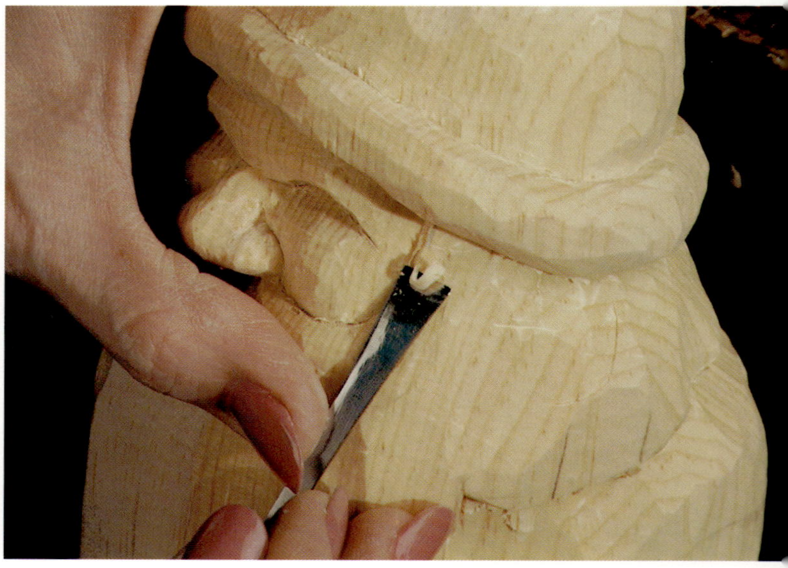

and hair line to the cheek.

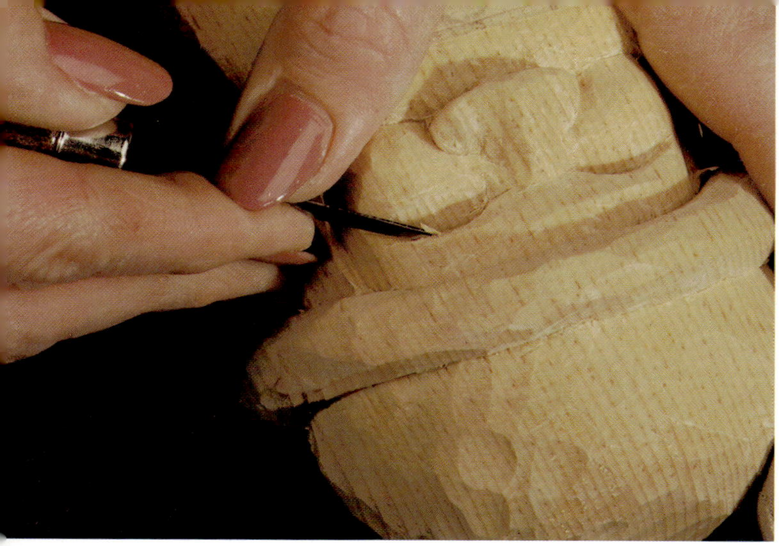

With a micro v-tool run a wrinkle over the eye...

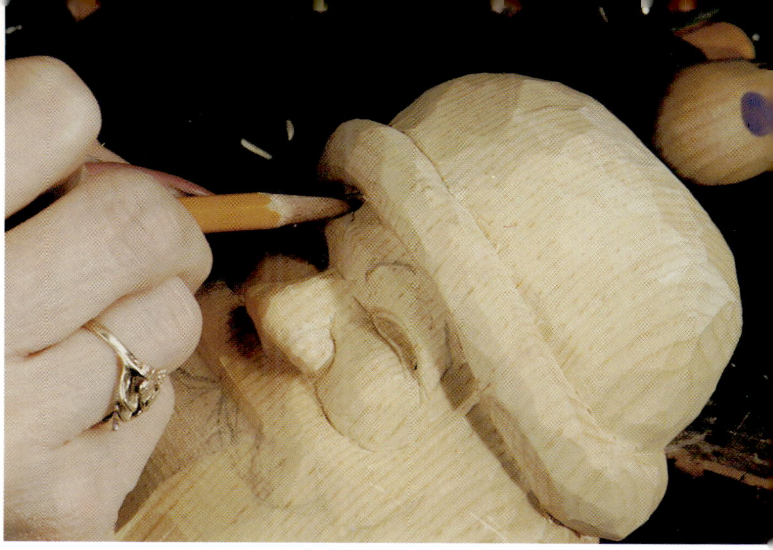

Draw in eyebrows running up under the hat.

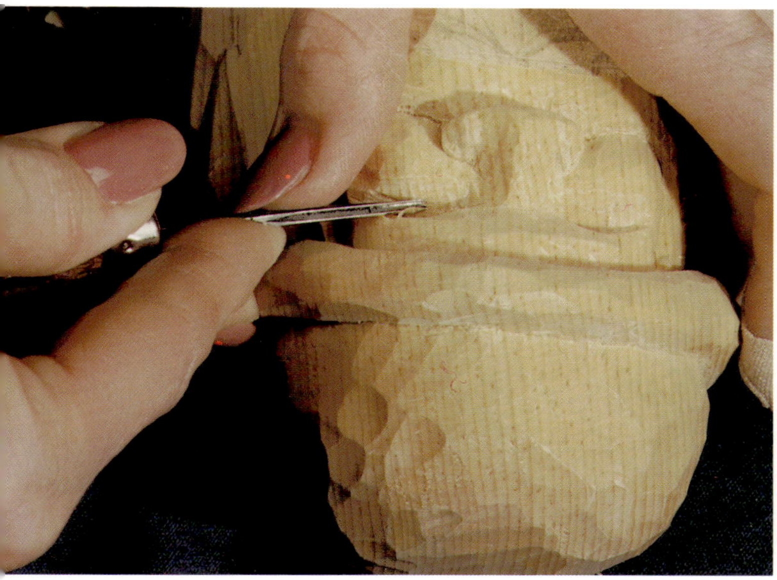

and one under. These character lines will be accentuated with the antiquing finish.

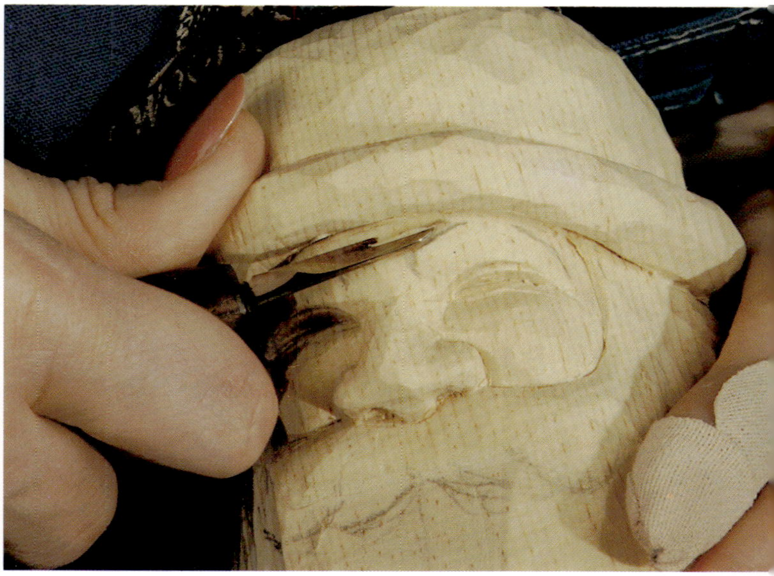

Starting with the knife on the line you drew, scoop out into the forehead to bring out the eyebrow.

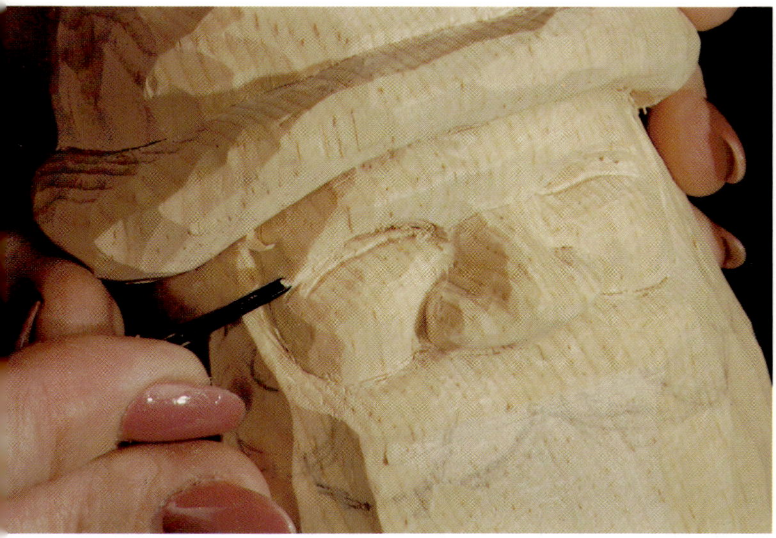

Add some crow's feet at the side.

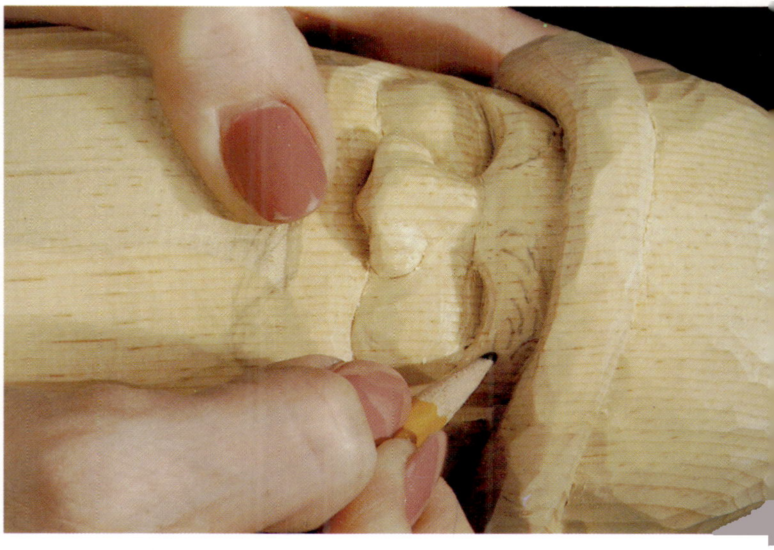

The lines of the eyebrow hair go up and out.

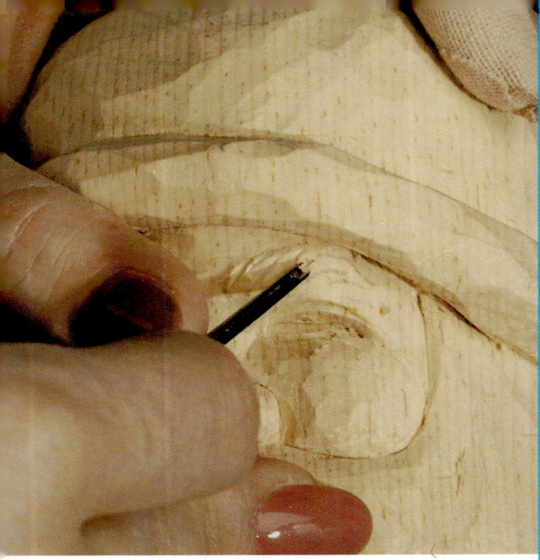

Create the eyebrow hair with the micro v-tool.

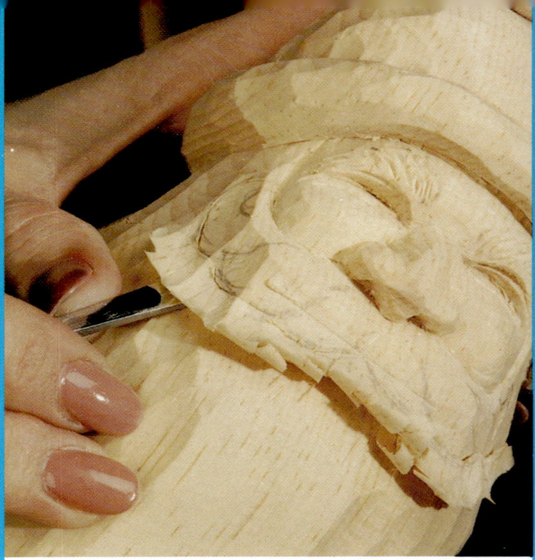

Cut back to it from the beard.

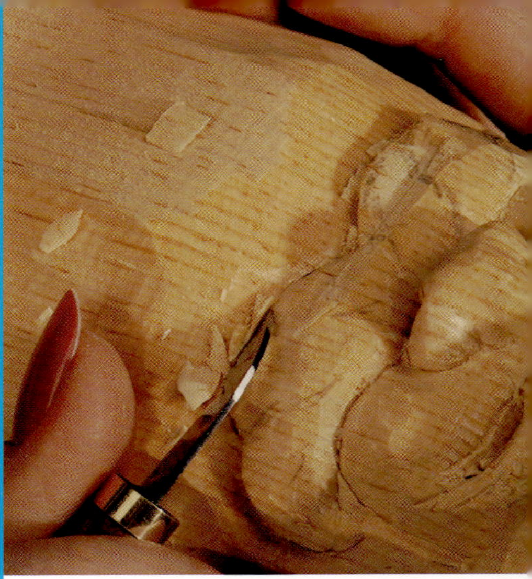

Round the moustache down to give it some shape.

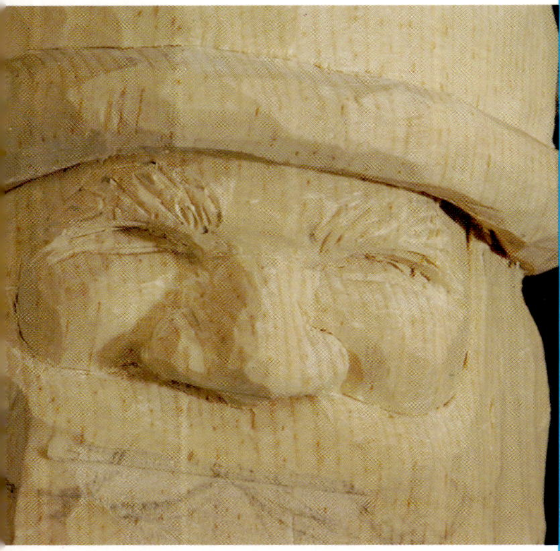

The result.

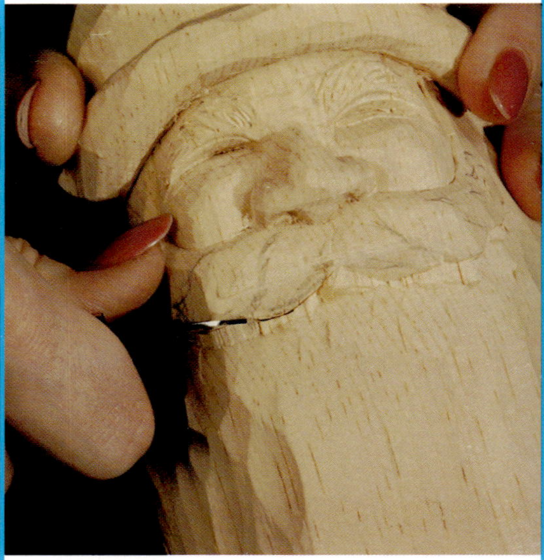

Repeat the process to take it deeper.

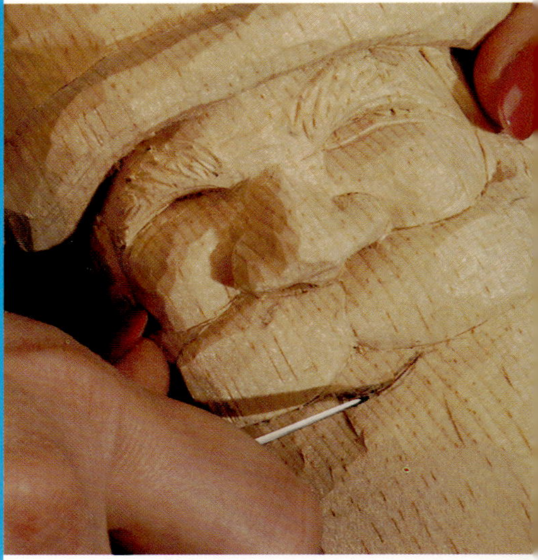

Draw and score the line of the lip.

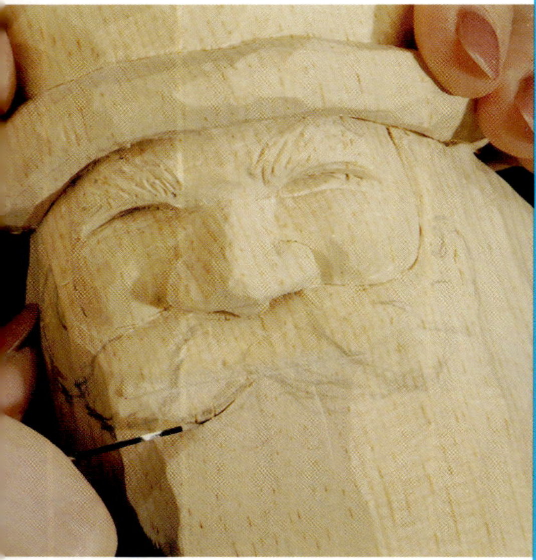

Redraw the moustache and score the lines.

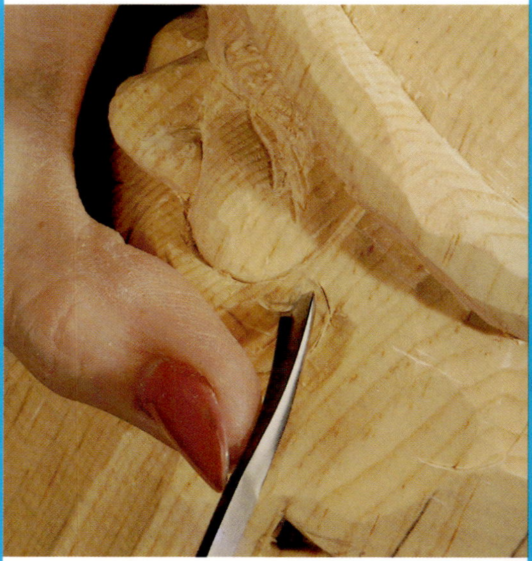

By rolling a curved gouge you get the curl at the end of the moustache.

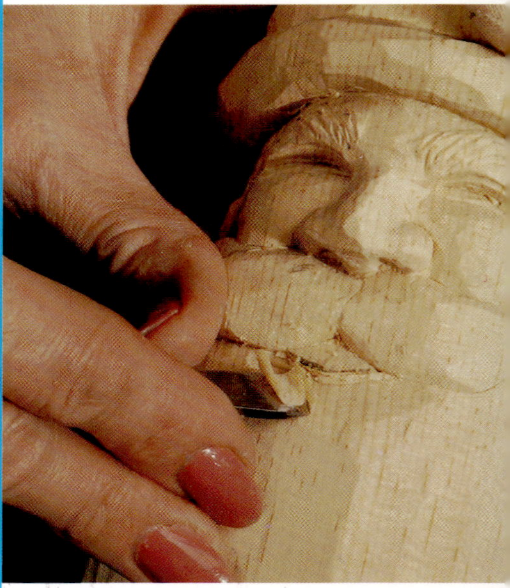

Trim back to it from the beard.

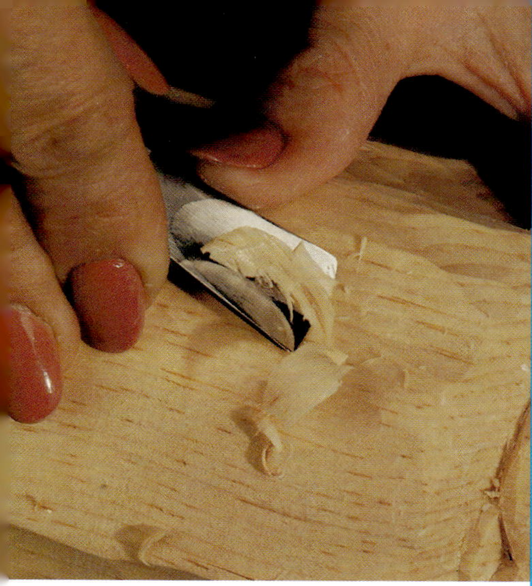

Shape the beard. It should come in a little under the chin. Remember to go with the grain or the wood will tear.

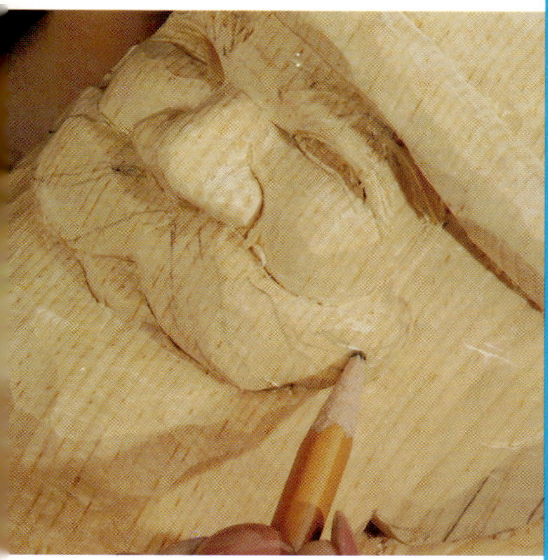

Referring to the pattern, redraw the hairlines of the moustache...

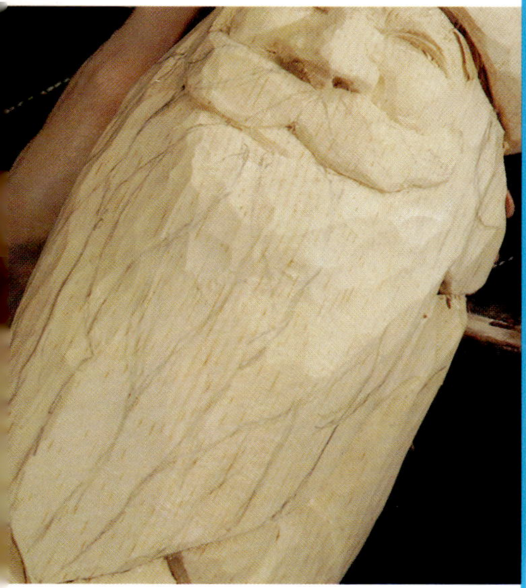

and the beard.

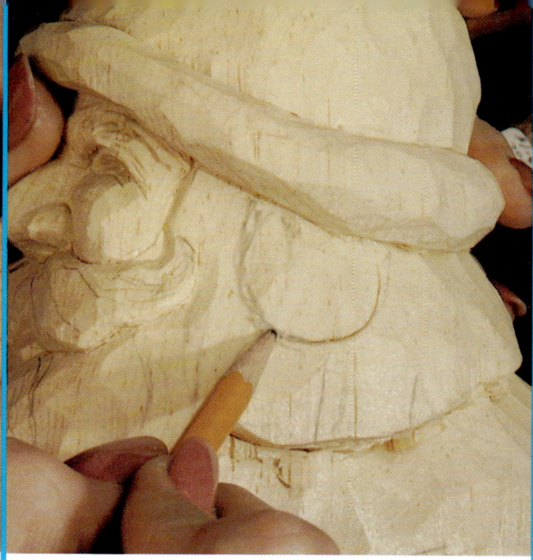

Redraw the earflaps.

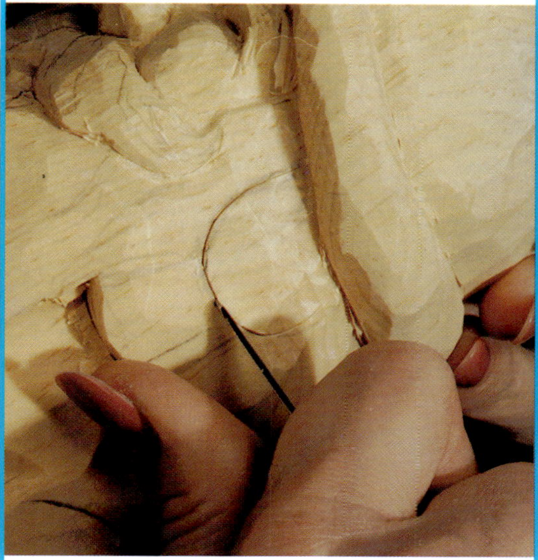

Score the lines of the earflaps.

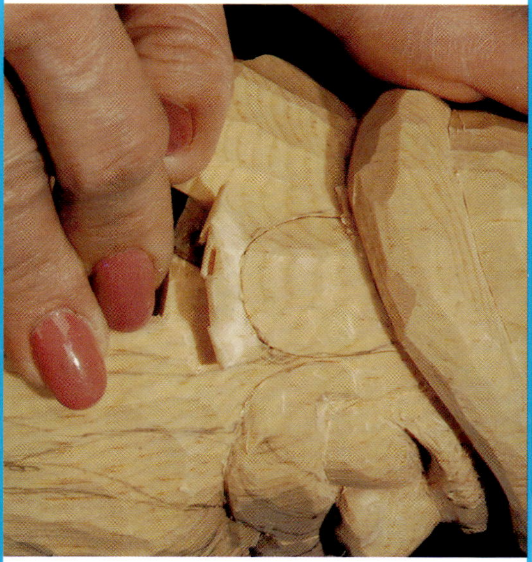

Trim back from the hair. These do not need to be real deep.

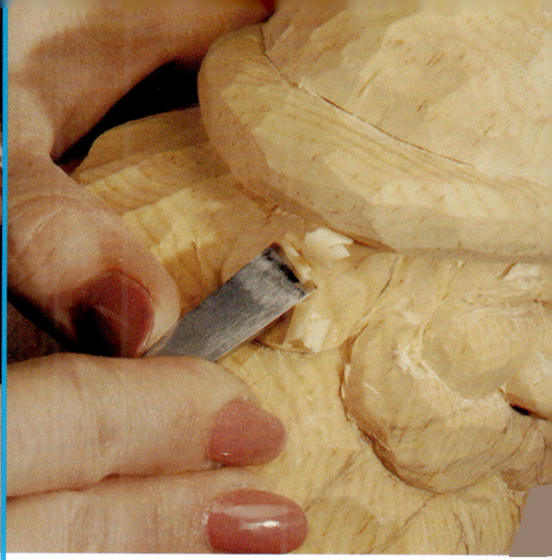

For decorative painting the flap need to be fairly flat. Smooth it out with a chisel.

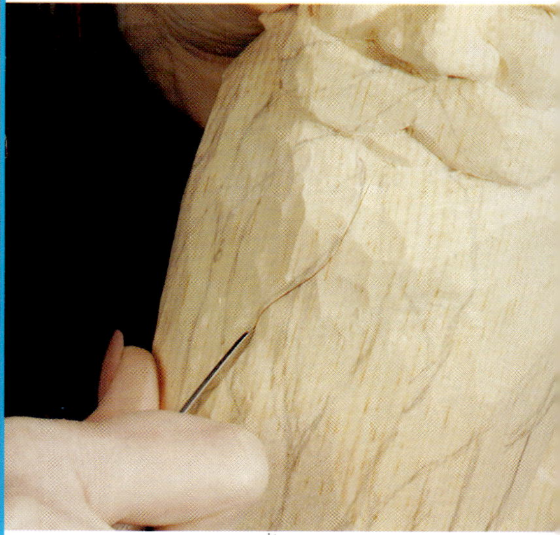

Score around the uppermost lock of beard.

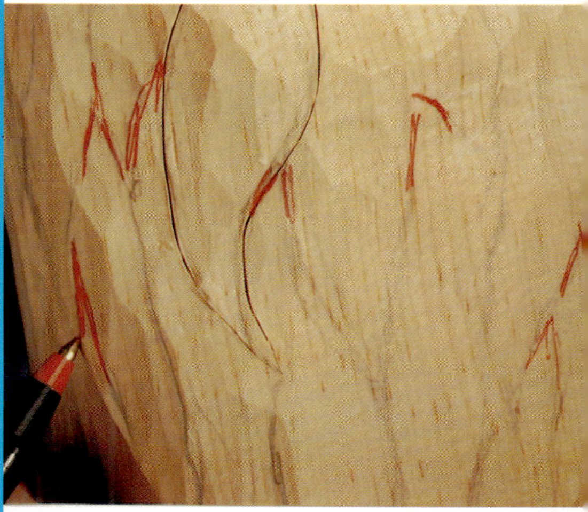

The corners marked in red will be extra deep because they go through more than one level. The depth at the end of a lock will be much shallower. This helps keep dimensionality in the wood.

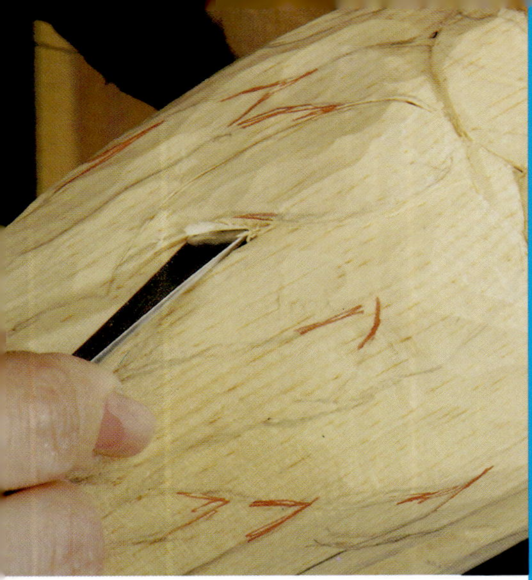

Cut stops in the corners and come back into them with a skew chisel.

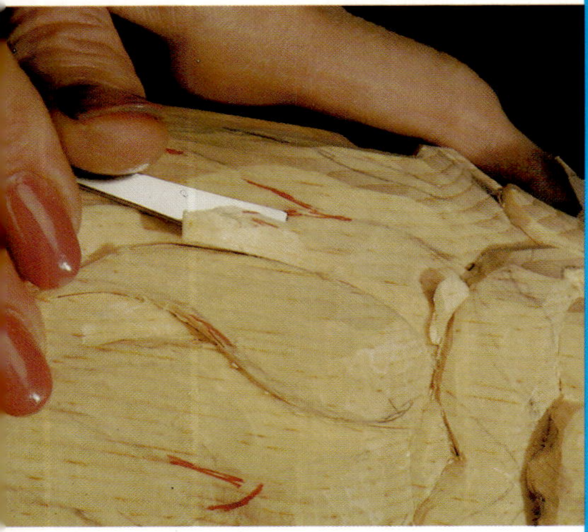

Continue to go around the lock. I generally do one lock at a time, bringing them out the first time around, then going back and shaping them.

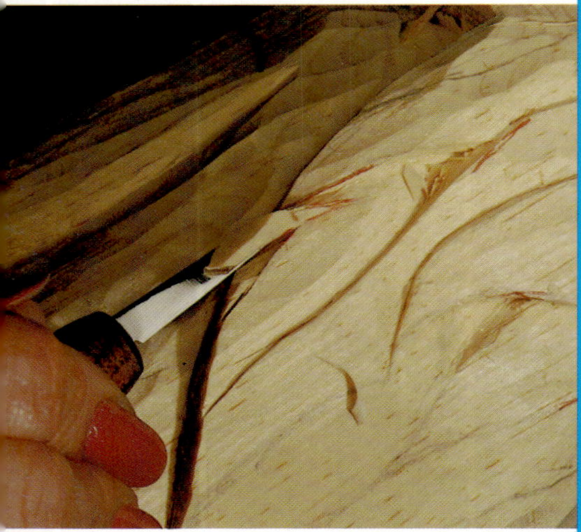

Along the edge you will want to break up the smooth line with a few locks coming into the line.

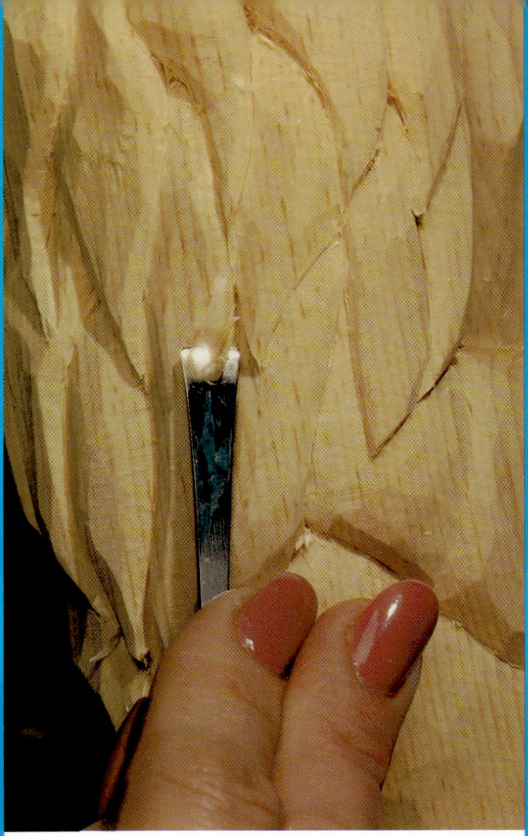

When the locks are defined, go back and round them off a little.

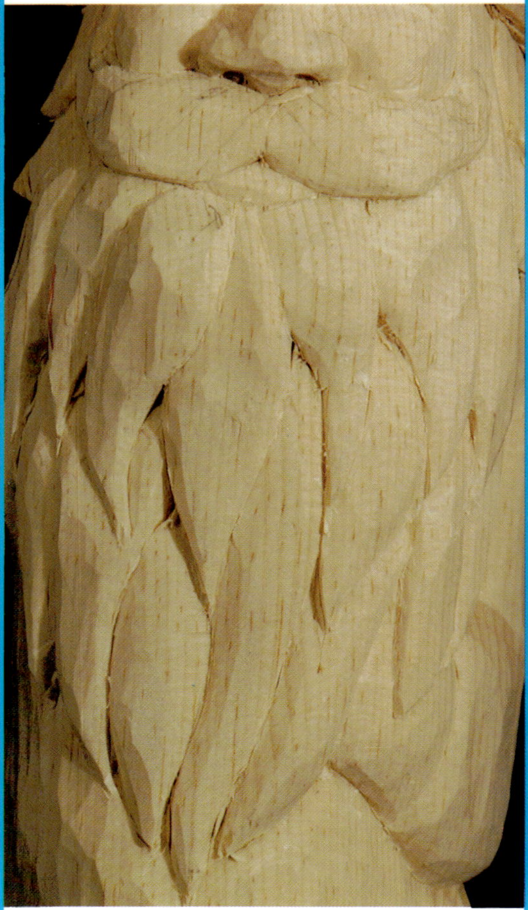

Progress.

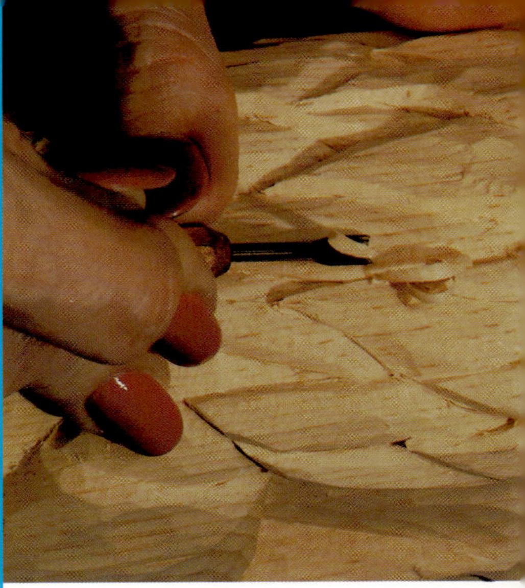

With a small gouge randomly add some texture lines to the beard.

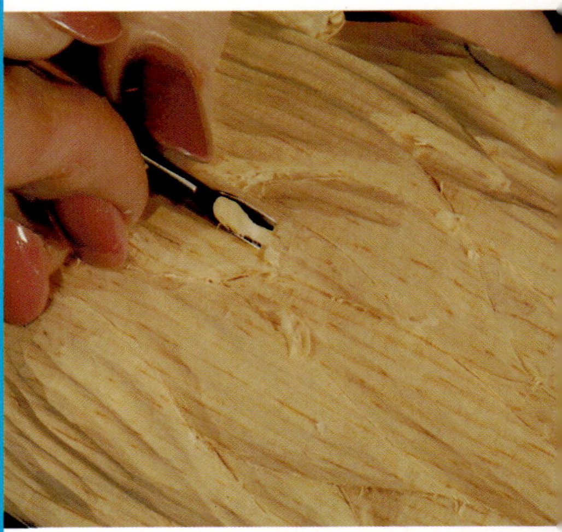

Continue up the beard.

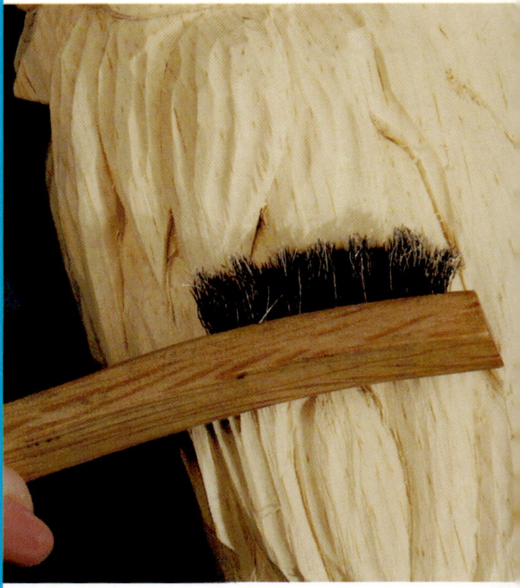

A light wire brushing will pop out the loose bits of wood.

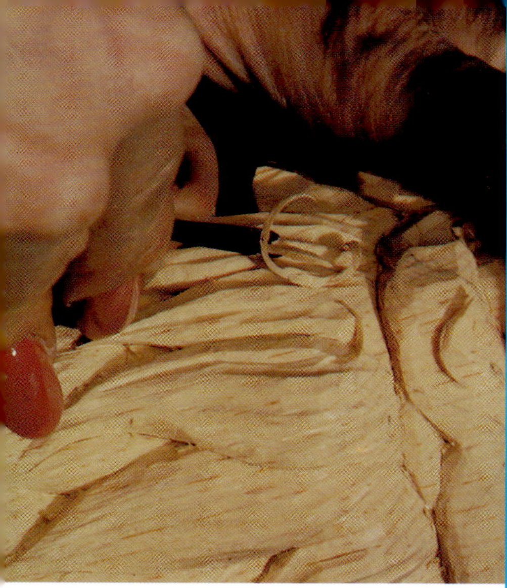

A little more detail can be added with the v-gouge.

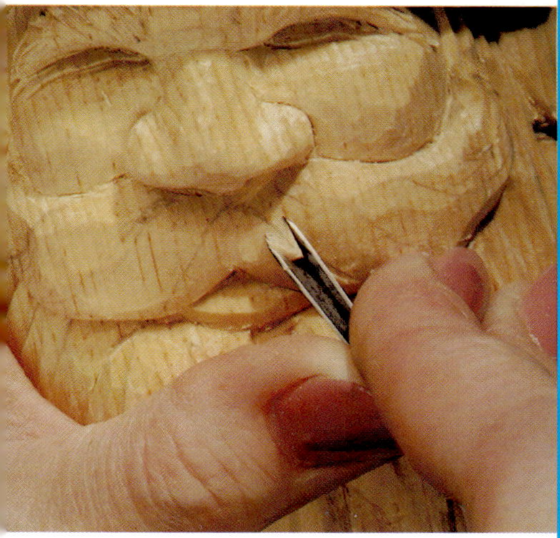

Make fairly deep v-tool cuts on the lines of the moustache.

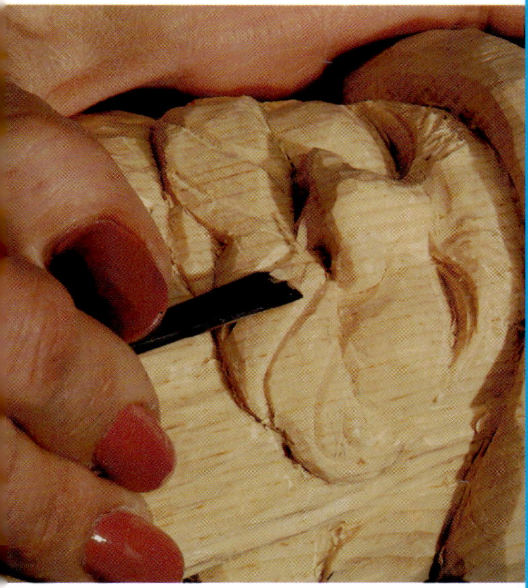

Shape the segments of the moustache with the straight chisel.

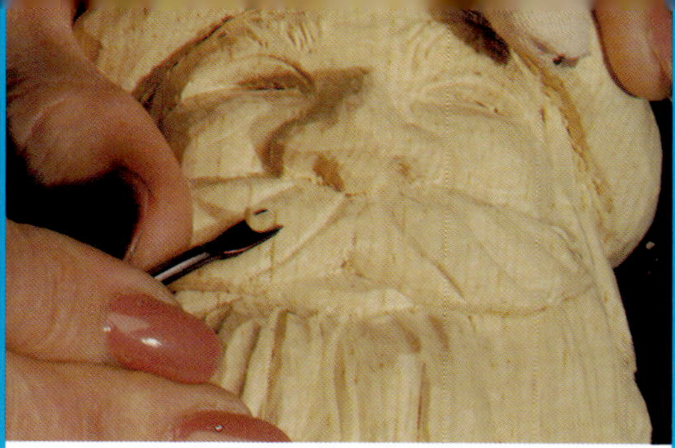

Add texture with the small gouge.

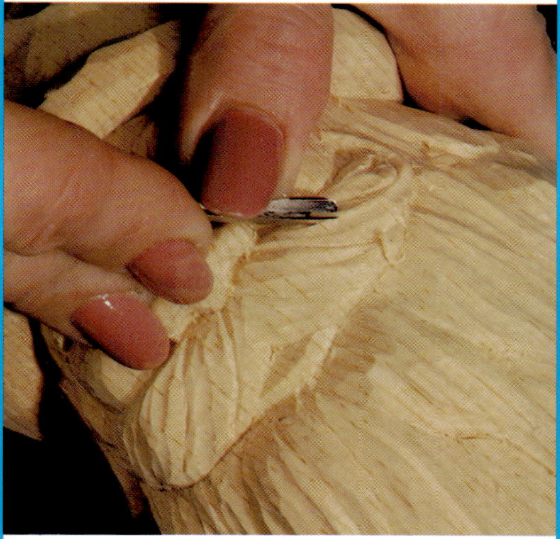

Finally create some detail with light v-tool cuts.

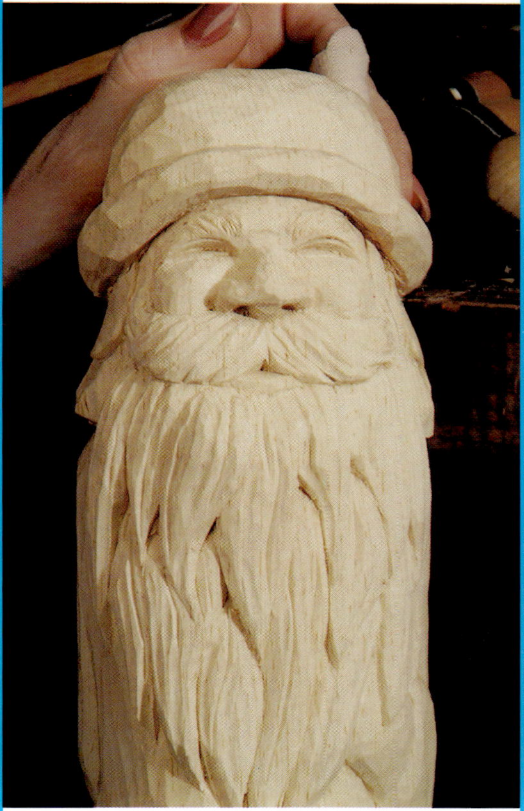

Progress.

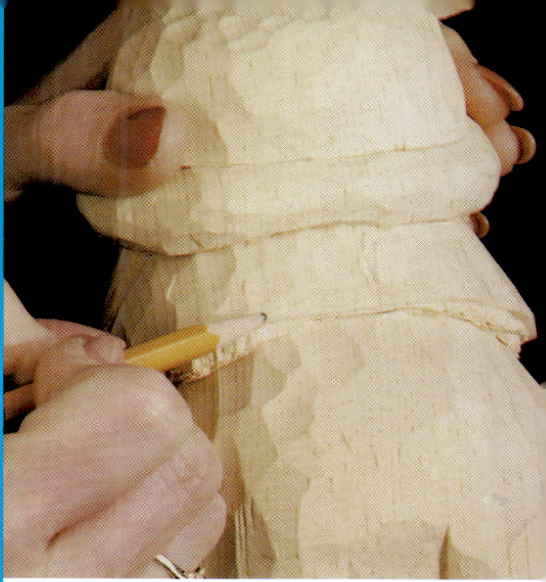

Draw in the main lines of the hair.

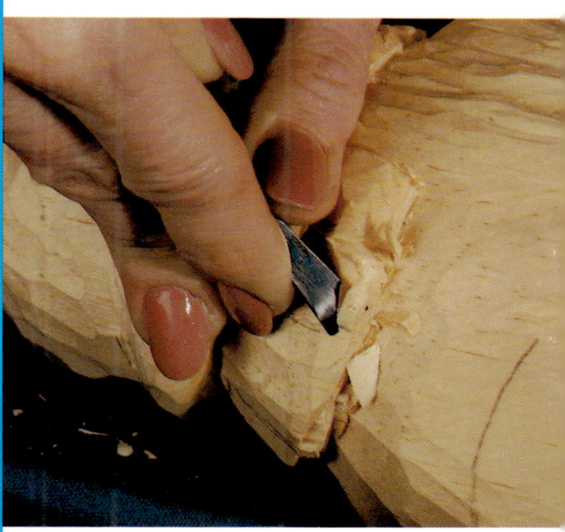

Round the bottom of the hair with a chisel.

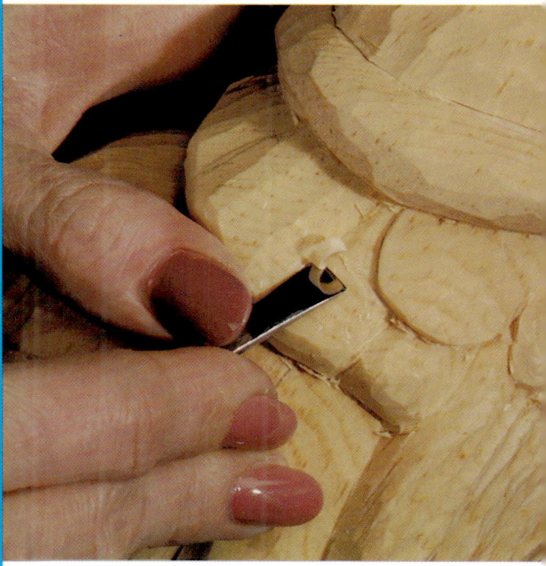

Use the chisel to wedge out some locks of hair and round them over.

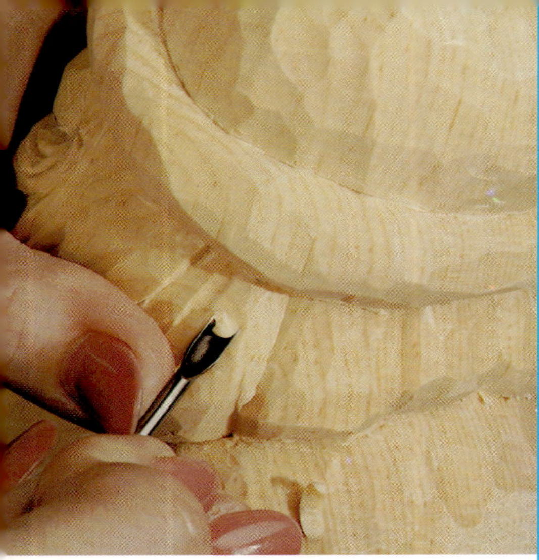

Add detail with the gouge.

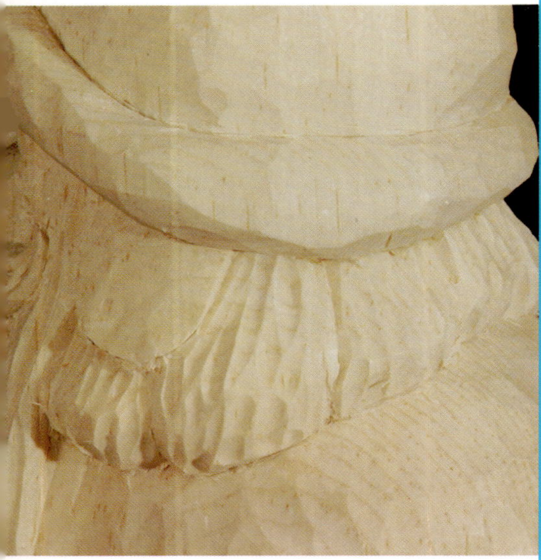

The result.

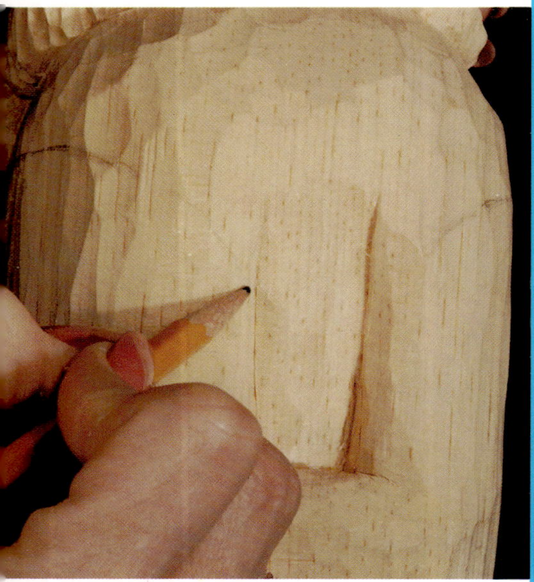

Draw the sleeves...

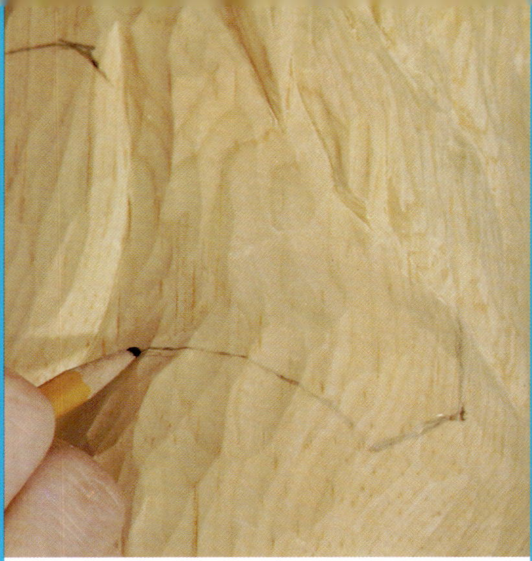

and bottom of the vest.

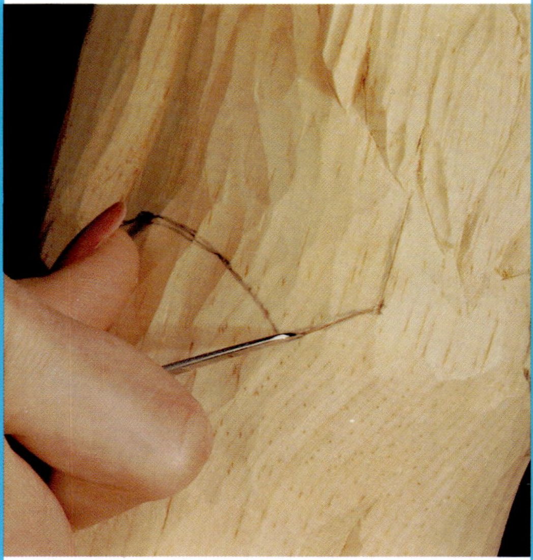

Cut shallow scores on the lines...

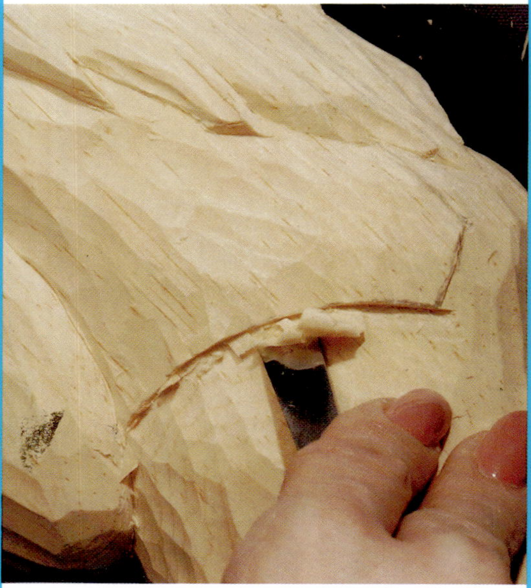

and chisel back to them from below.

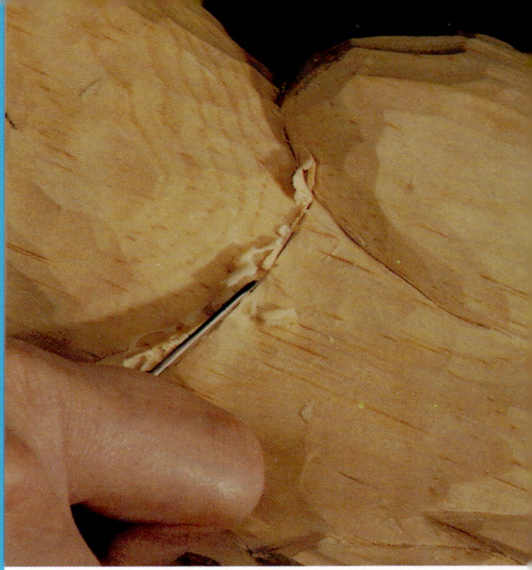

Clean things up with a knife.

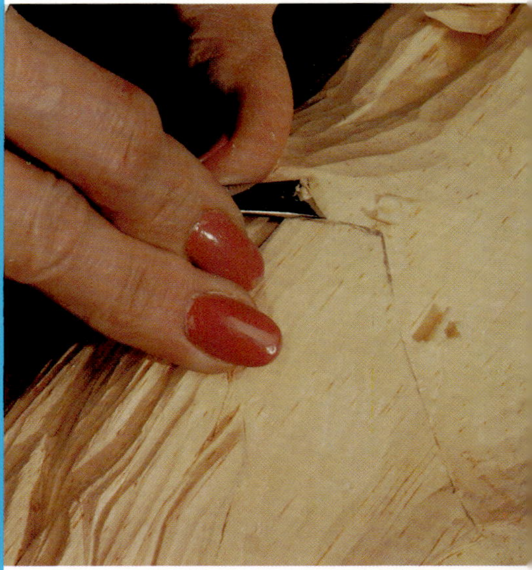

You may need to do some shaping to make things look right.

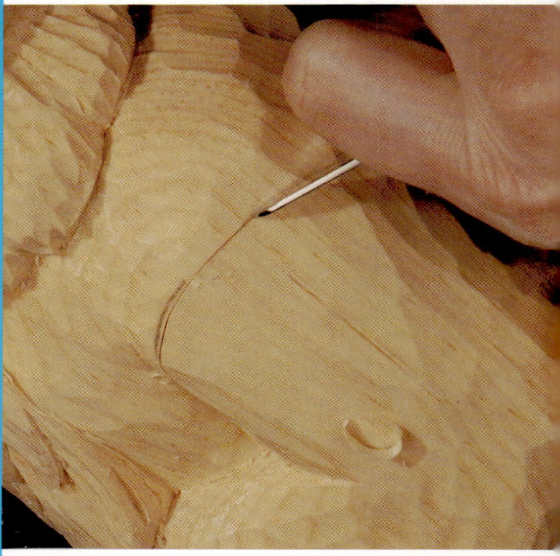

Do the same thing at the shoulders. The edges around the vest should stay nice and crisp.

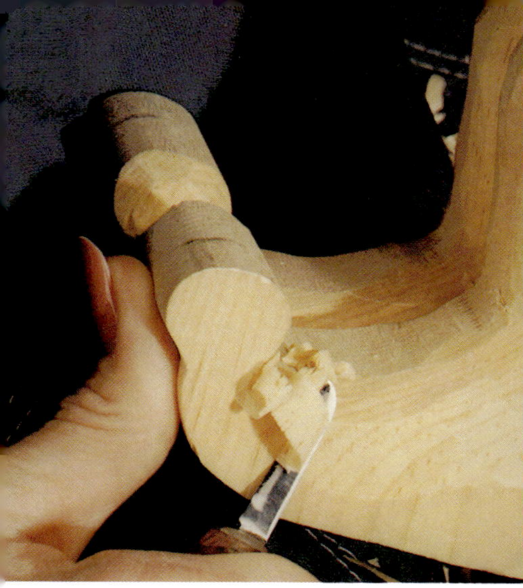

Return to the shoes and begin rounding off the top.

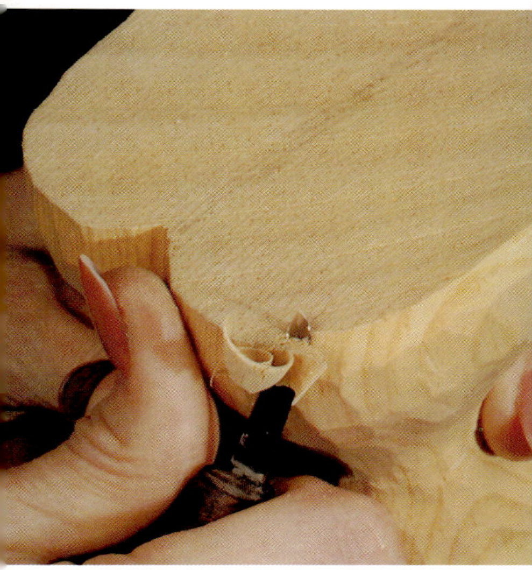

Knock off the edge of the soles.

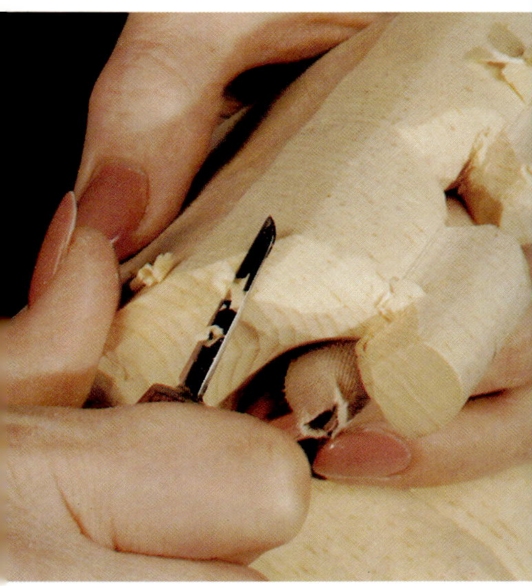

Begin to round the toe. The underside of the toe can be rounded more than the sole was.

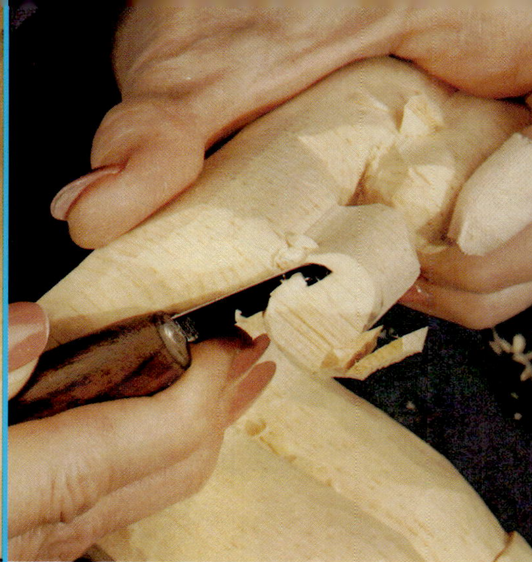

Knock off the sides of the pom-pom.

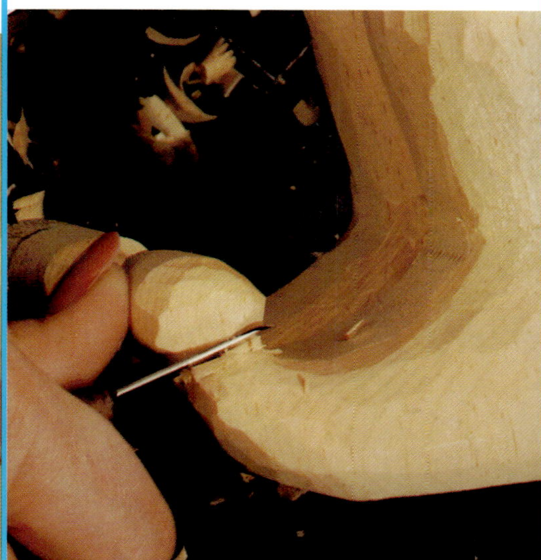

Start shaping the pom-pom to round.

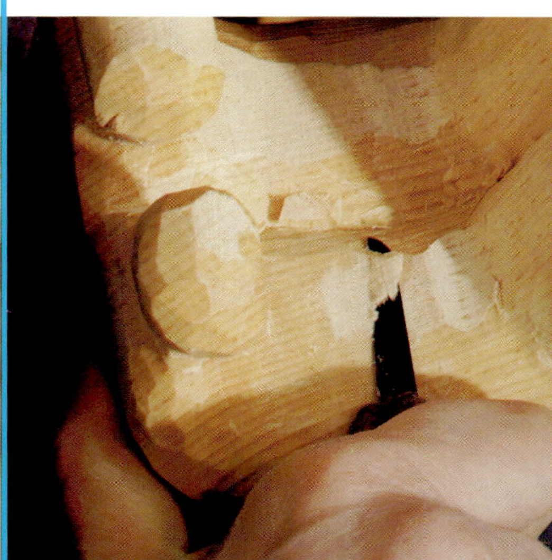

Continue to shape the shoes and the pom-poms until you are satisfied with the result.

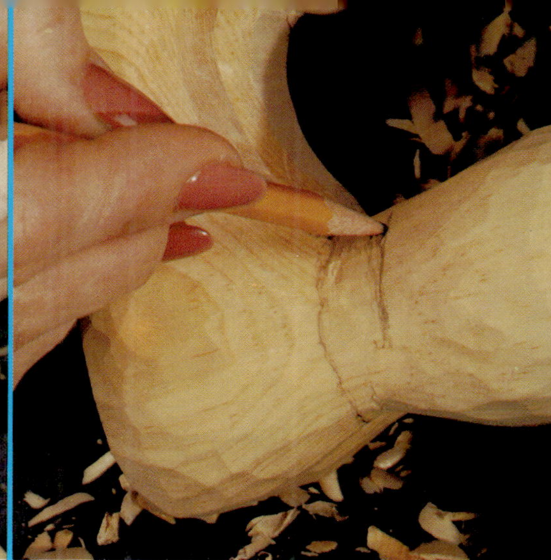

Draw in the band at the top of the shoe.

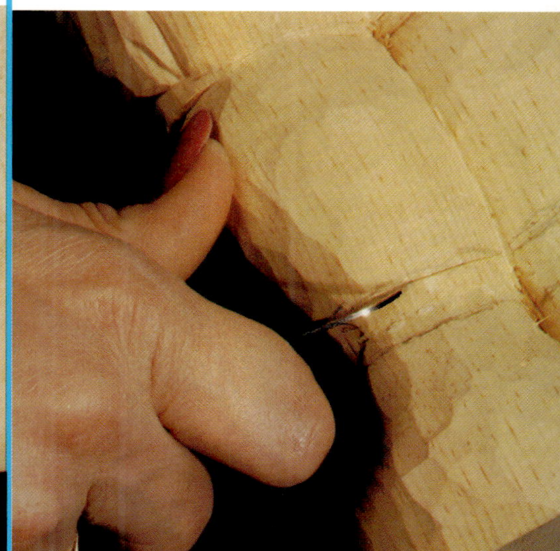

Score around the band, above and below.

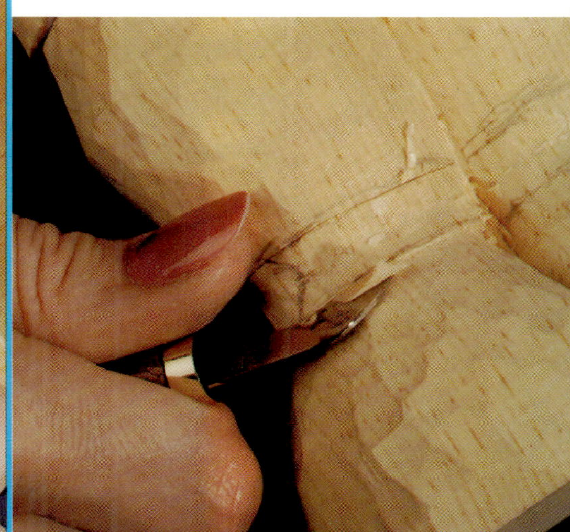

Trim back to it all around. This is a thin piece of leather, and, like the clothing, is a shallow cut.

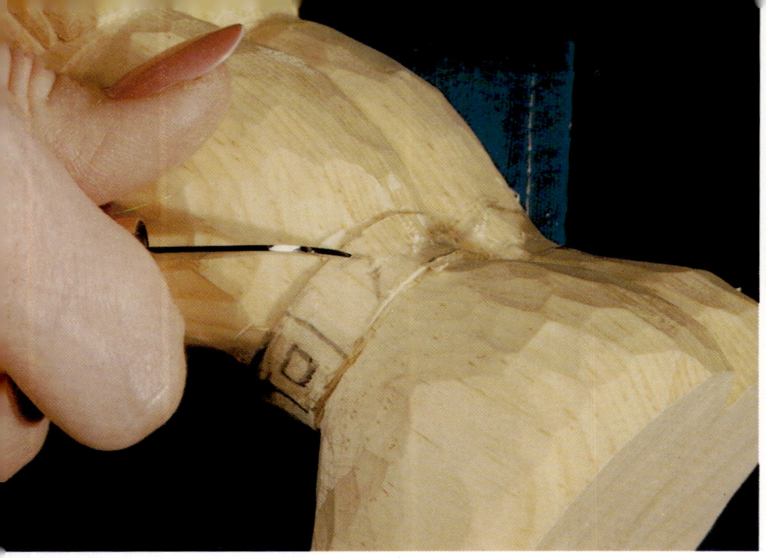

Score the ends of the bands...

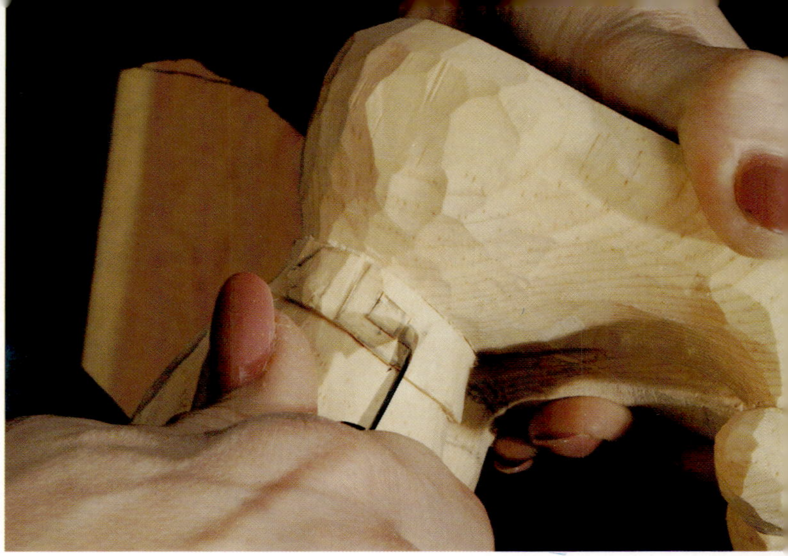

Score around the inside of the buckle...

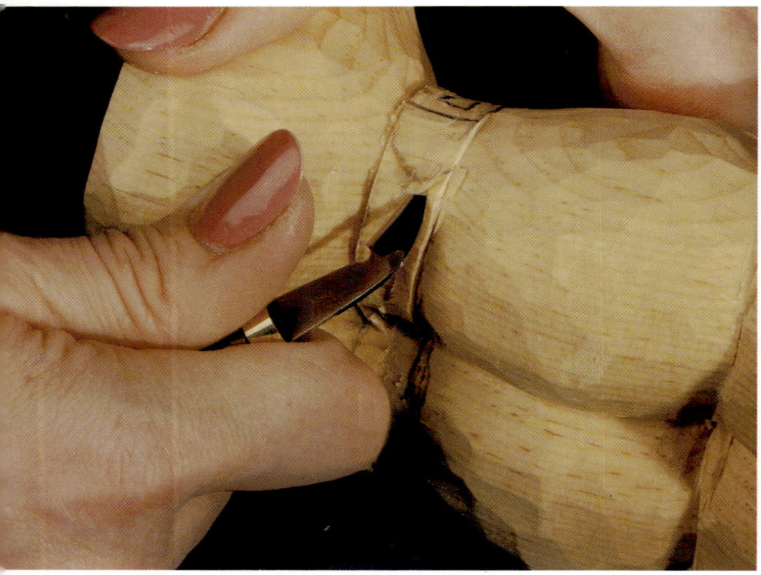

and trim back to them from the band.

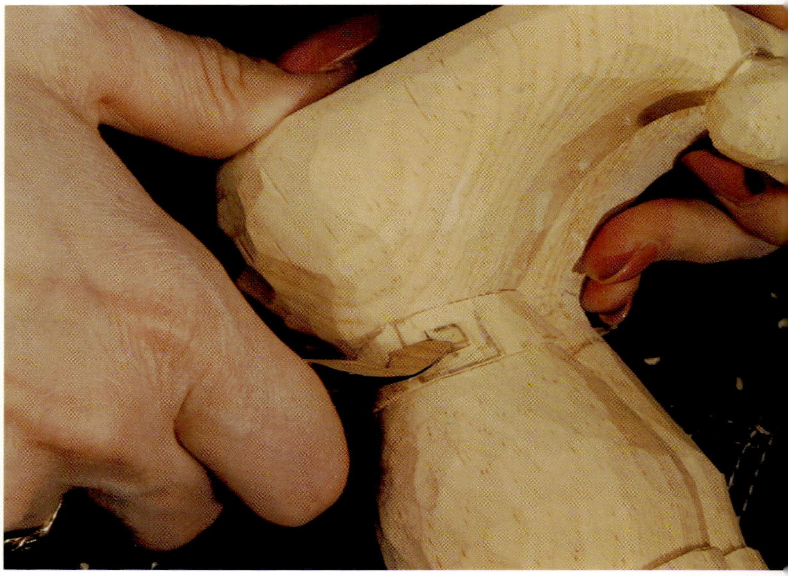

and slice back to the score line from the center.

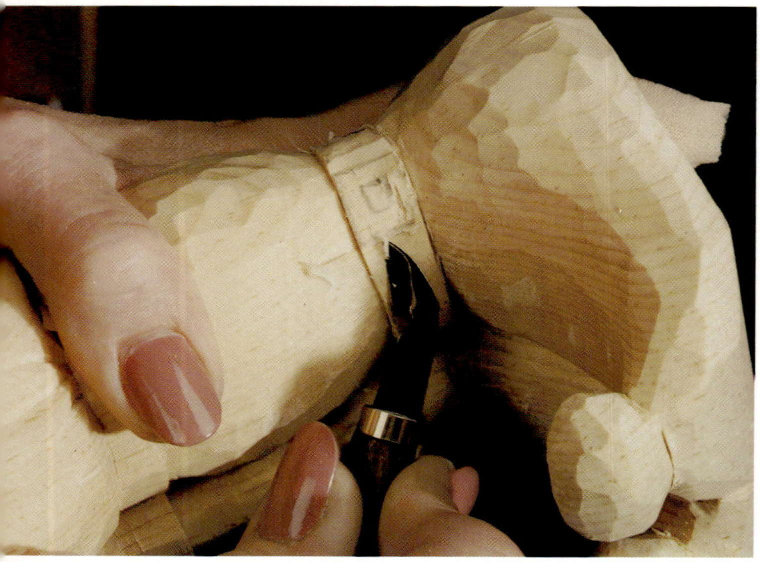

Do the same at the edges of the buckle.

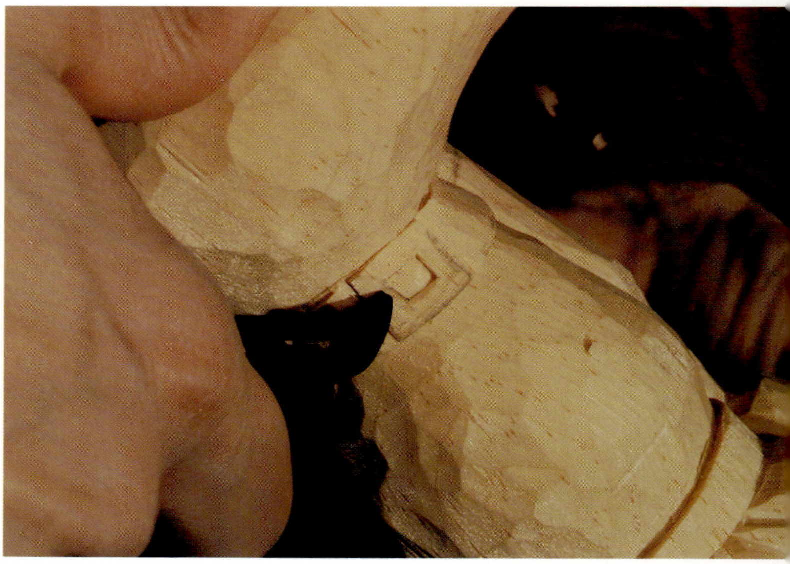

Slightly round the edges of the buckle, inside and out.

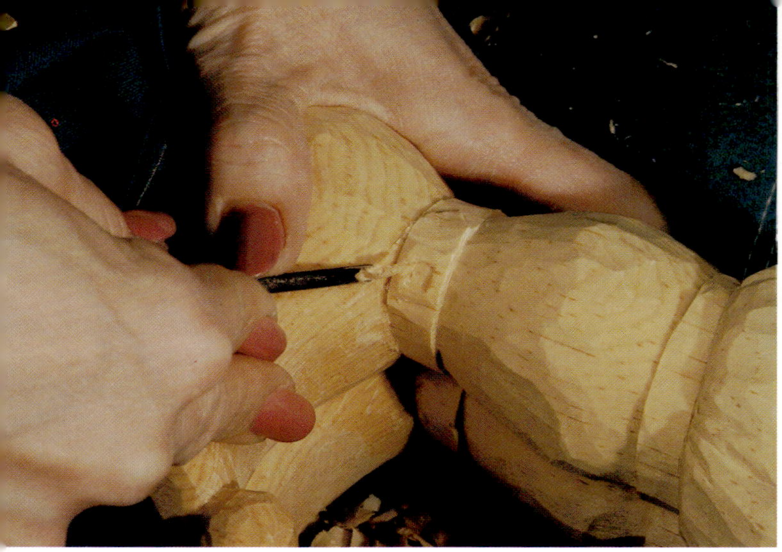

We need to add some tucks to the top of the shoes under the straps. These are easily done with a v-tool. There are three at the front outside corner...

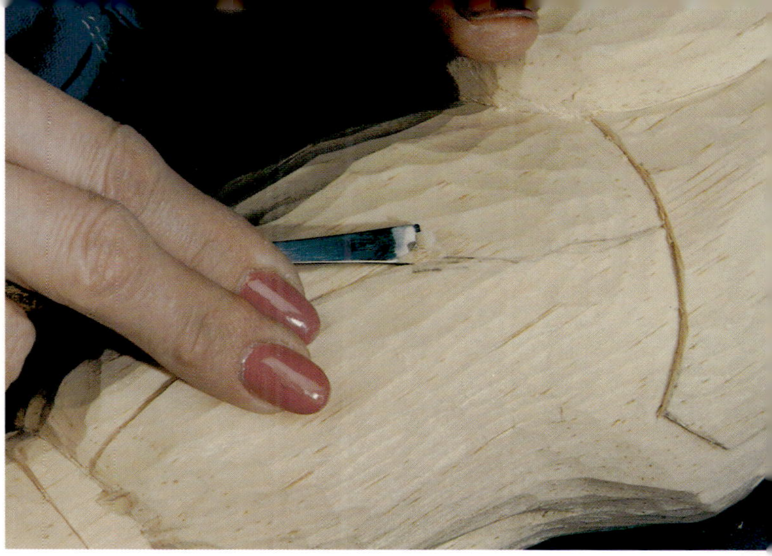

Trim back to the line from the back.

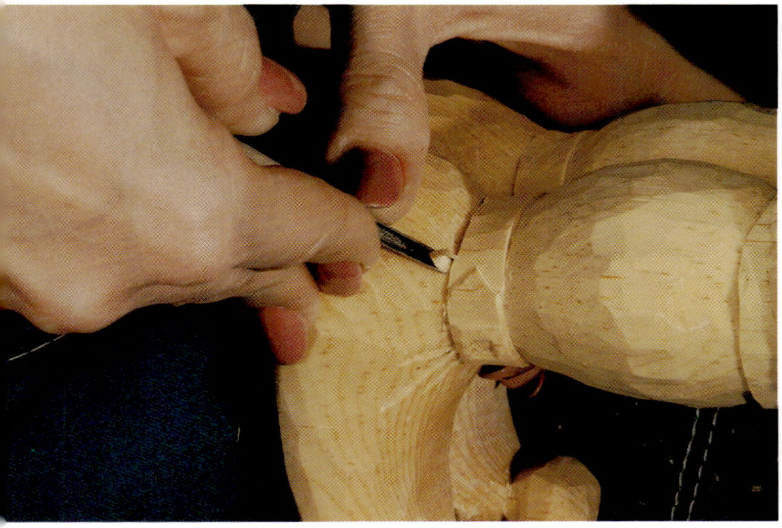

and one or two at the back corner.

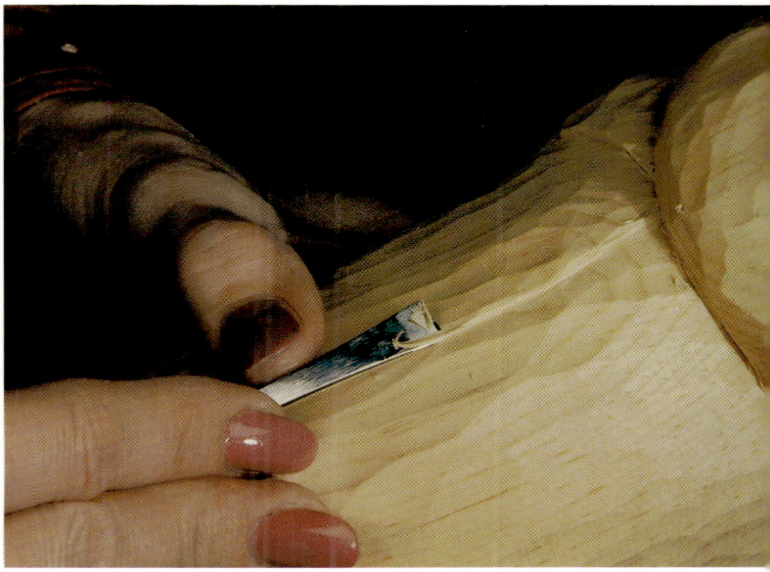

Round the edge of the seam just a little bit.

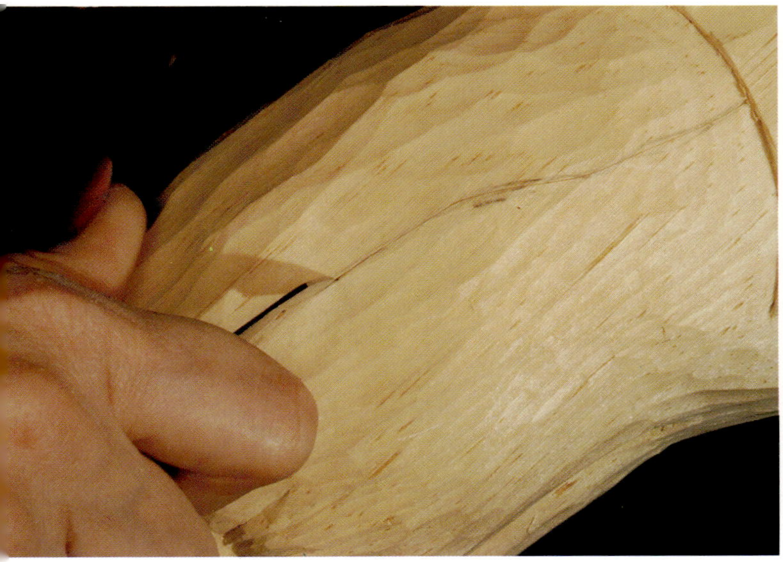

Draw and score the side seams of the pants.

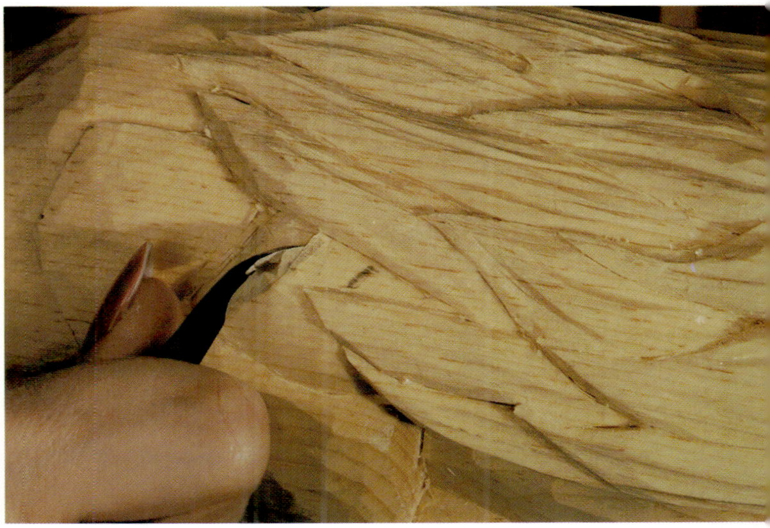

Cut a wedge between the fingers where they show through the beard.

Painting the Elf

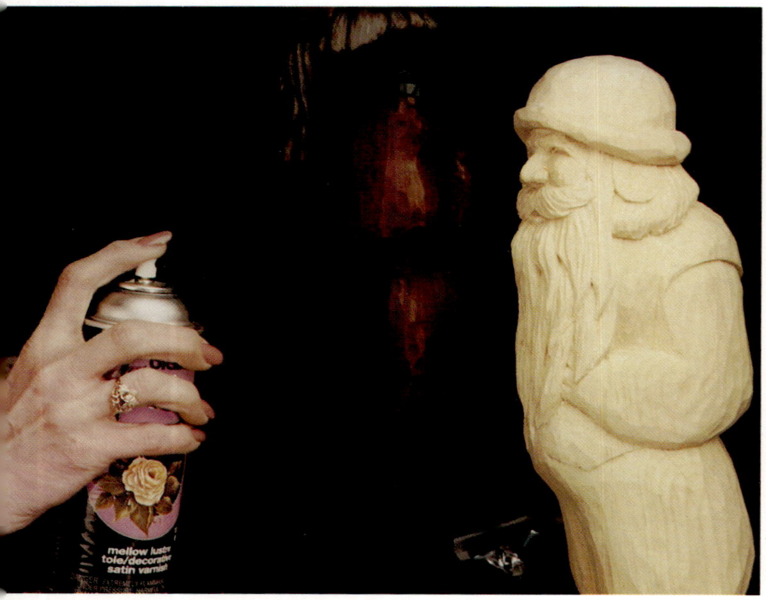

Mist the piece with a satin finish varnish.

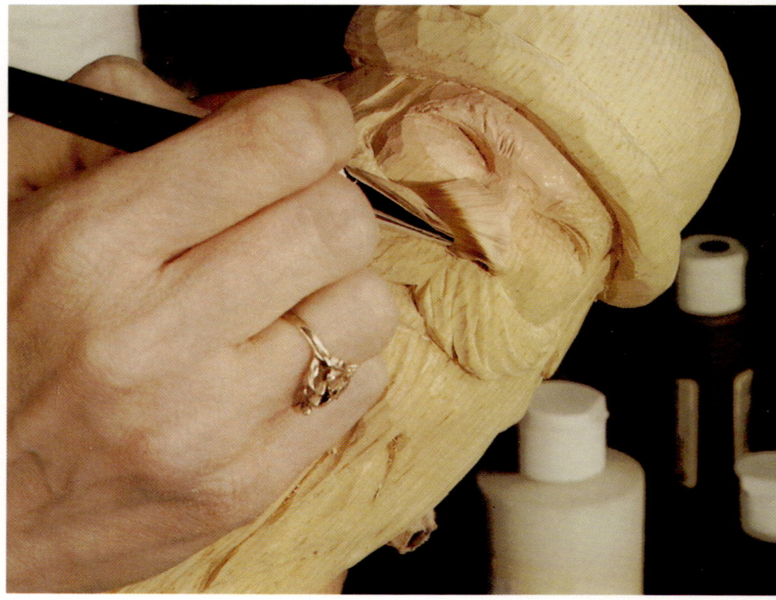

Paint the face with flesh, including the eyebrows.

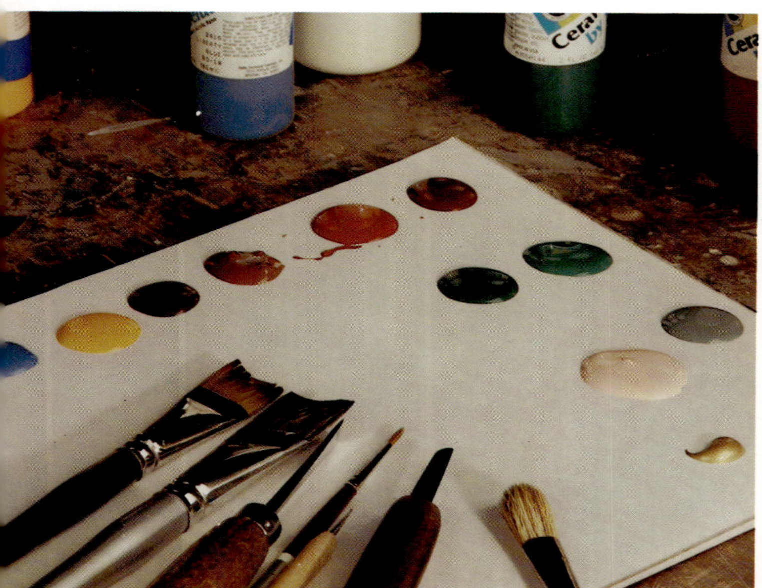

The palette.

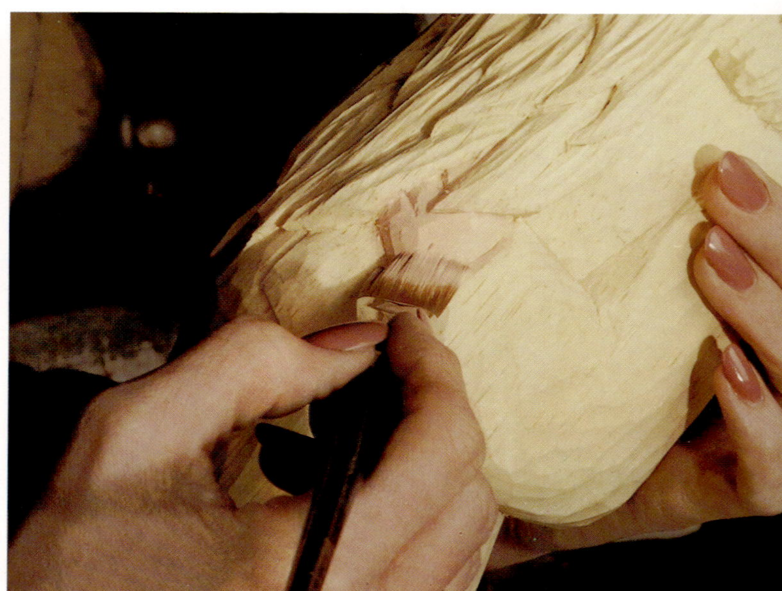

Use the same color on the hand.

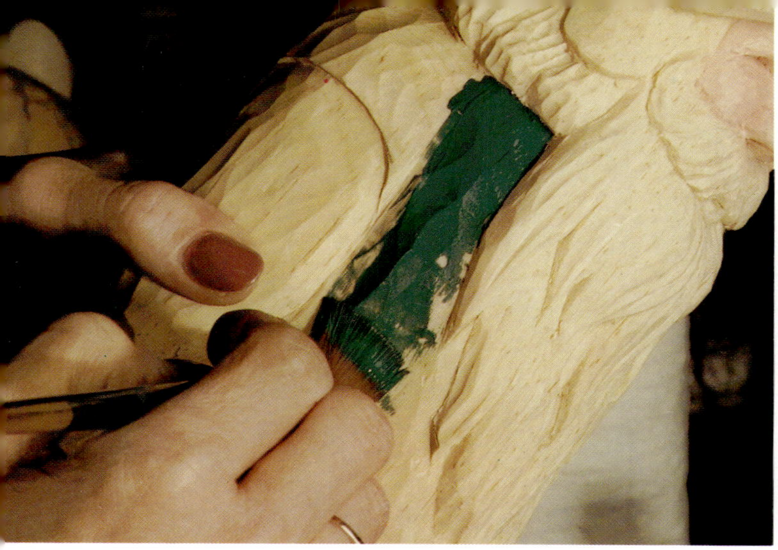

The base coat of the vest is a bluish green.

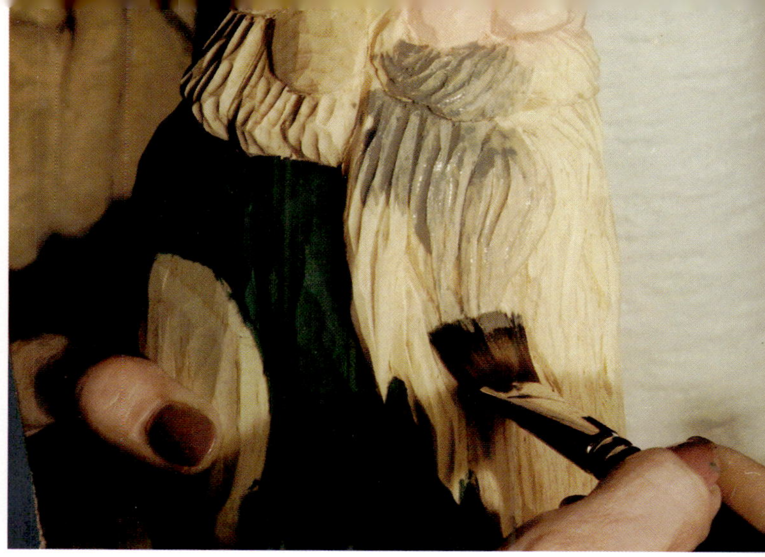

Undercoat the beard and hair with gray.

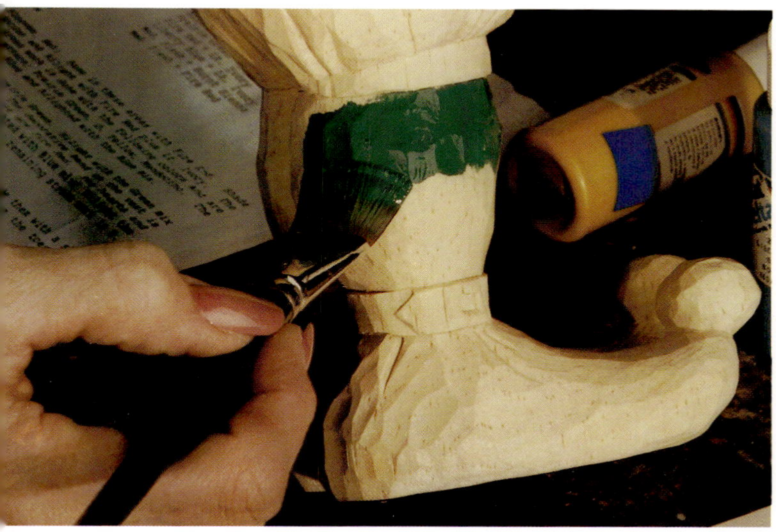

Continue the same green on the socks.

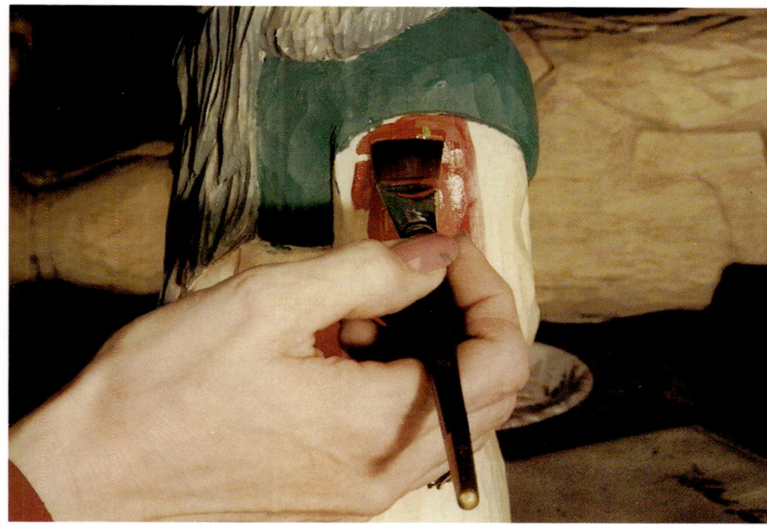

Apply an undercoat of red to the sleeves pants and hat.

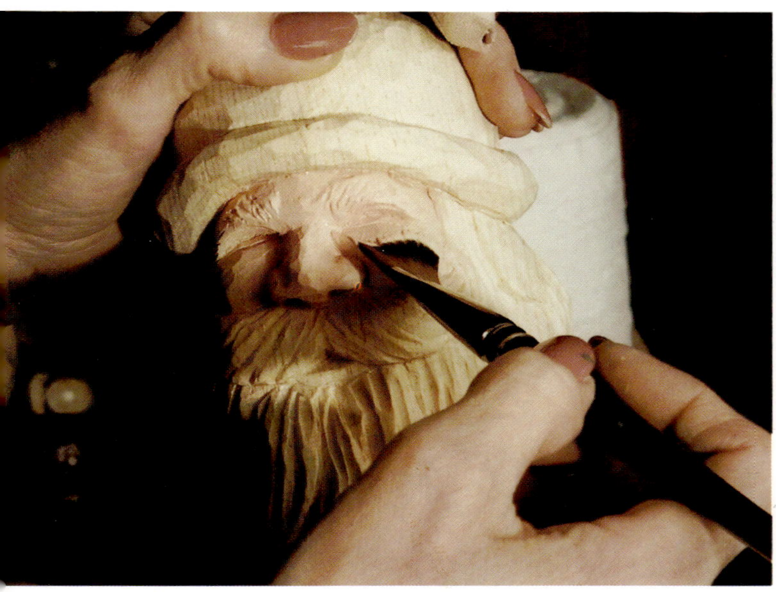

Do a second coat of flesh to insure that the wood is sealed so the antiquing doesn't grab too heavily.

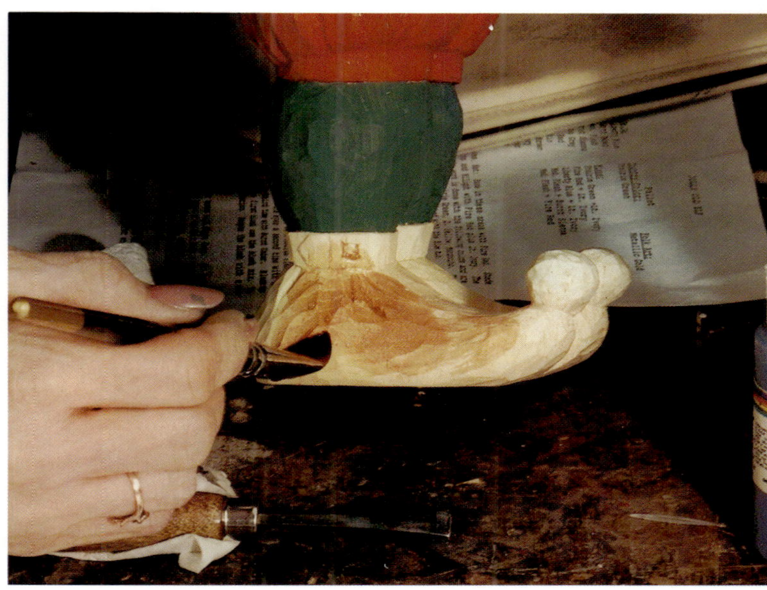

Apply a wash of burnt sienna to undercoat the shoes.

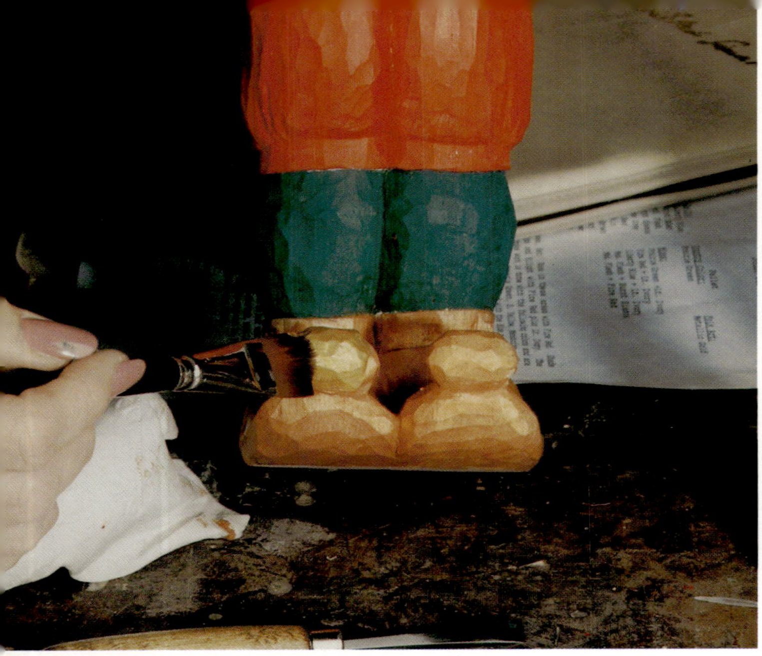

Go over the pom-poms and the buckles with metallic gold.

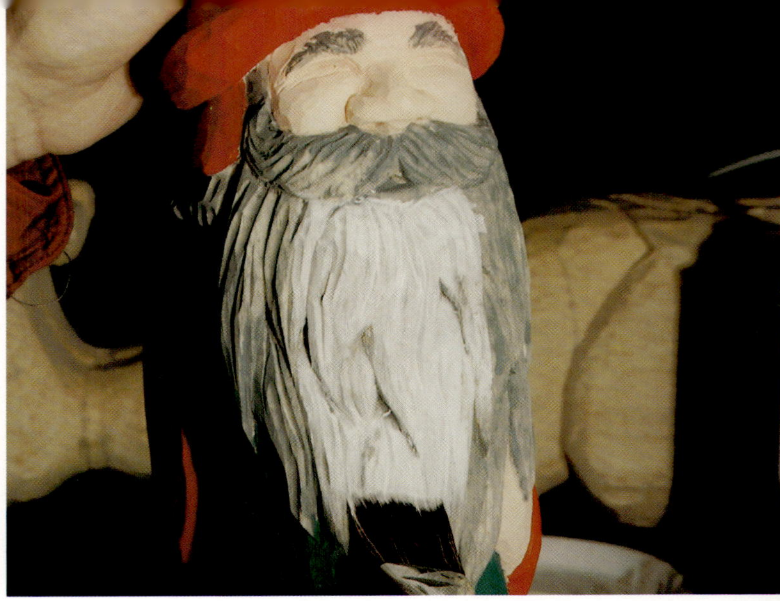

With diluted off-white go over the hair with a wash. Brush over the top and don't worry about trying to get the white into the deeper areas which are to be dark anyway.

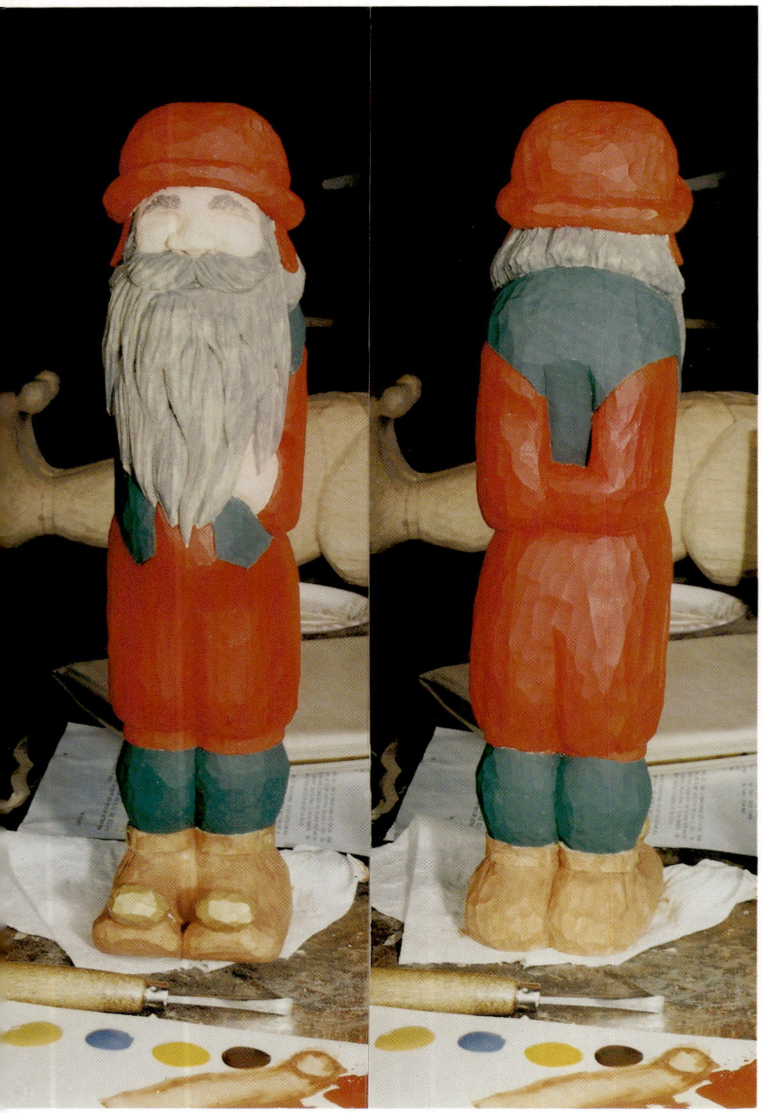

The base coat complete.

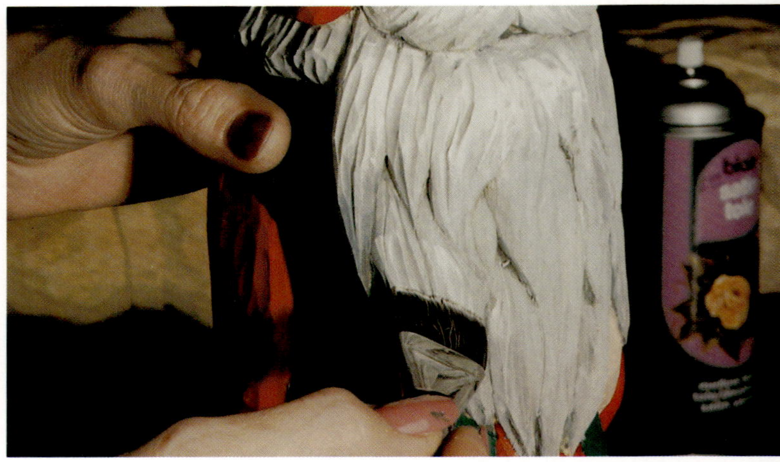

Go over the hair again, this time with a thicker off-white paint, hitting just the high points of the hair.

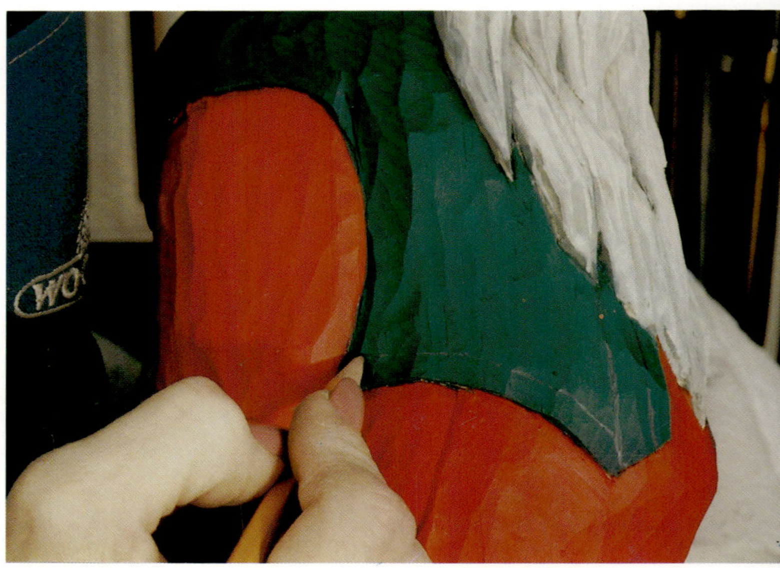

Draw in the lines of the red trim on the vest.

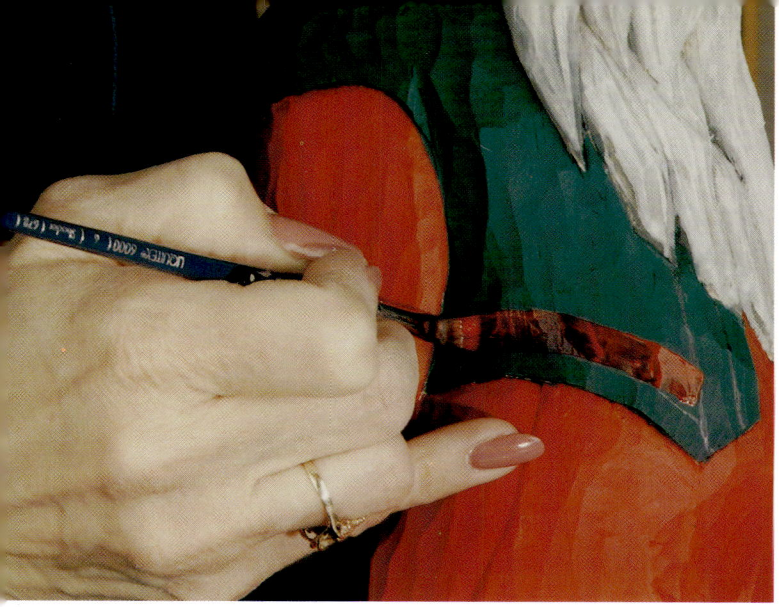

Apply red paint to the trim. It may take several coats to get the color you want.

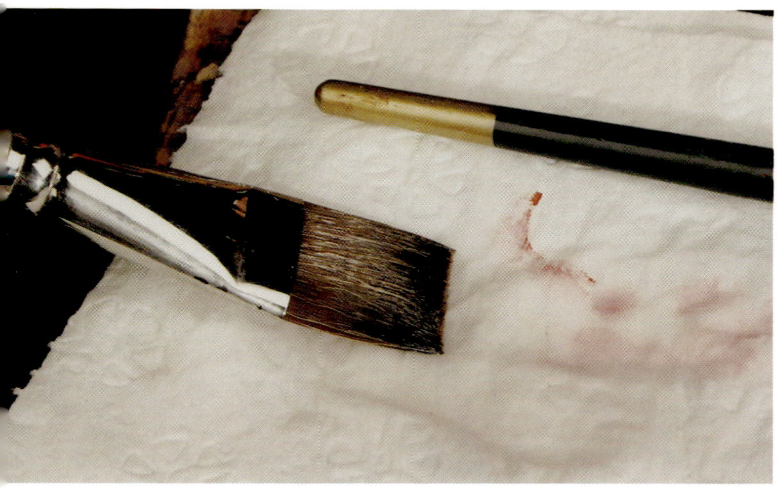

To add some dark highlight to the beard you need to corner load the brush. You begin by lightly blotting a wet brush.

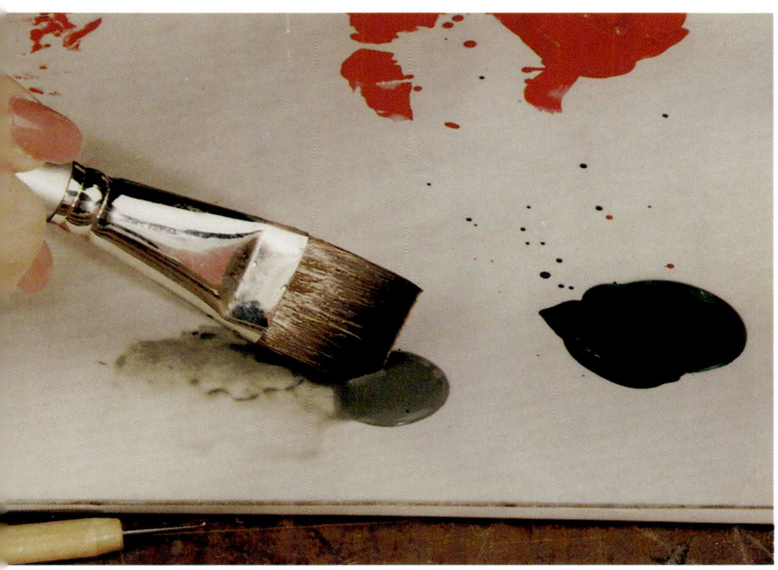

Dip one corner into the paint.

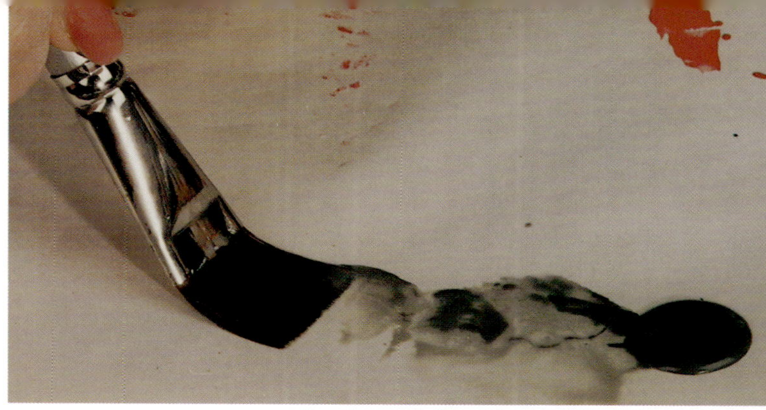

On the palette work the paint with the brush so that there is a decreasing range of pigment on the brush, from heavy on the dipped side to almost none on the other side.

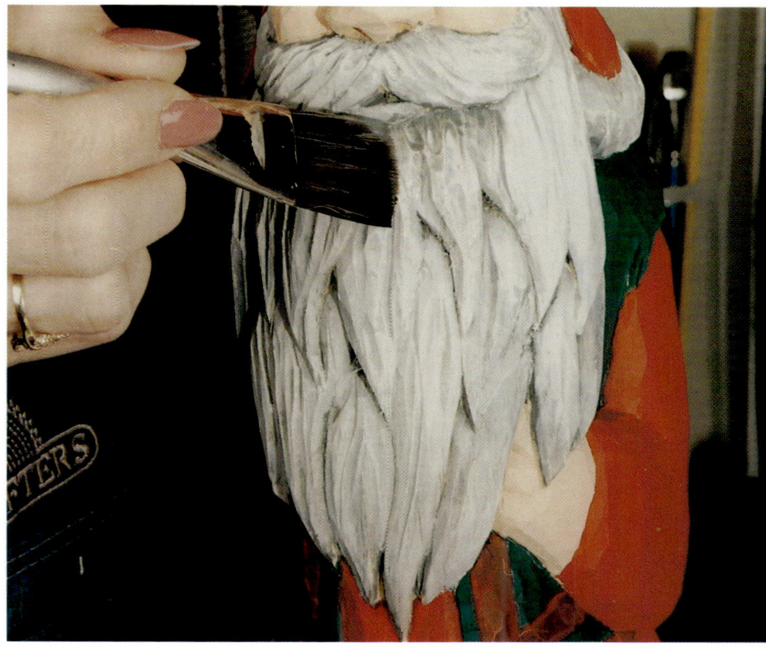

Hold the heavily pigments edge of the brush at the top of the beard, and walk the brush across. This will create a shaded highlight.

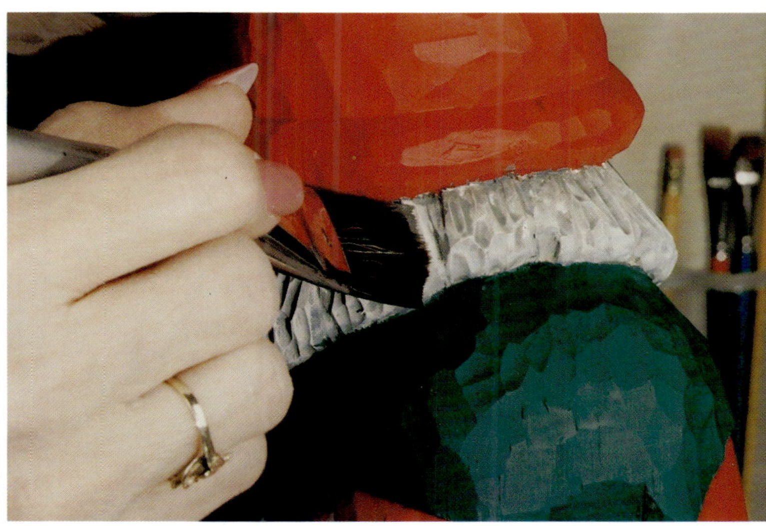

Do the same on the hat, with the pigmented edge of the brush under the brim.

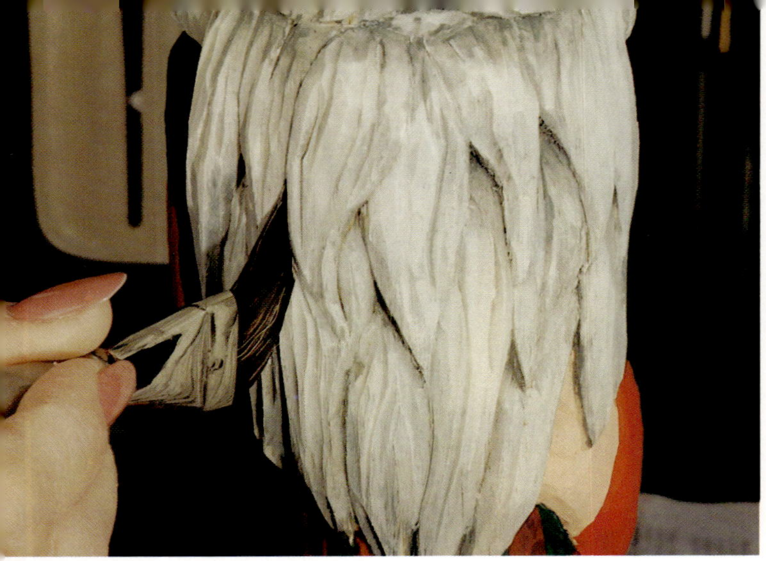

Finally do the deep corners of the beard.

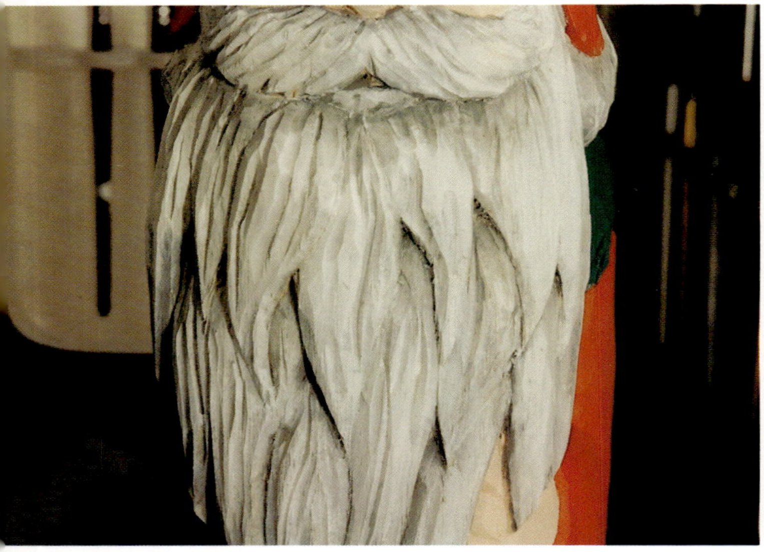

You can see the graduated effect.

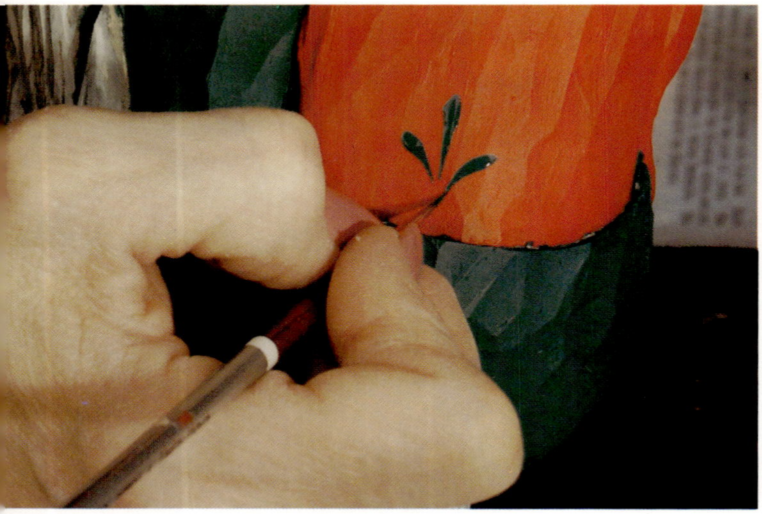

The decorative painting on the arm begins with three leaves. These are created by setting a loaded round brush down at the thicker point of the leaf and pulling it to the thinner, letting up on the pressure as you go.

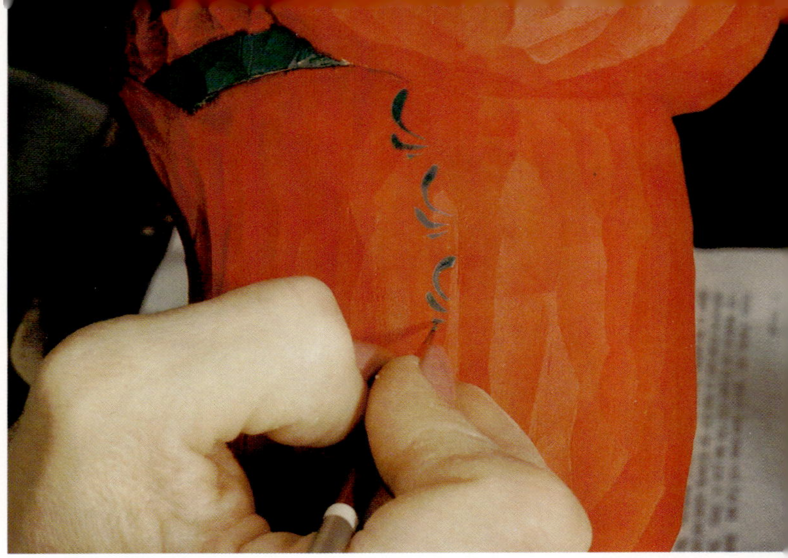

Use the same technique to create the pattern down the seam. It, too, is a pattern of three leaves, but they have a different configuration.

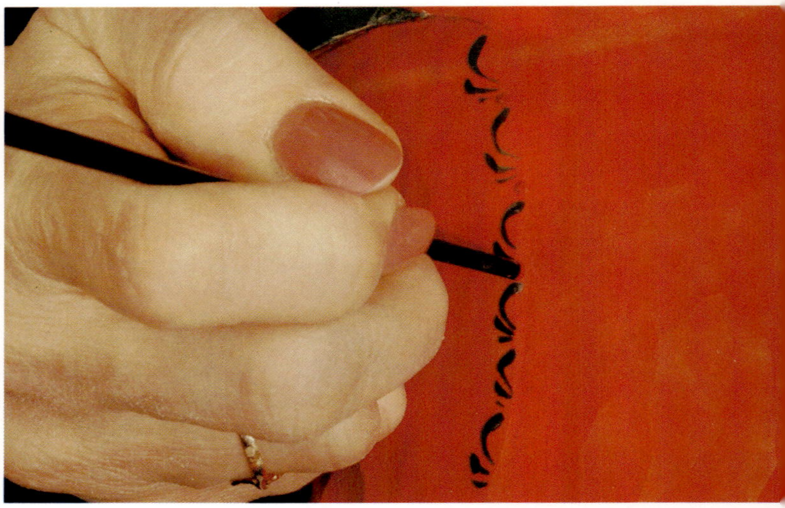

With the end of a paint brush handle, add a dot of a darker red at the small end of each group of leaves on the seam.

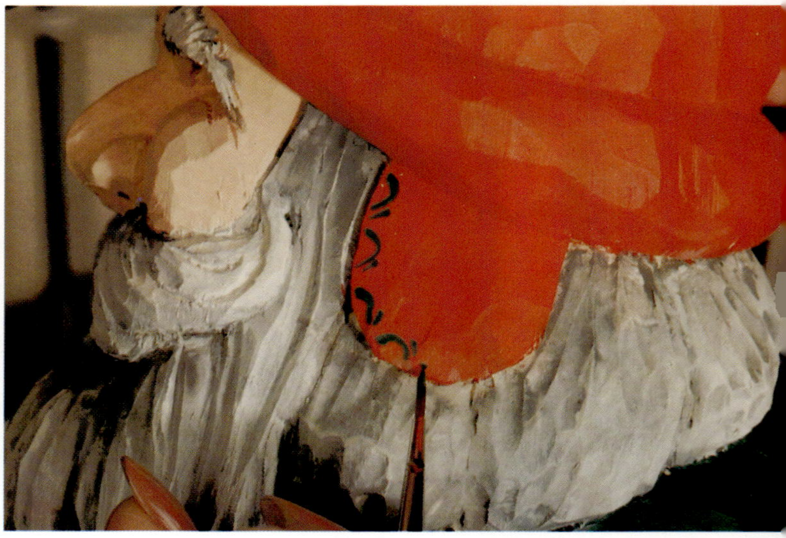

A pattern of two leaves borders the ear flap. This uses a finer brush because the space is smaller.

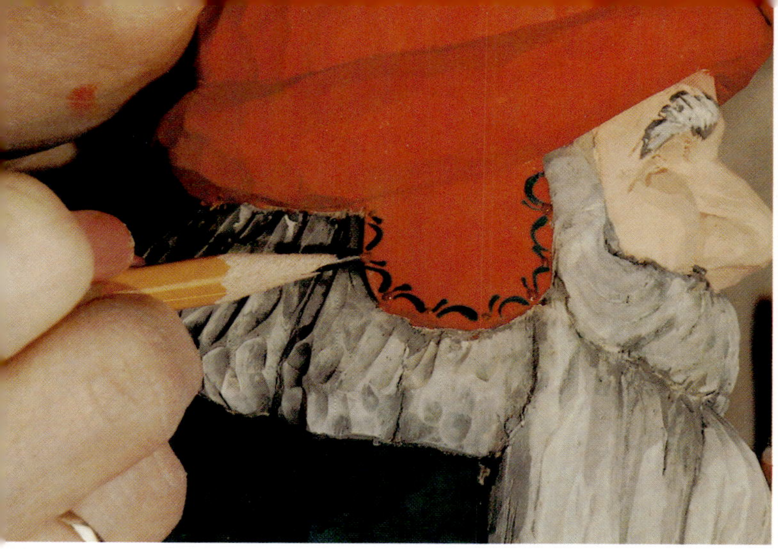

These leaves get a dot of red too. Use the point of a sharpened pencil or a stylus to apply a small berry.

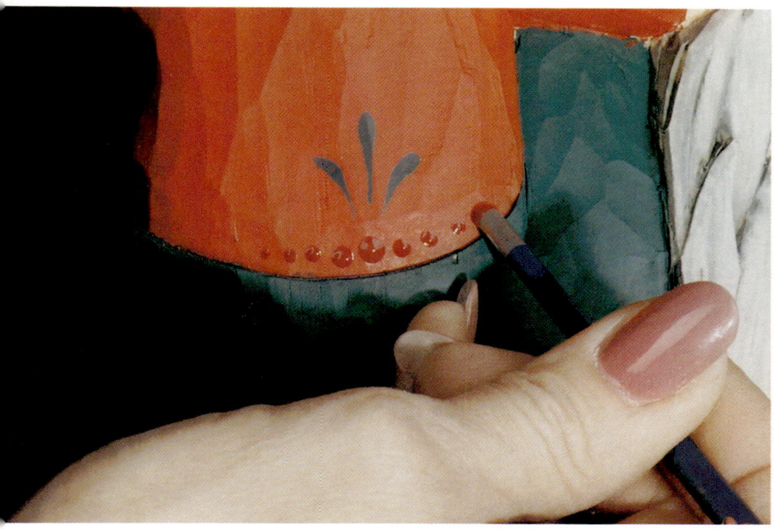

A pattern of darker red dots goes above the leaves on the sleeve as well. These get smaller as they move out in each direction from the center.

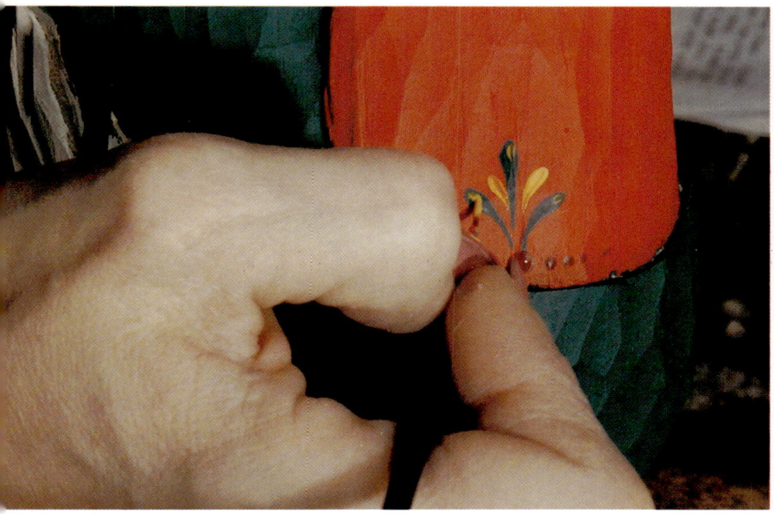

On the shoulders create yellow leaves between the green, and add some yellow highlights to the green leaves.

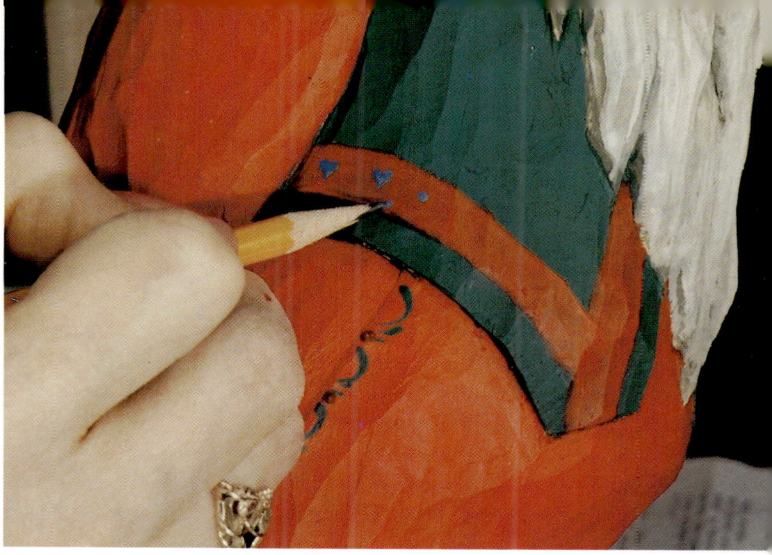

The trim of the jacket is decorated with a series of light blue hearts. These are easy to create using the pencil point or stylus. Make two dots...

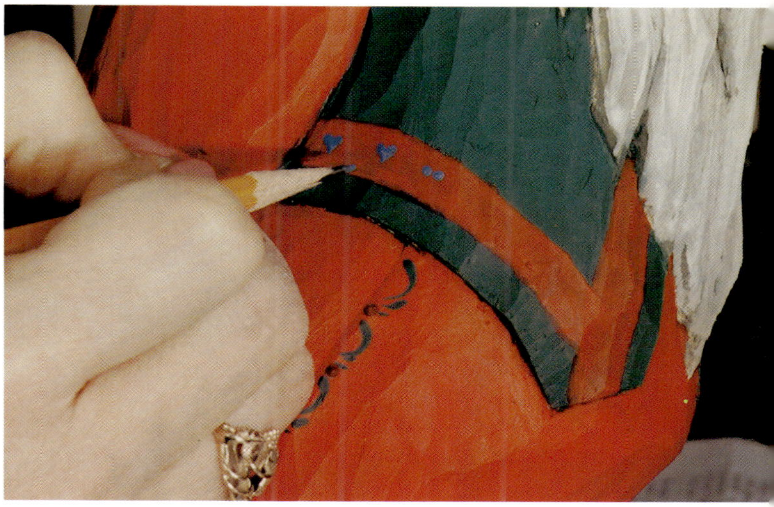

side-by-side...

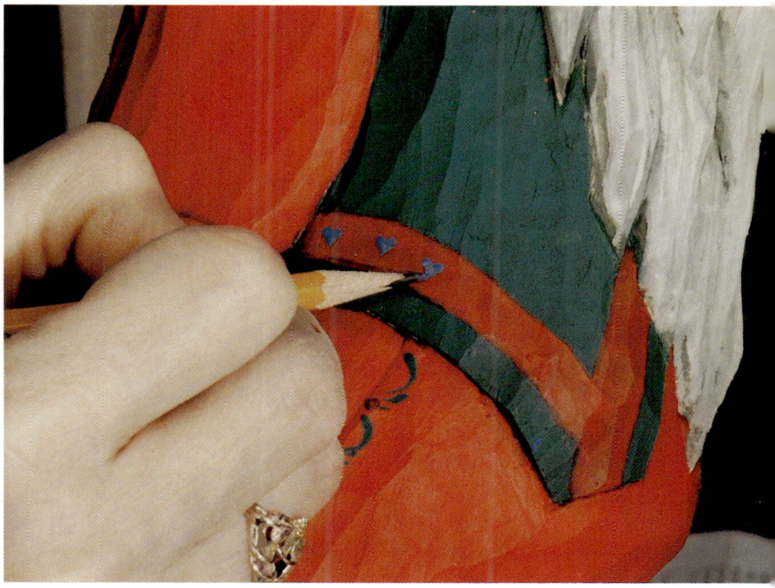

and pull from each down to the point of the heart.

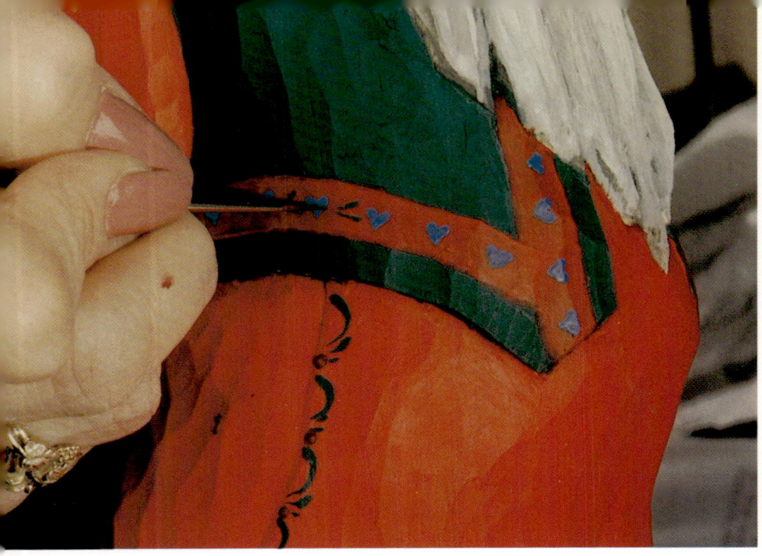

Between the hearts add two green leaves...

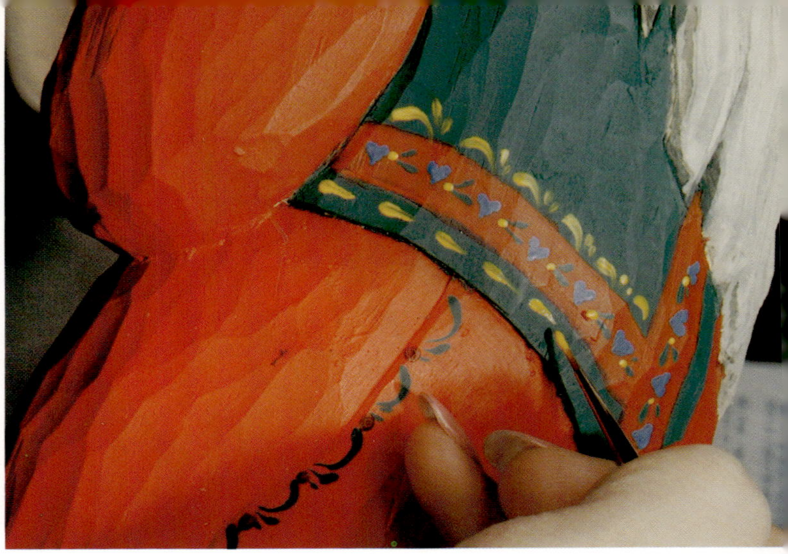

Below the trim create a line of single yellow leaves.

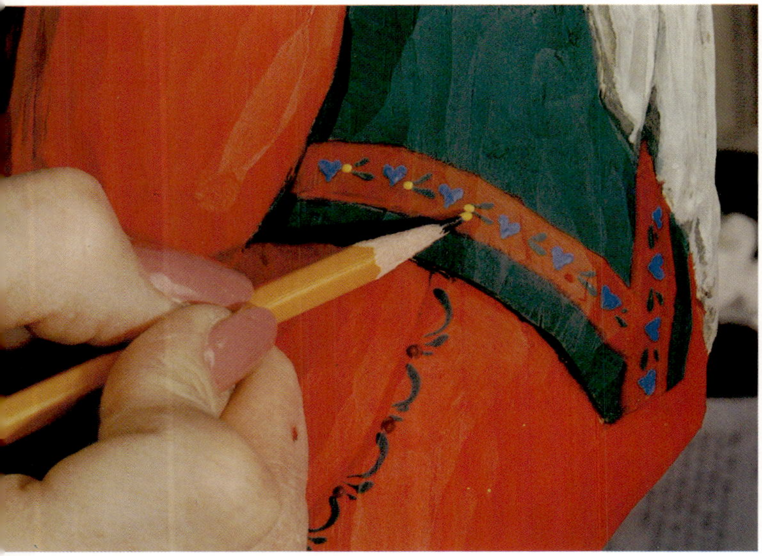

with a yellow berry where the come together.

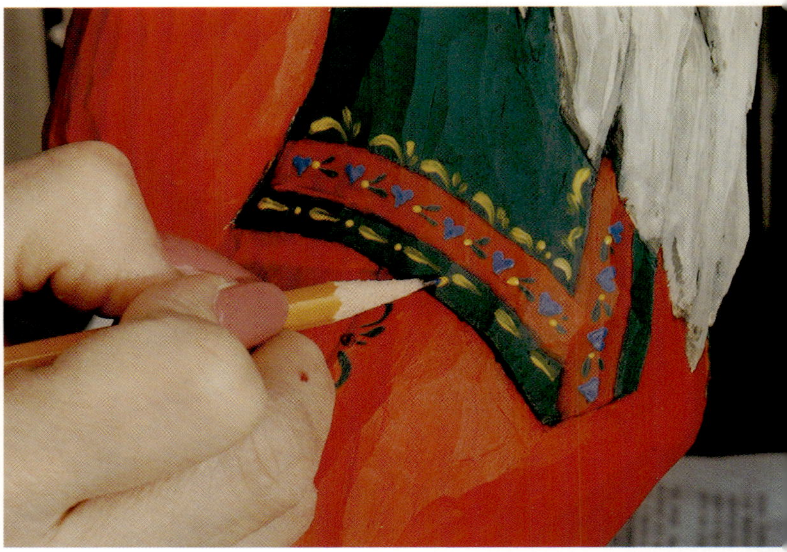

Add dots between the leaves below...

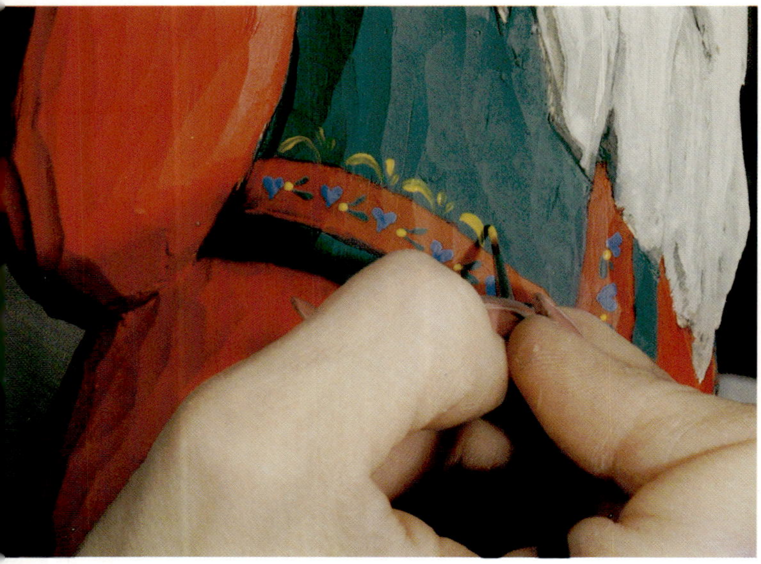

Along the top side of the jacket trim create a pattern of three yellow leaves, like those along the seam.

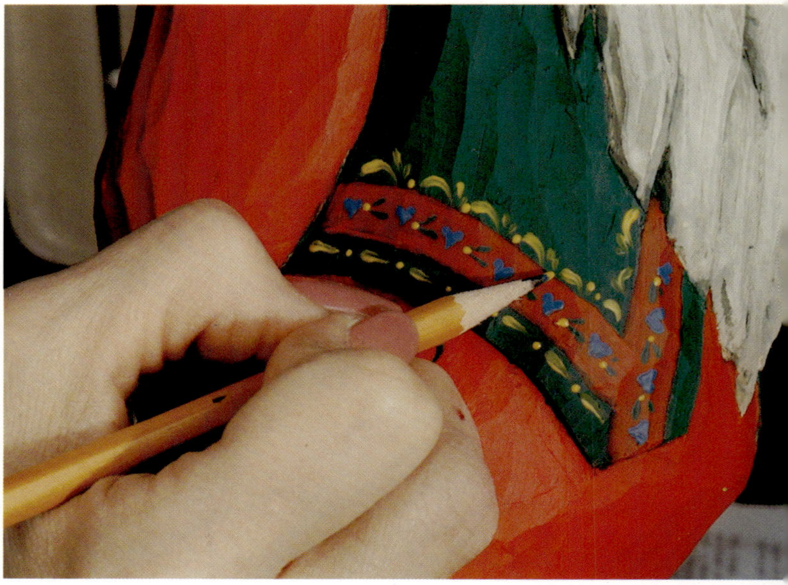

and above.

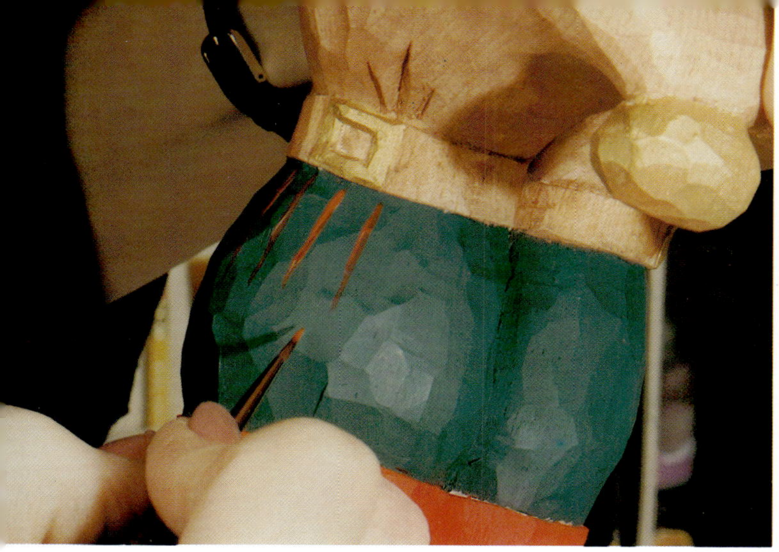

Add red stripes to the socks, coming about halfway up the calf from the shoe tops.

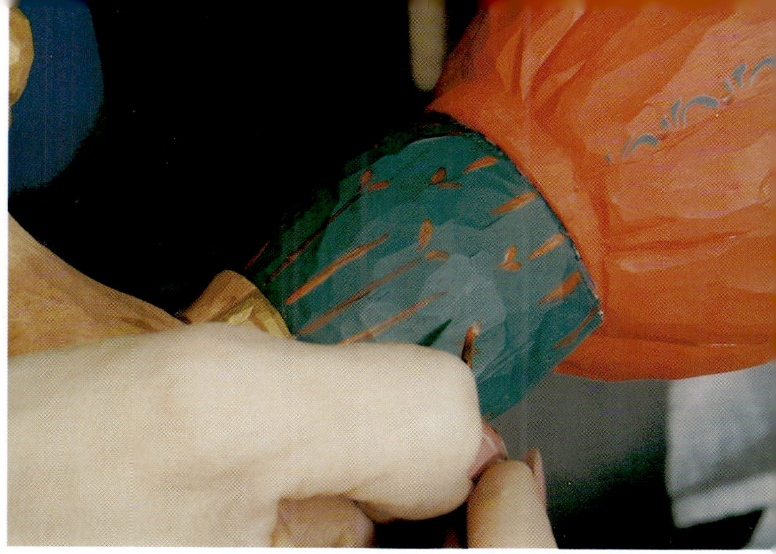

Do the same at the bottom of every other upper stripe, so they are staggered.

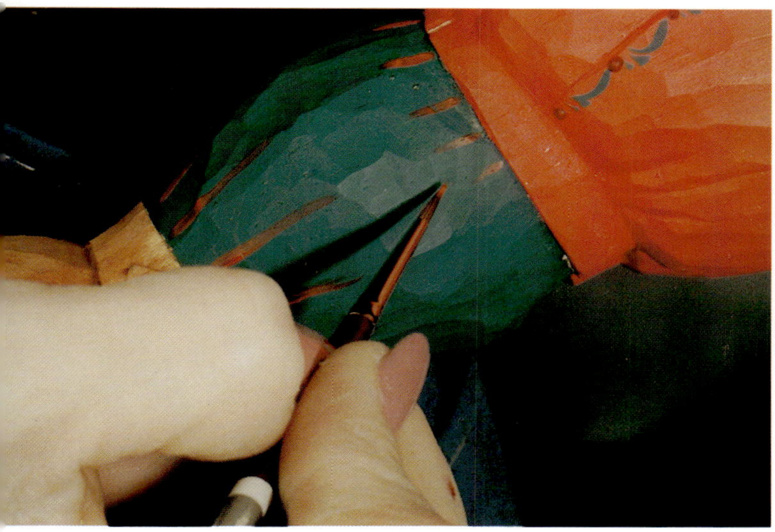

Paint a shorter stripe from the top of the sock.

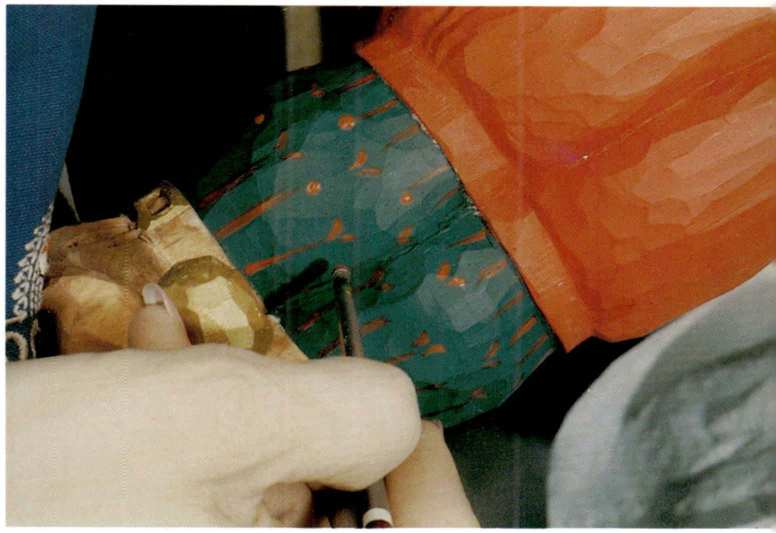

At the tips of the remaining stripes, upper and lower, make a dot of red.

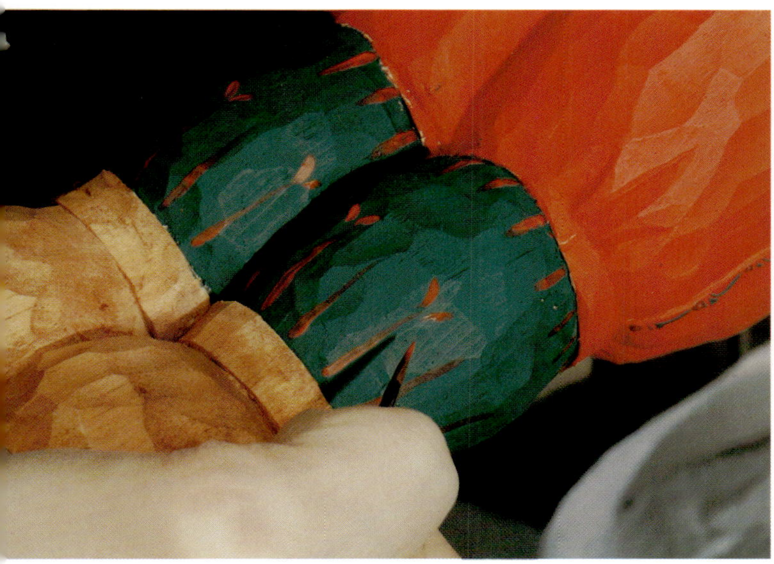

At the top of every other lower stripe, paint a pattern of two leaves.

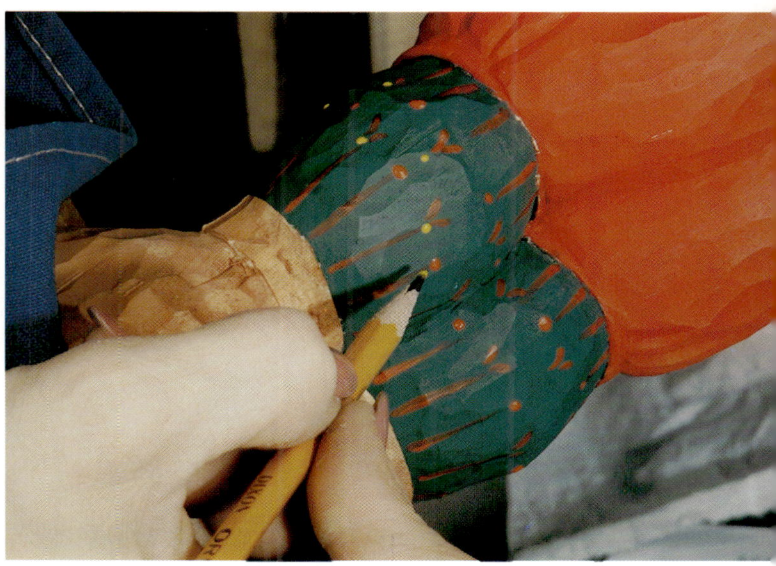

Put a yellow dot at the point of each leaf pattern.

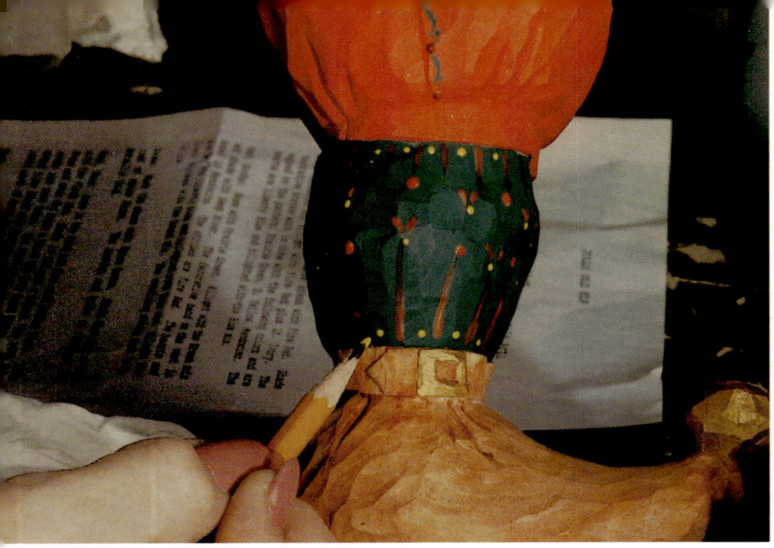

Add dots between the stripes at the top and at the bottom.

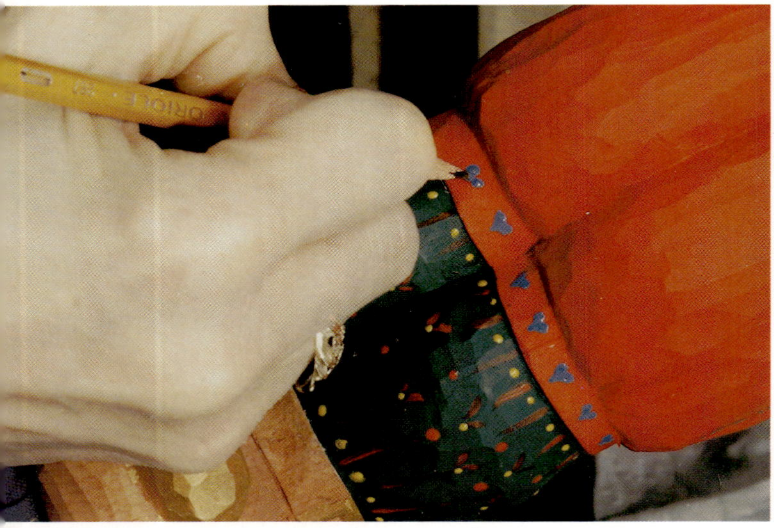

Paint hearts around the cuff.

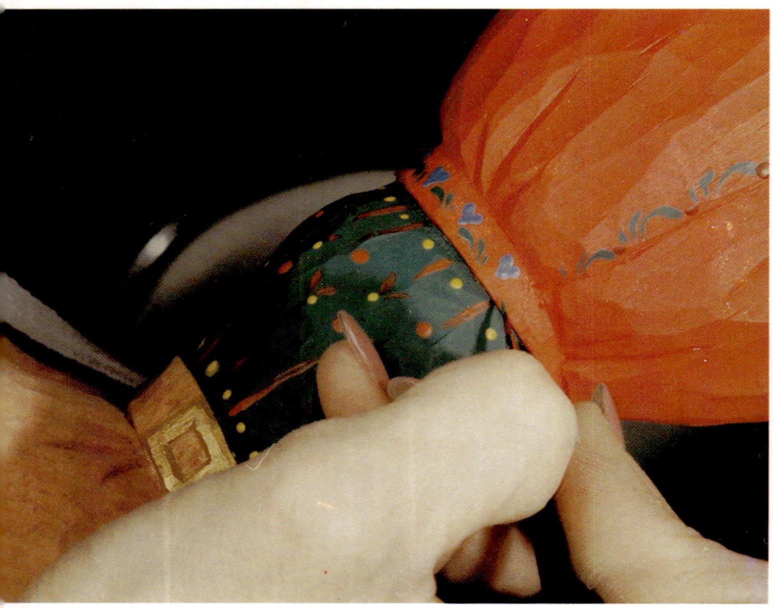

Between the hearts paint a pattern of three leaves.

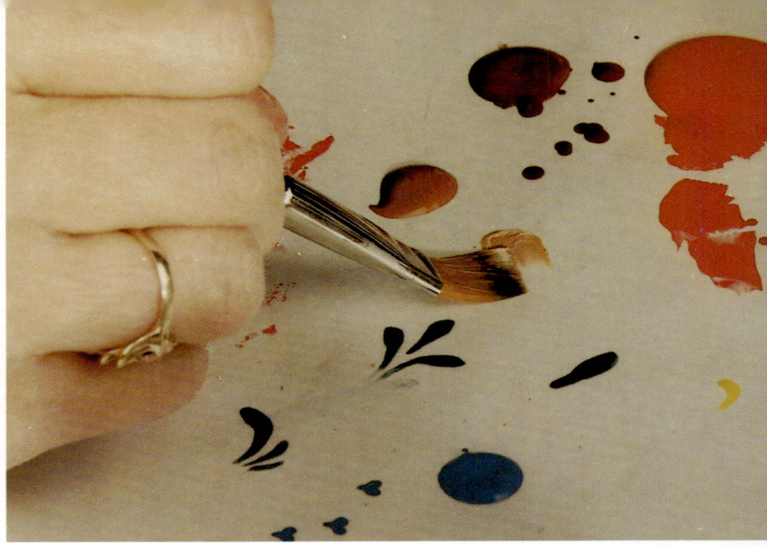

Tint some flesh paint with a touch of burnt sienna.

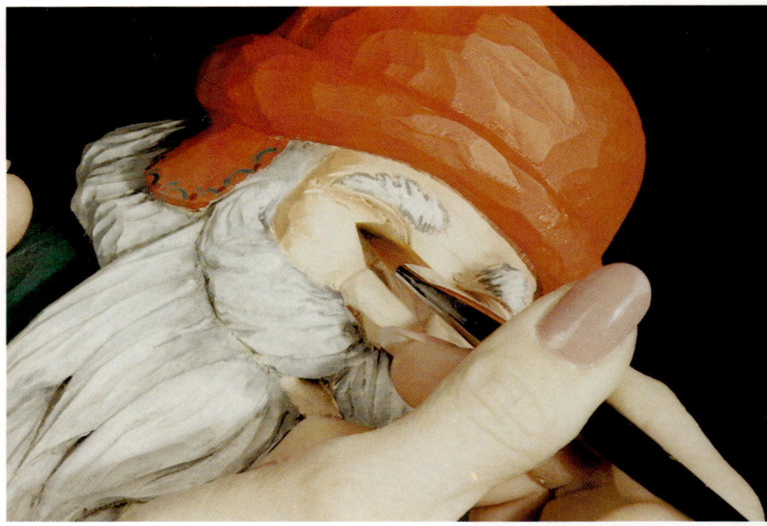

Use it to shade the eyes and the sides of the face. Corner load the brush to do this, and paint with the heavily loaded part of the brush against the hairline and in the upper part of the eye.

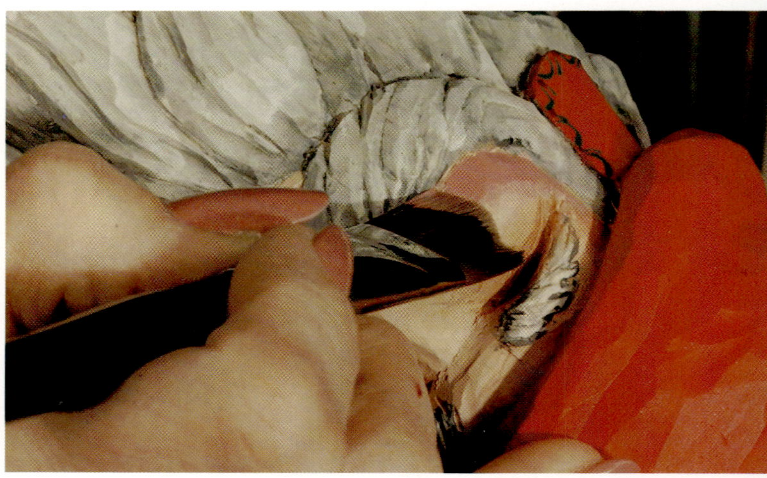

Mix some red with flesh to get a blushing pink. Corner load the brush and run it across the lower cheeks and nose, with the loaded side against the hair line. The elf will look pretty garish before adding the antiquing.

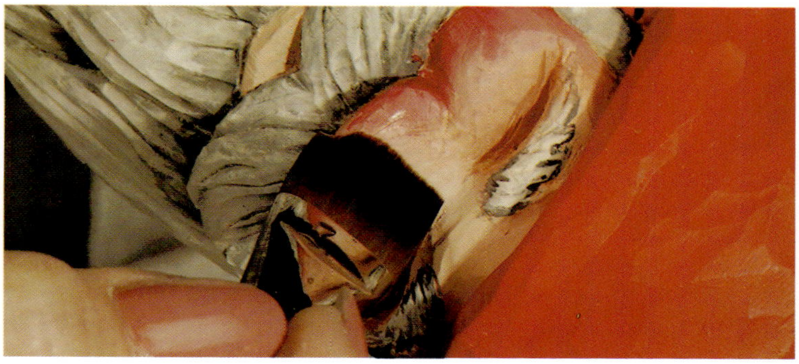

Go over the same area with a darker red, again with the brush corner loaded.

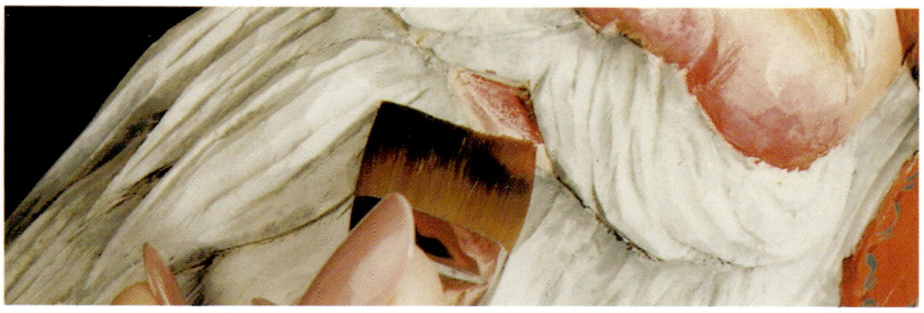

Go over the lip with the dark color.

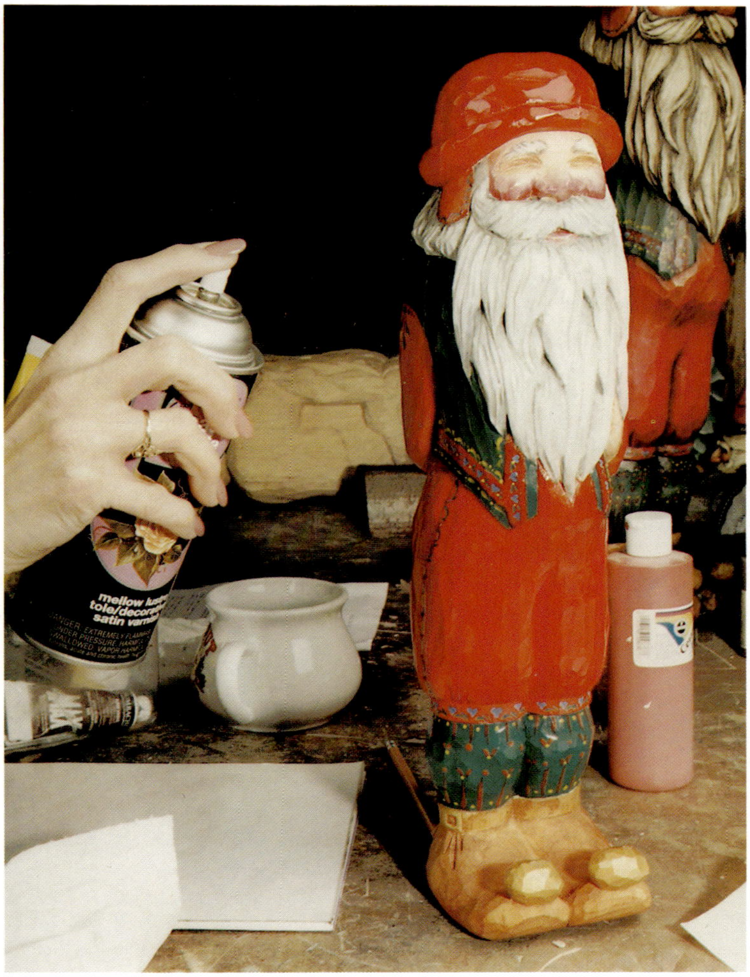

Apply three coats of satin varnish, letting the each coat dry thoroughly before applying the next.

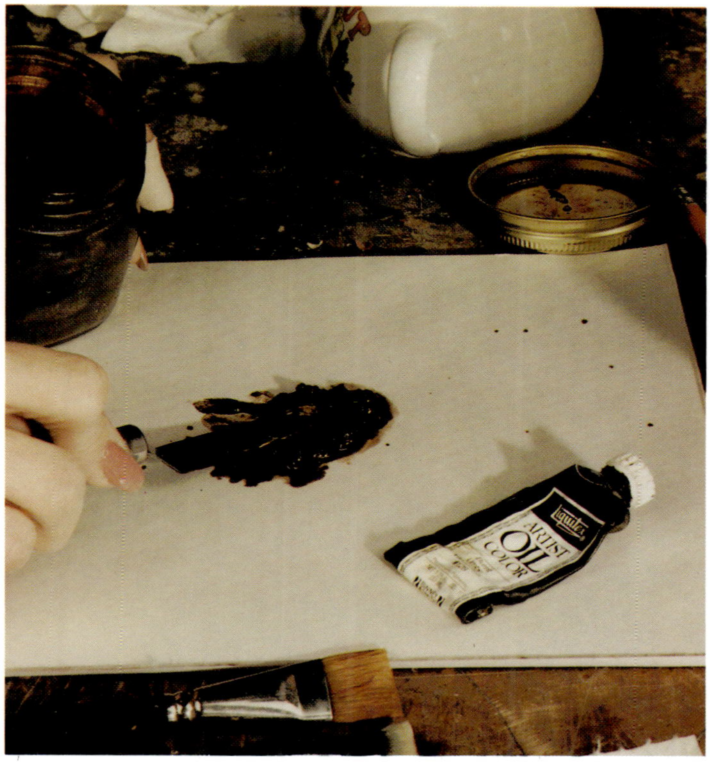

The antiquing is done with burnt umber oil paint, thinned to the consistency of melted chocolate chips. If thinned too much the paint loses its adhering properties and when it dries will come off like dust.

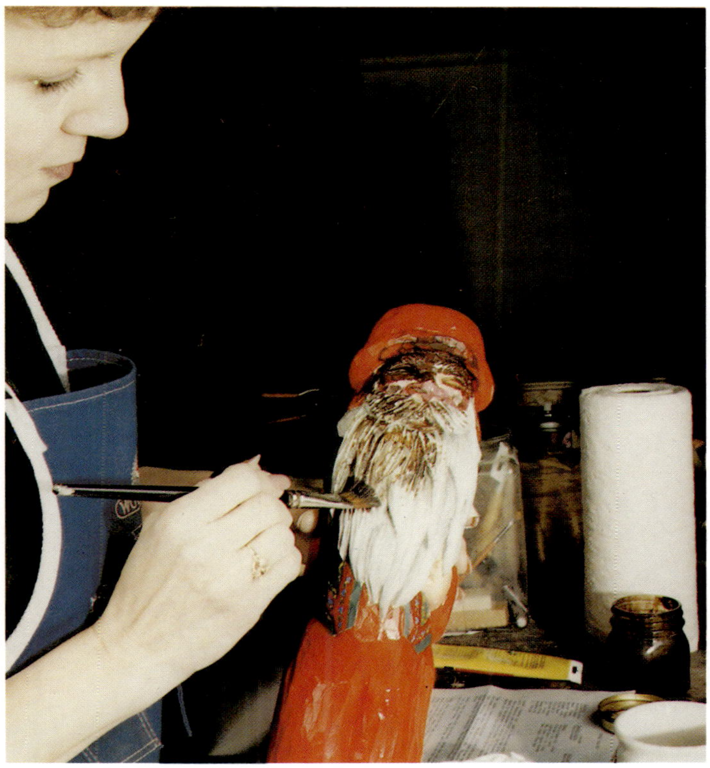

Apply the antiquing to the whole piece, covering it completely.

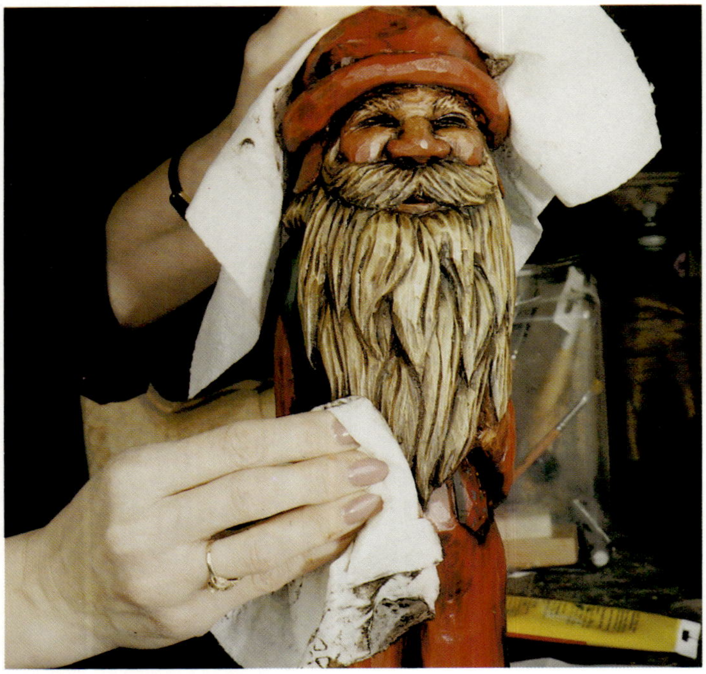

After it is completely applied, rub it off with paper towel. (The oily towel can spontaneously combust, so dispose of it properly and safely).

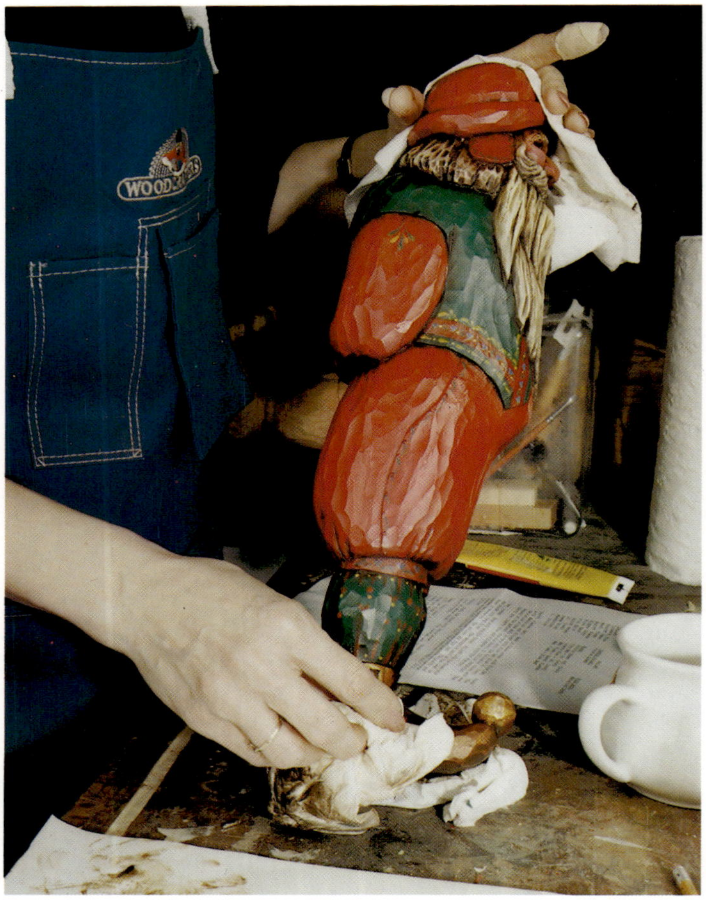

On antiques the high spots tend to be shiny because the are most handled, while the deeper spots tend to get dark from neglect. To simulate this, rub the higher spots the most, the recesses the least, and blend between the two.

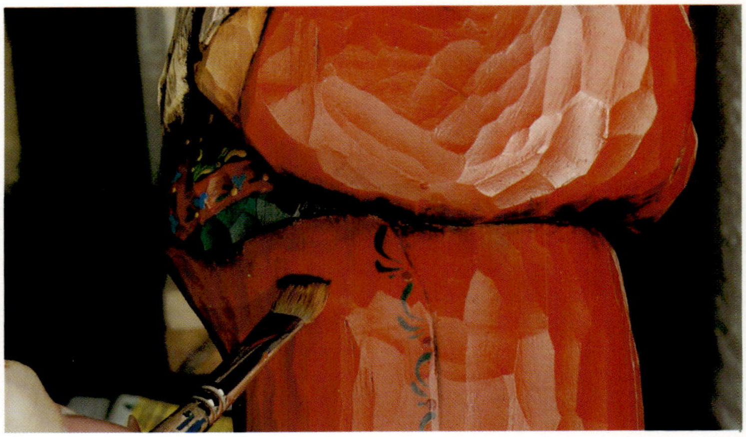

In some of the creases where the antiquing is still heavy after rubbing, take an old dry brush with nothing on it, and blend the antiquing out. Go over the whole piece with the blending process.

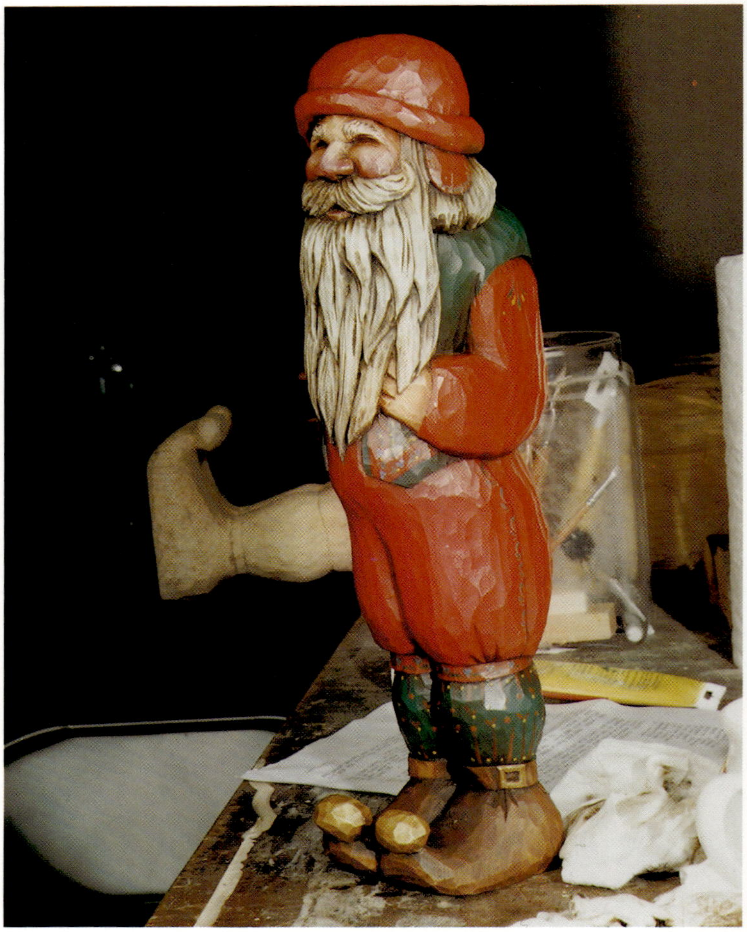

The antiquing will enhance the look of your carving by making the cuts appear deeper, highlights the carving strokes, and accenting the lines of your design.

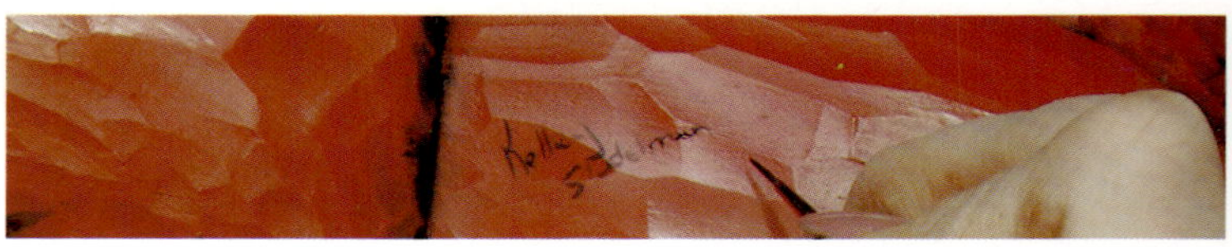

Sign the work.

The Gallery

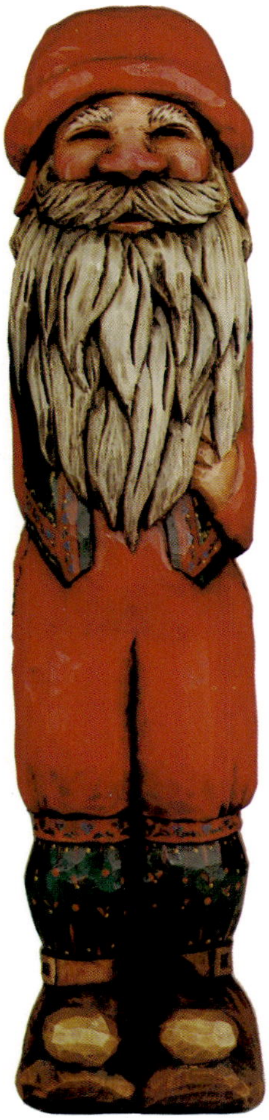

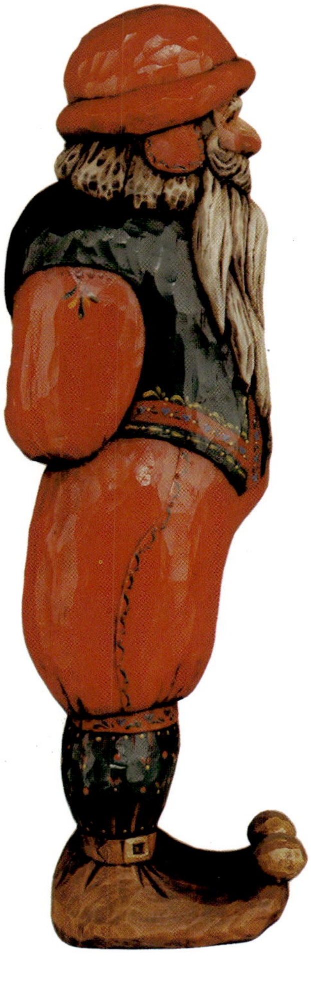

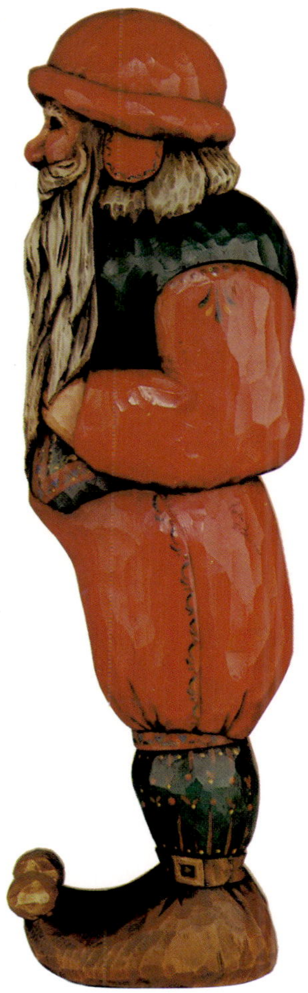

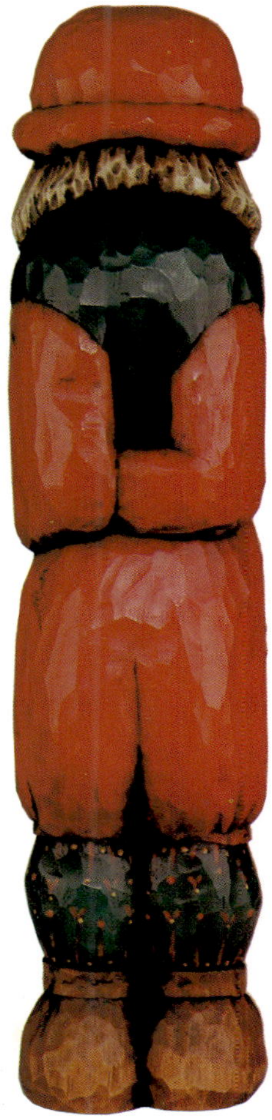

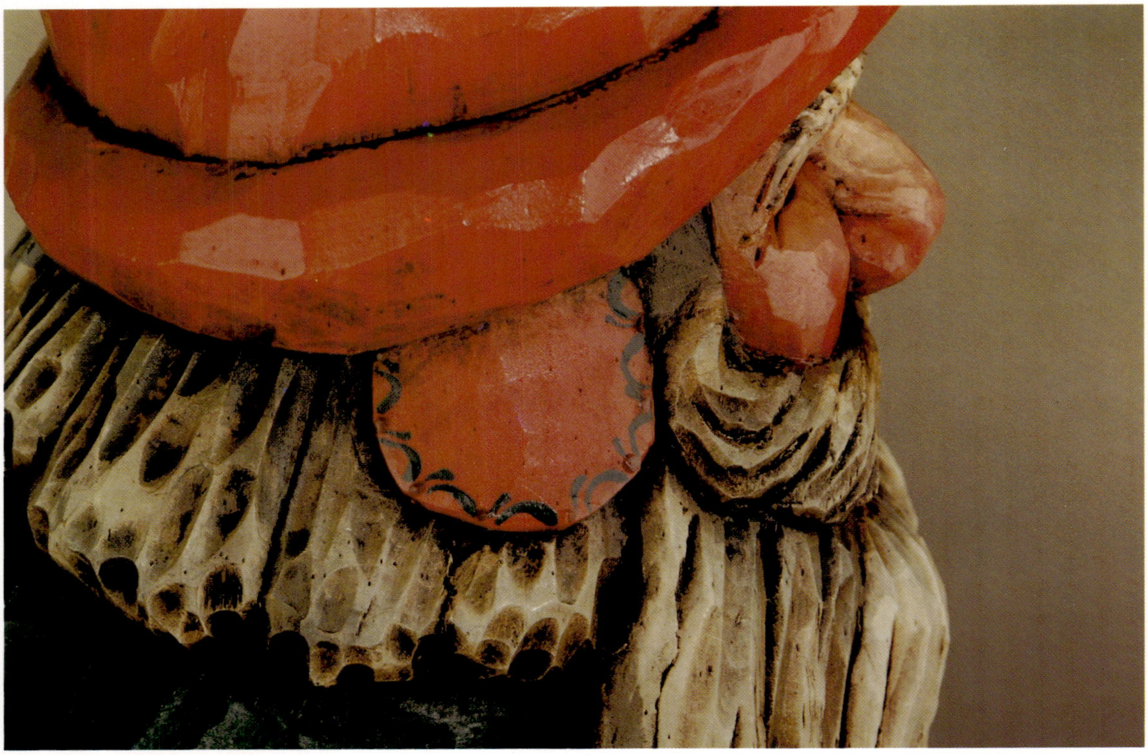

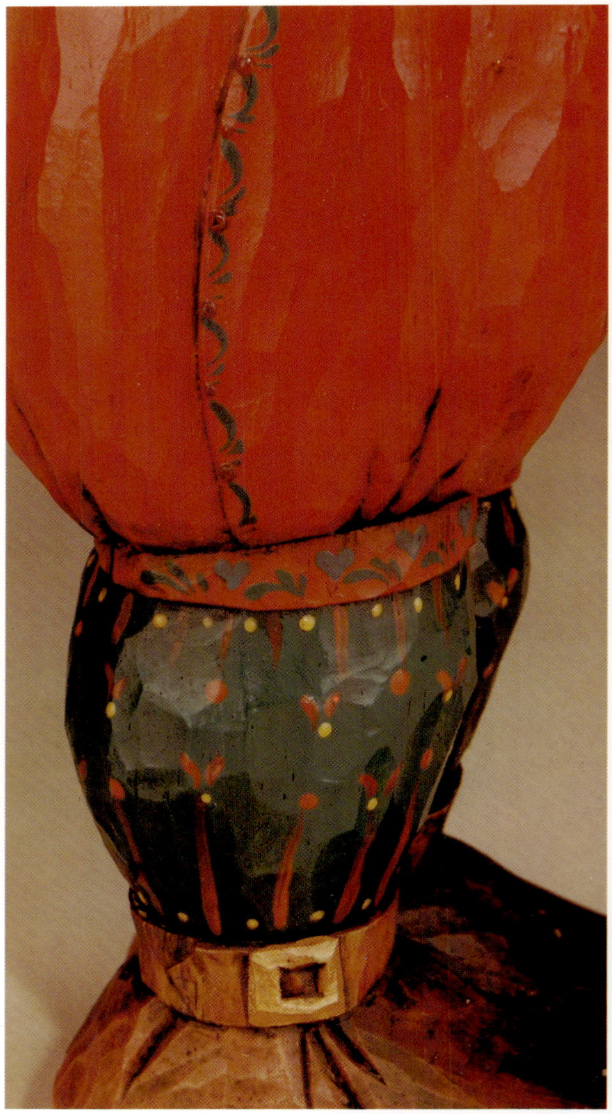

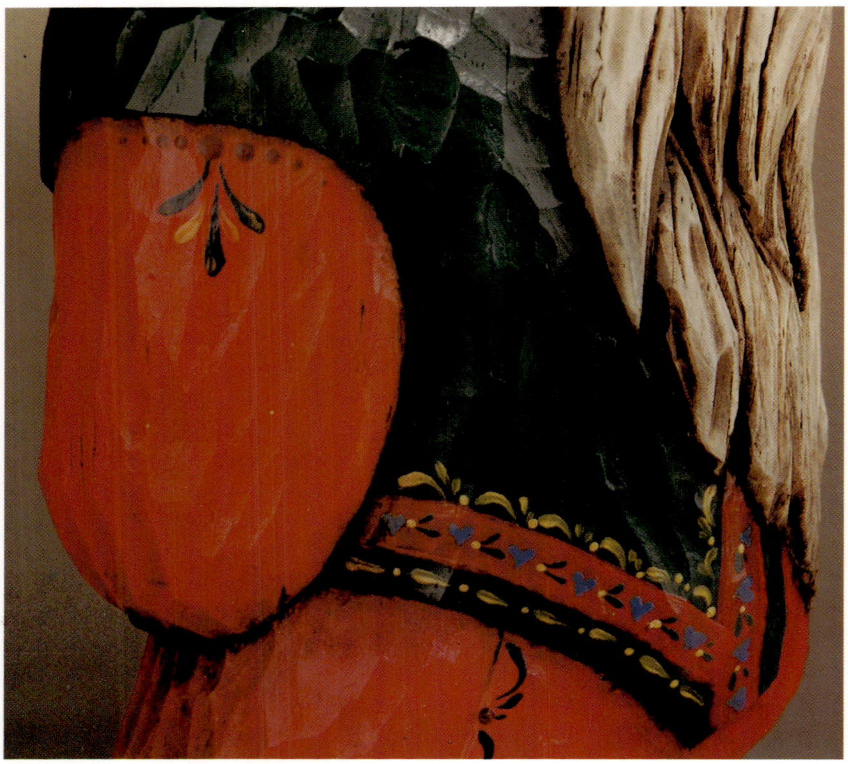

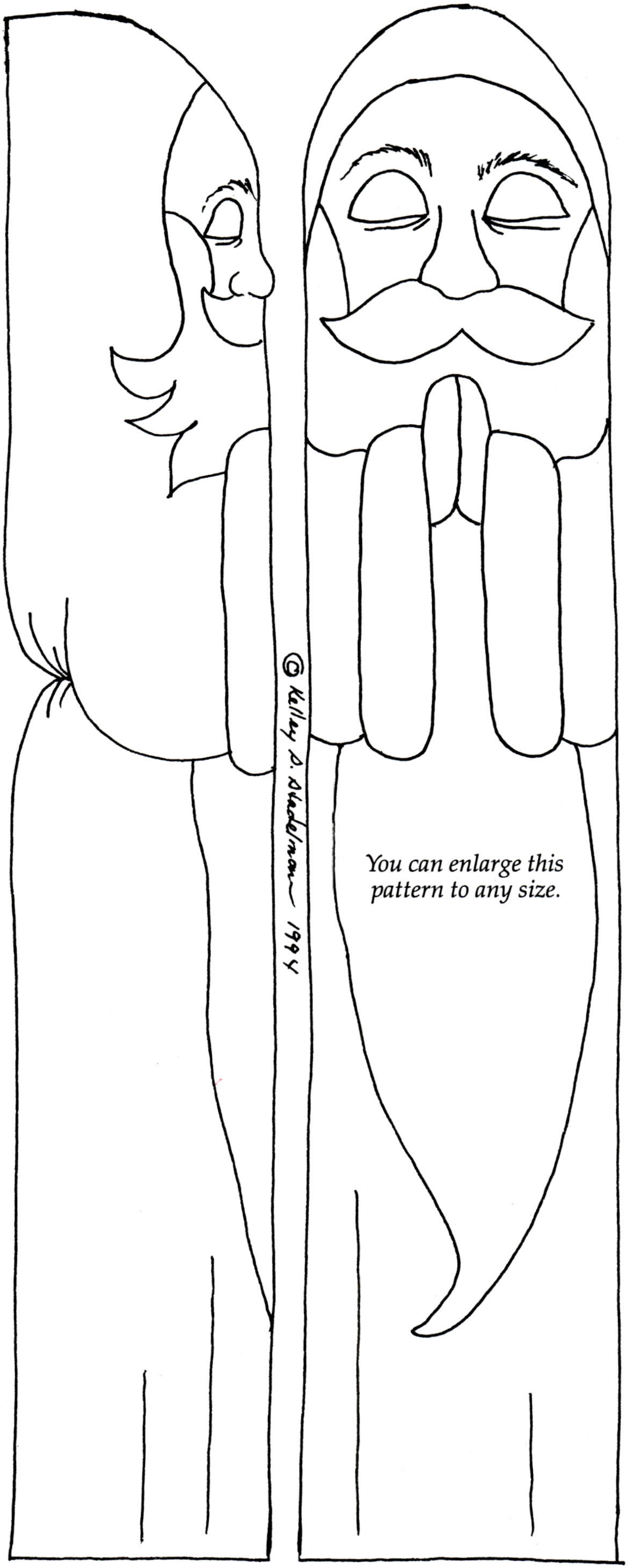
© Kelley D. Stadelman 1994
You can enlarge this
pattern to any size.

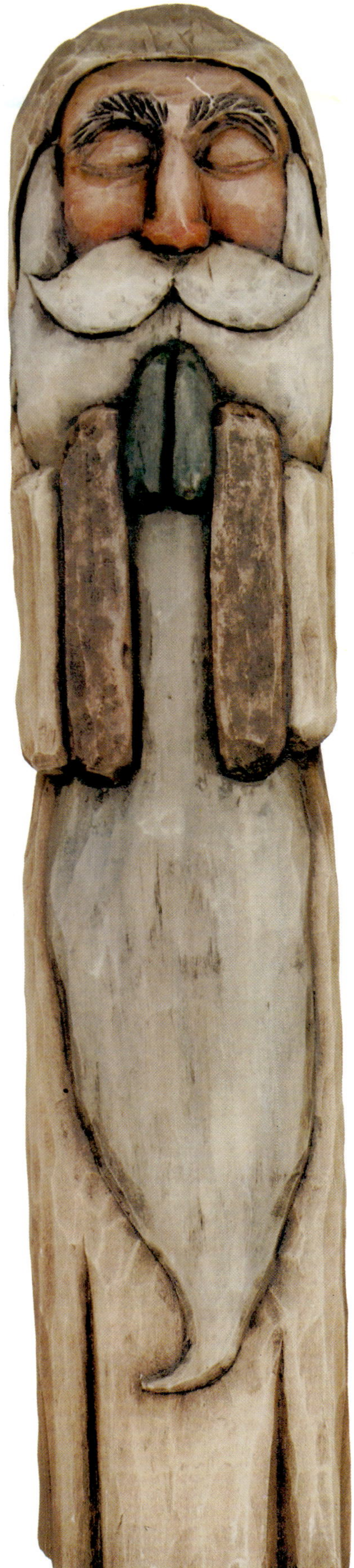

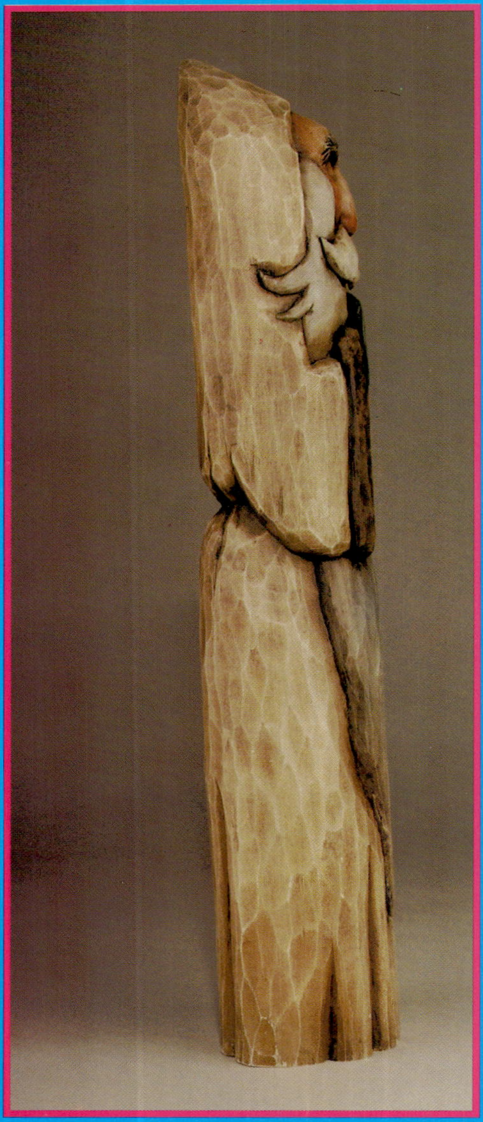

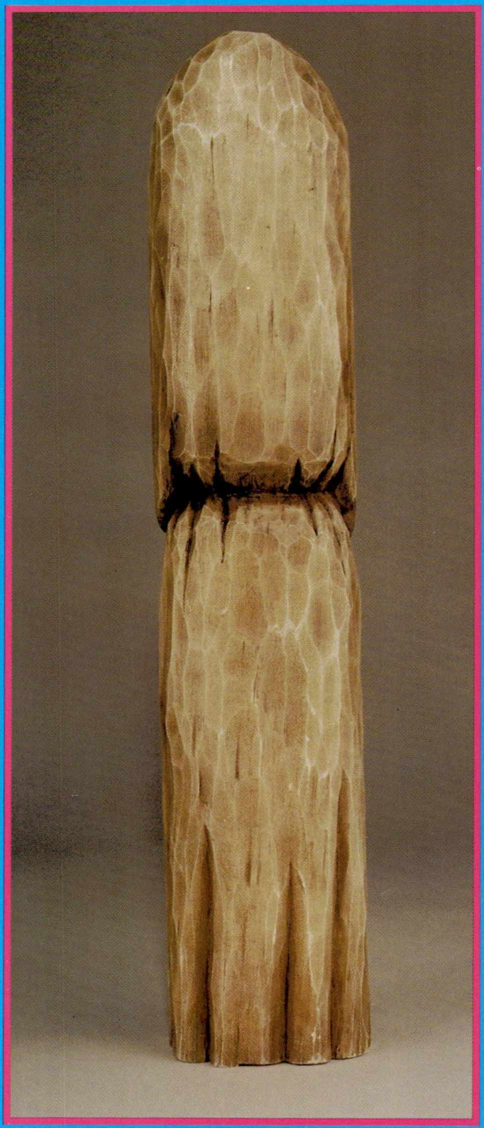

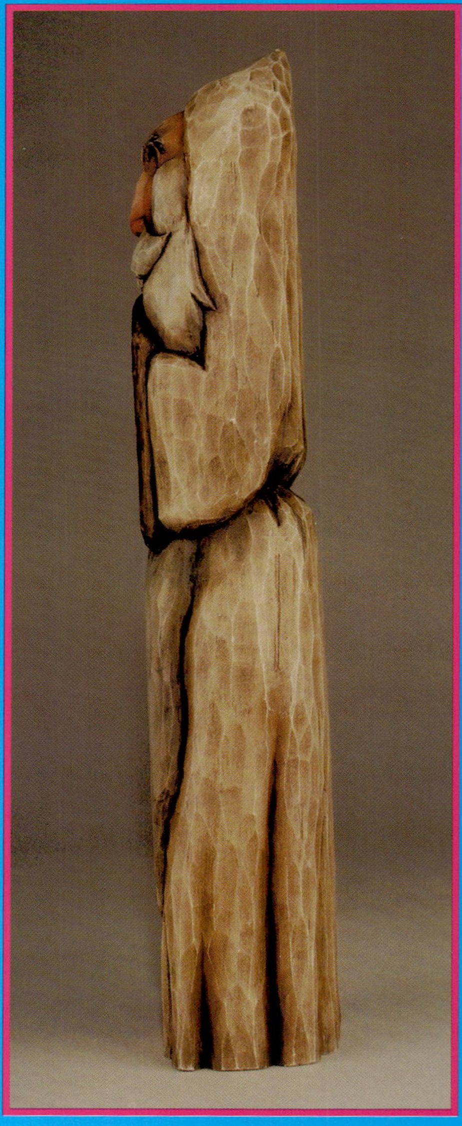

You can enlarge this pattern to any size.

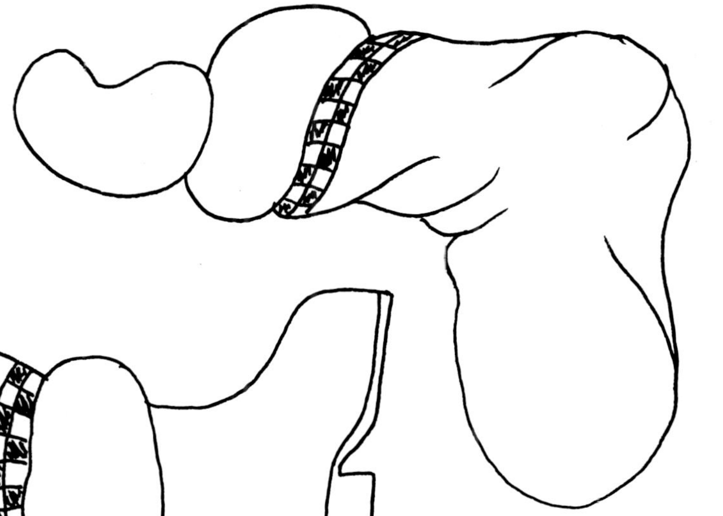

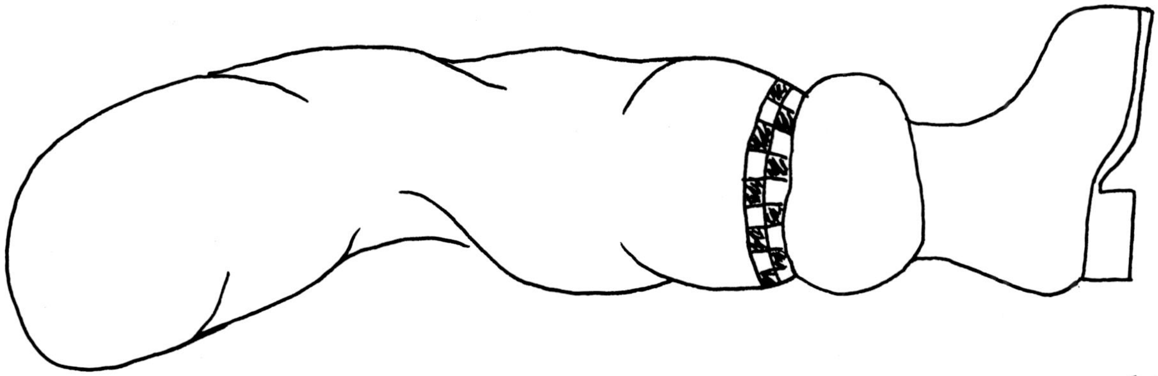

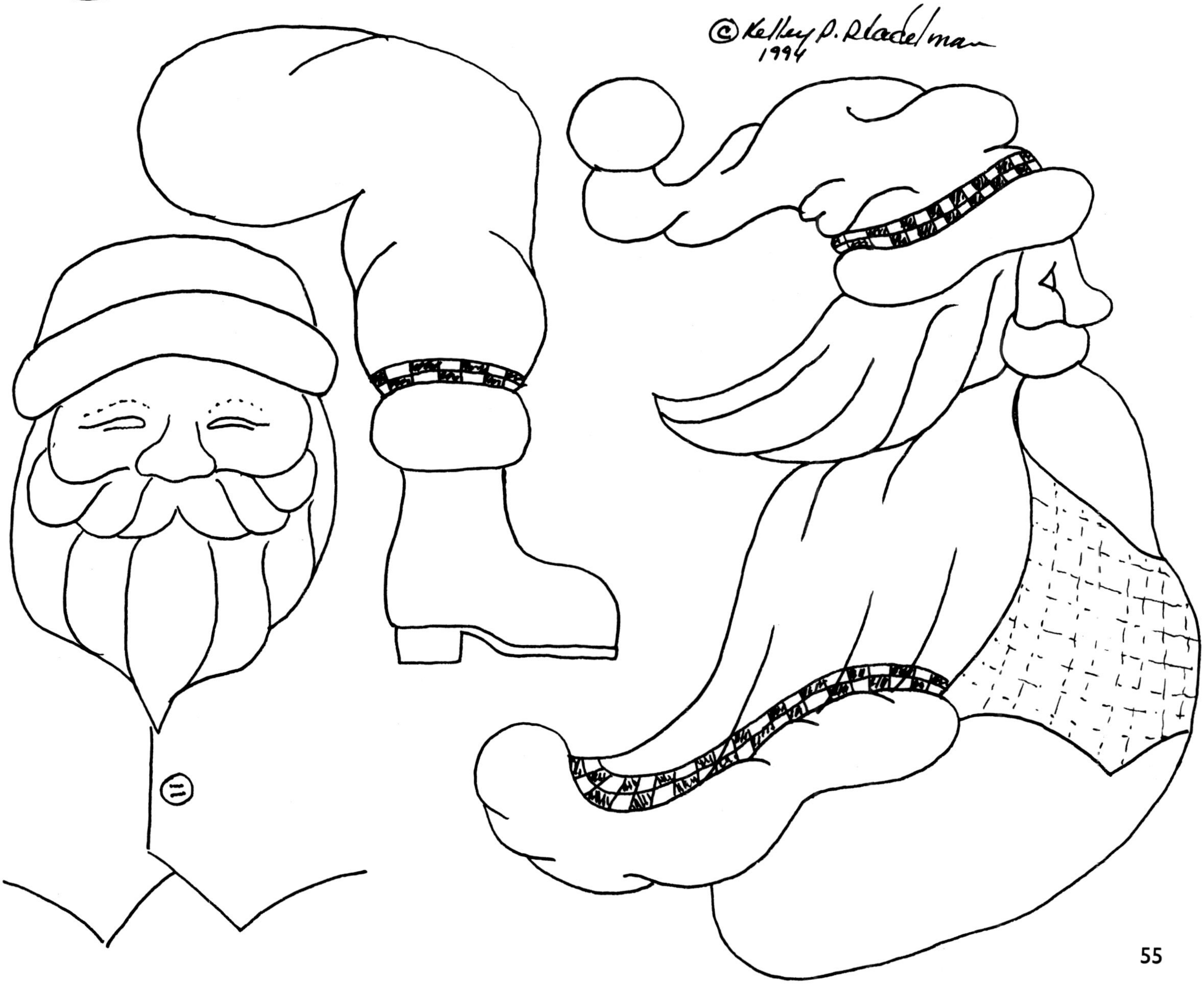

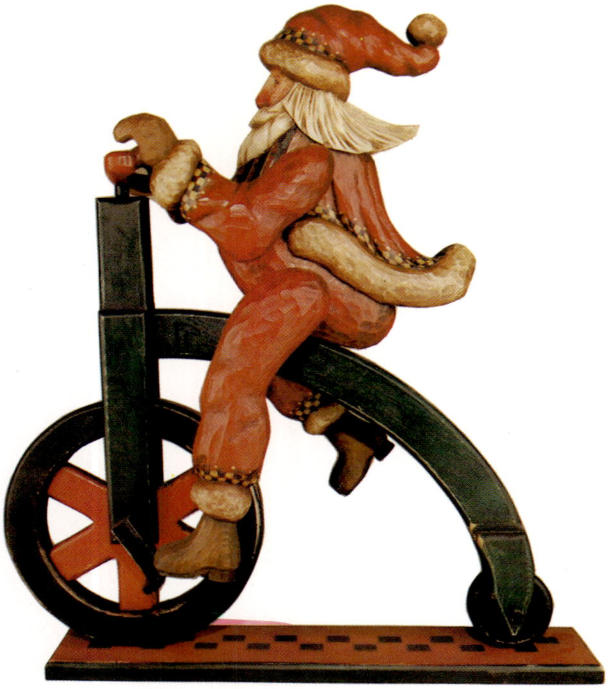

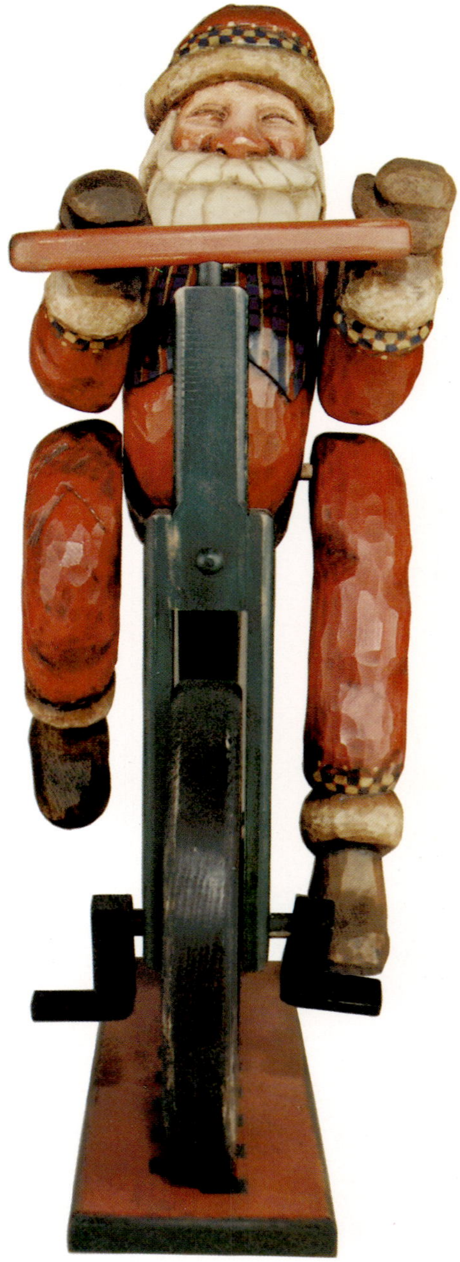

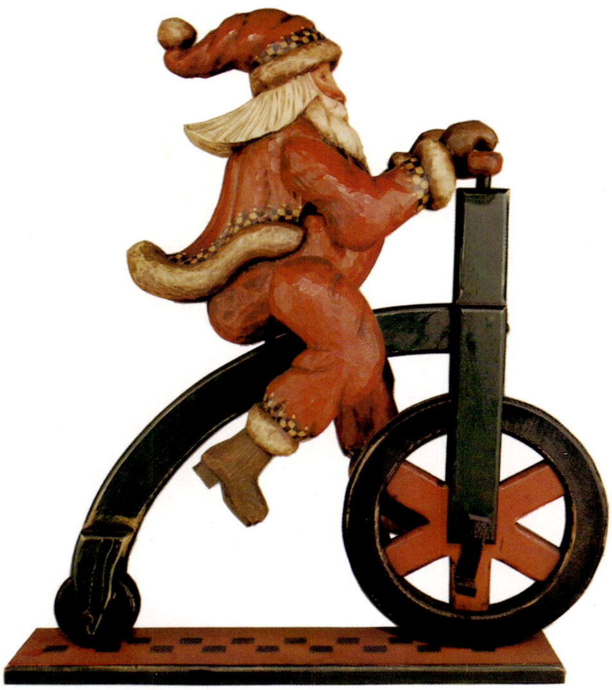

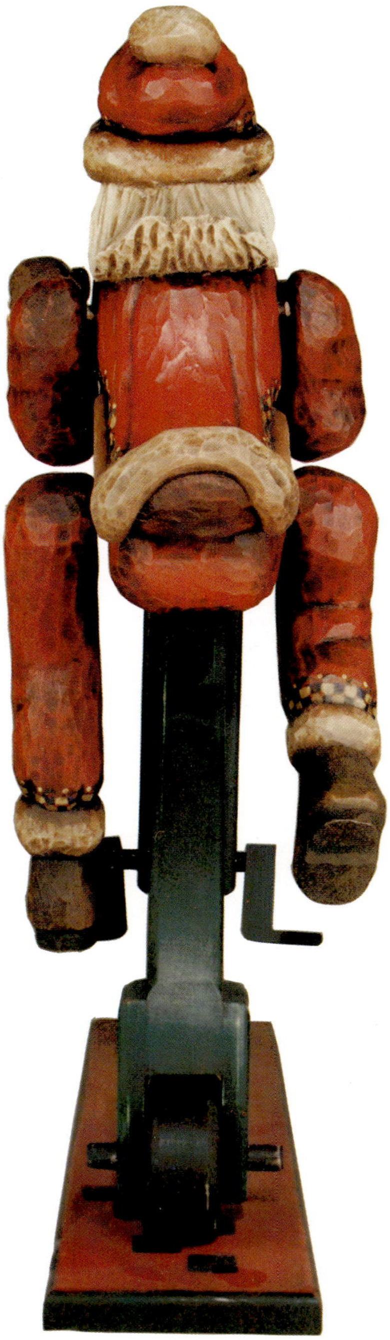

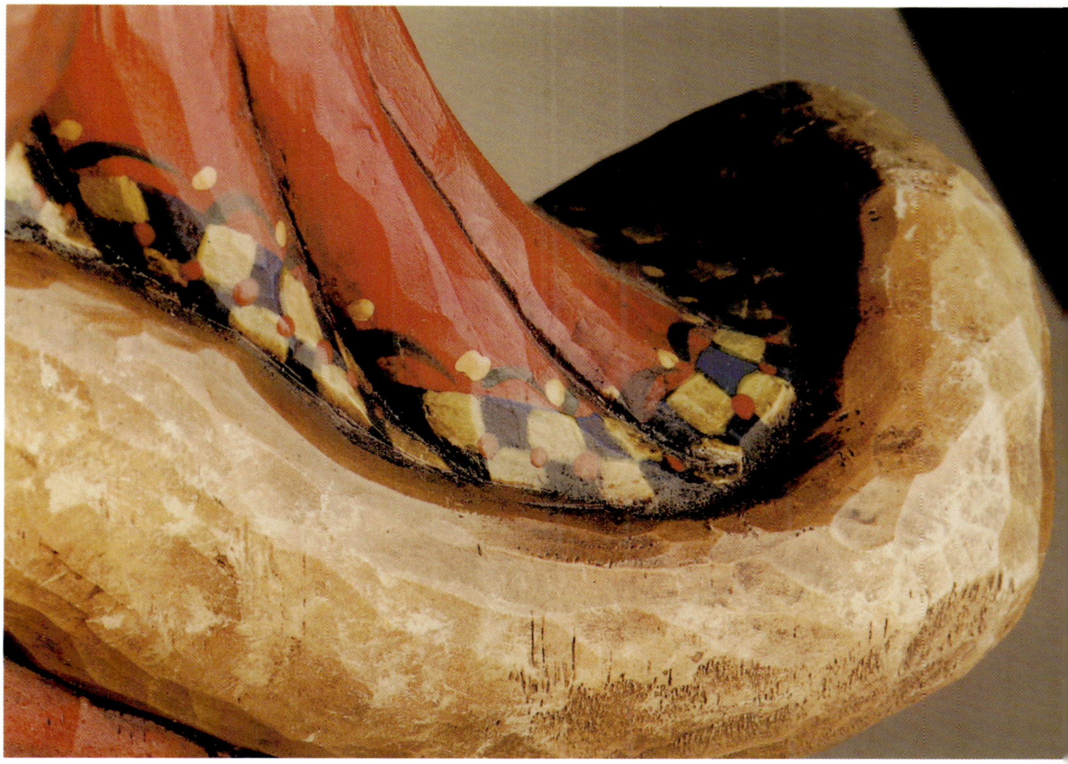

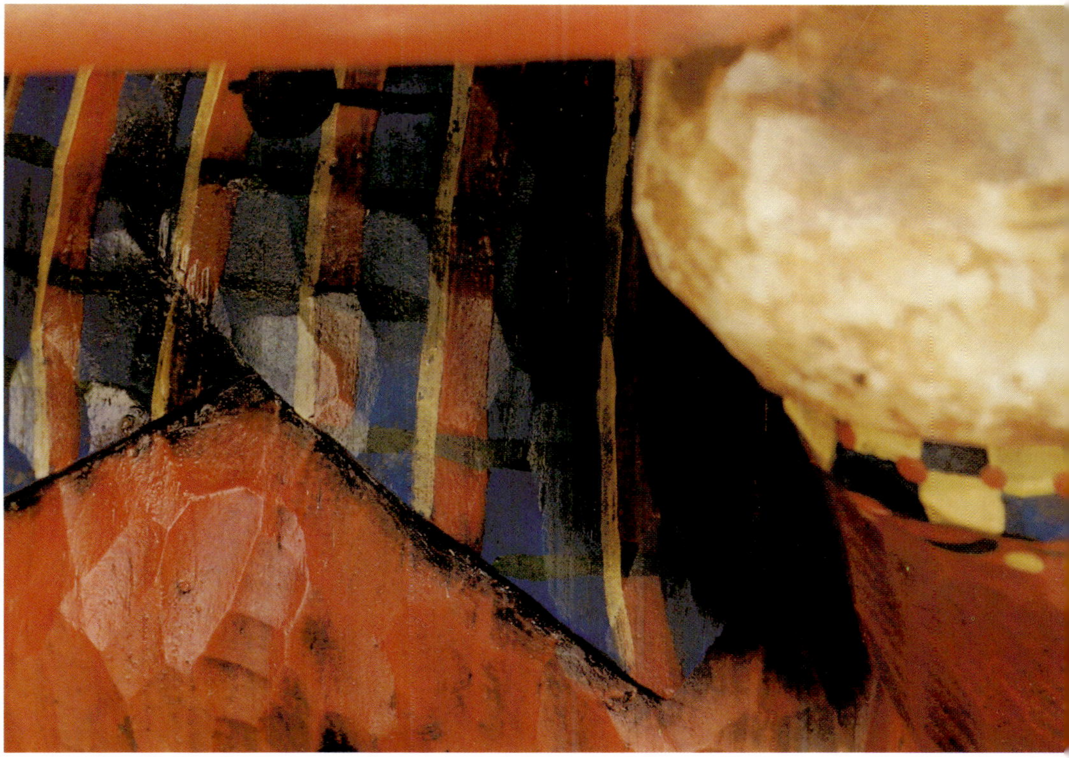

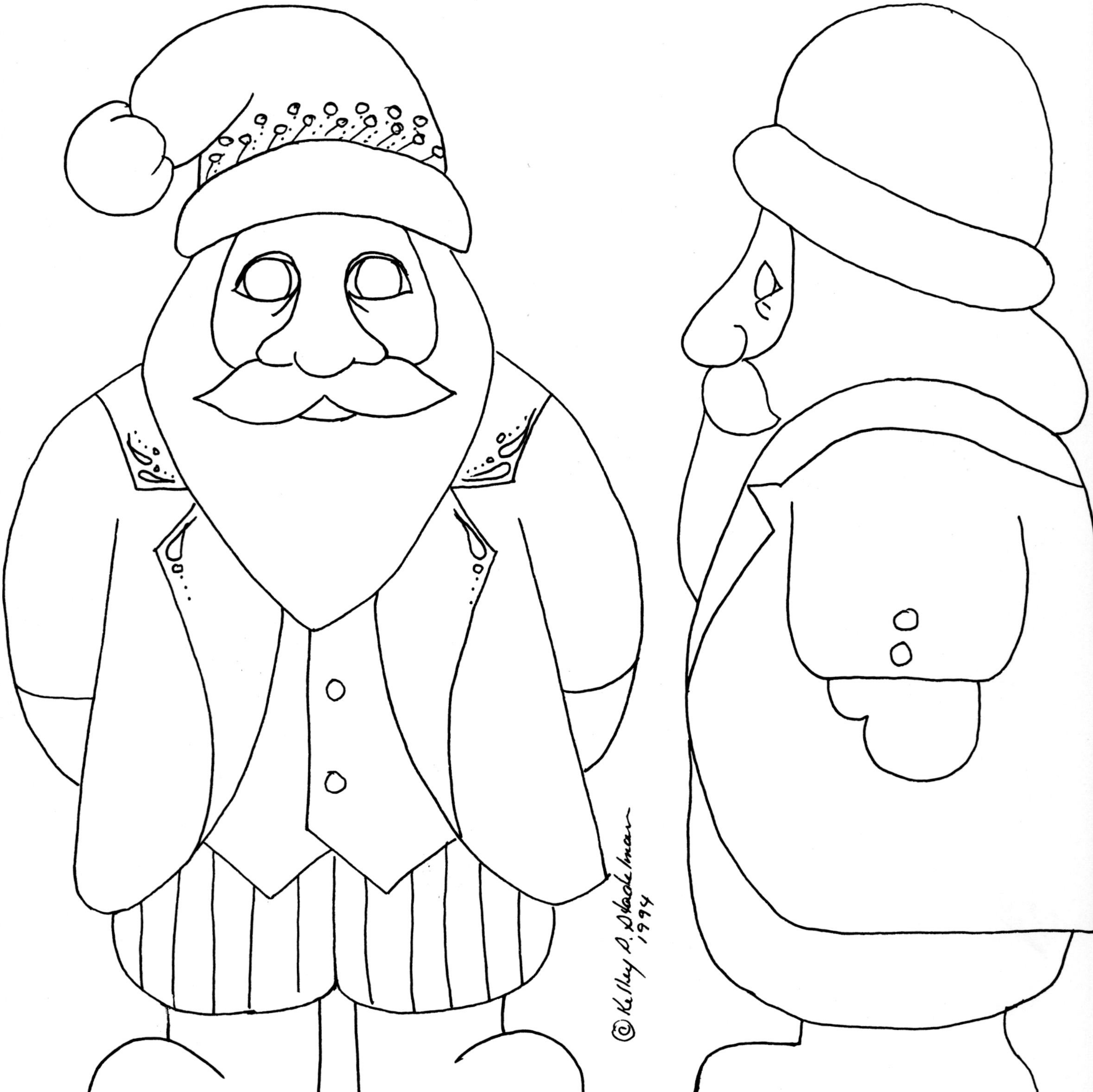
© Kelley D. Stadelman
1994

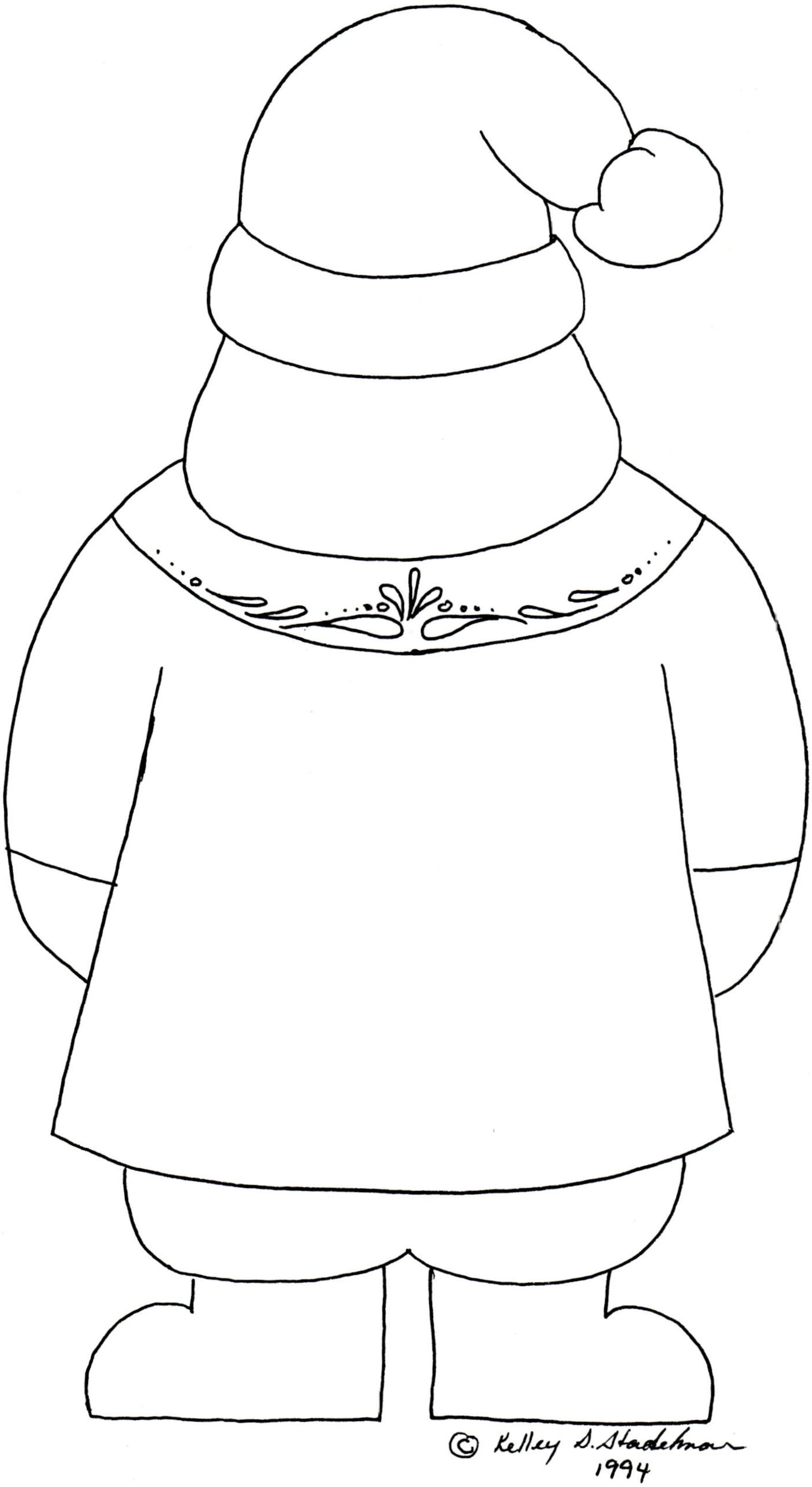

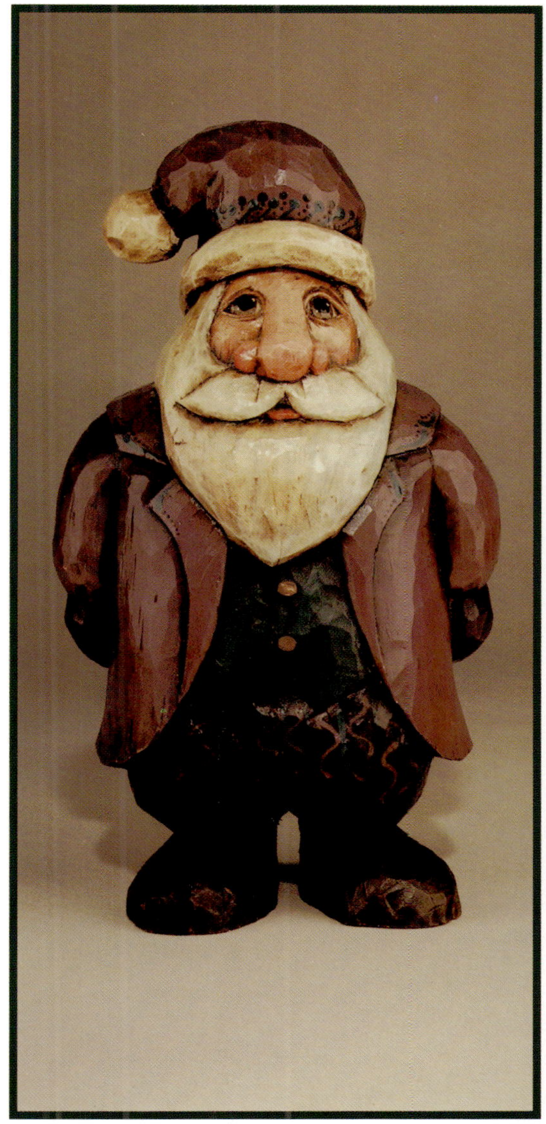

You can enlarge this pattern to any size.

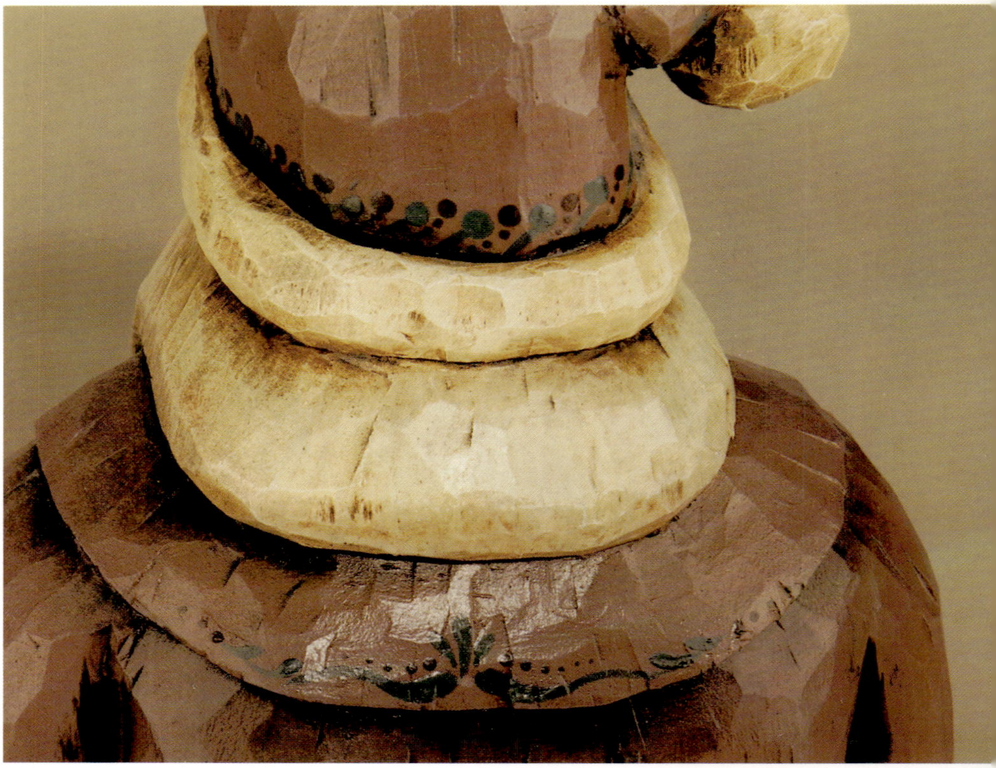

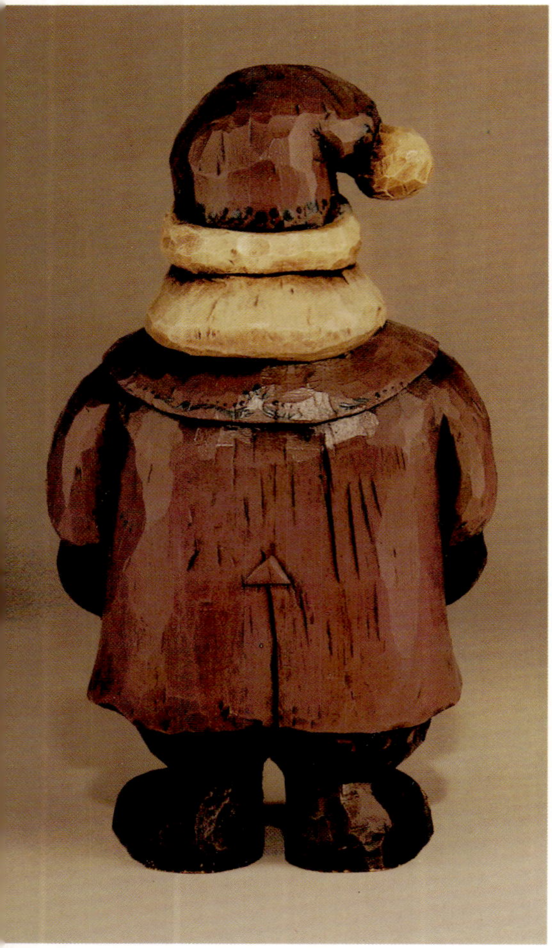

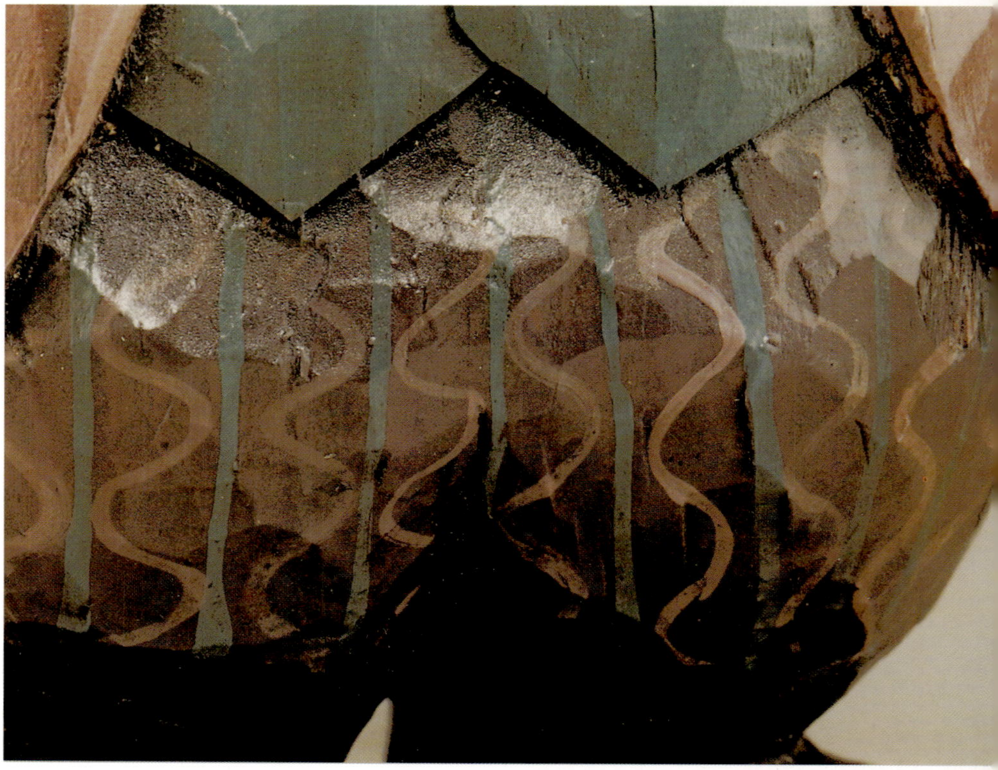

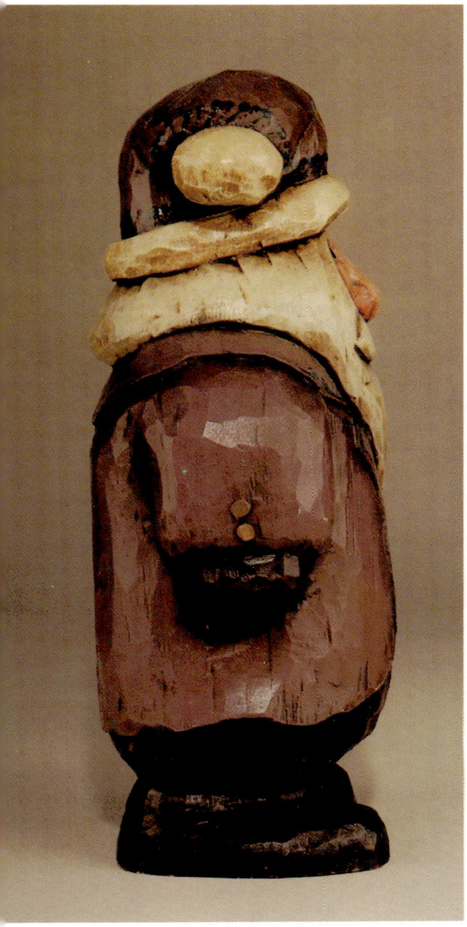

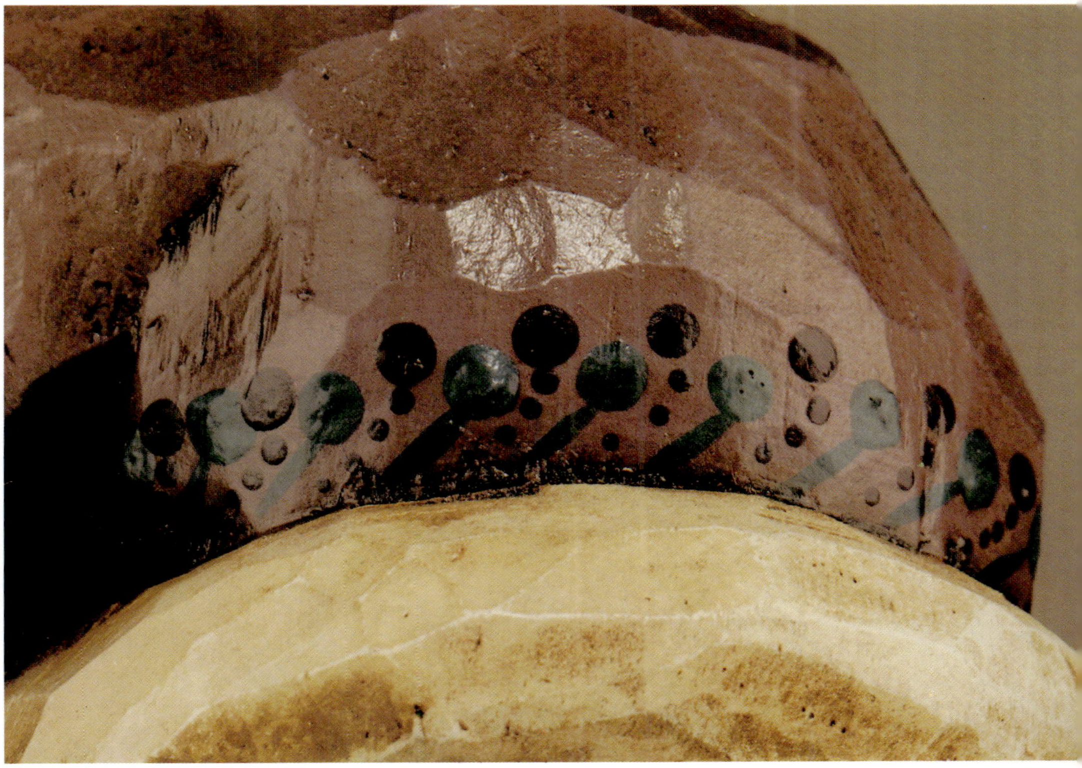

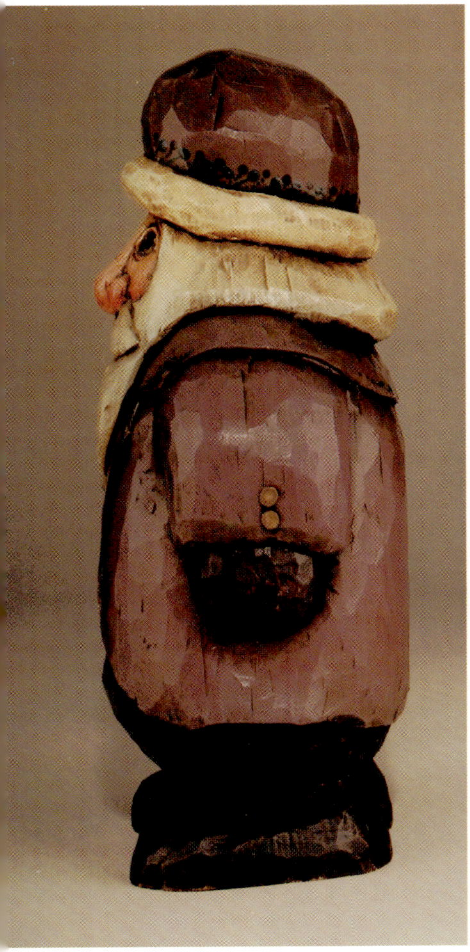

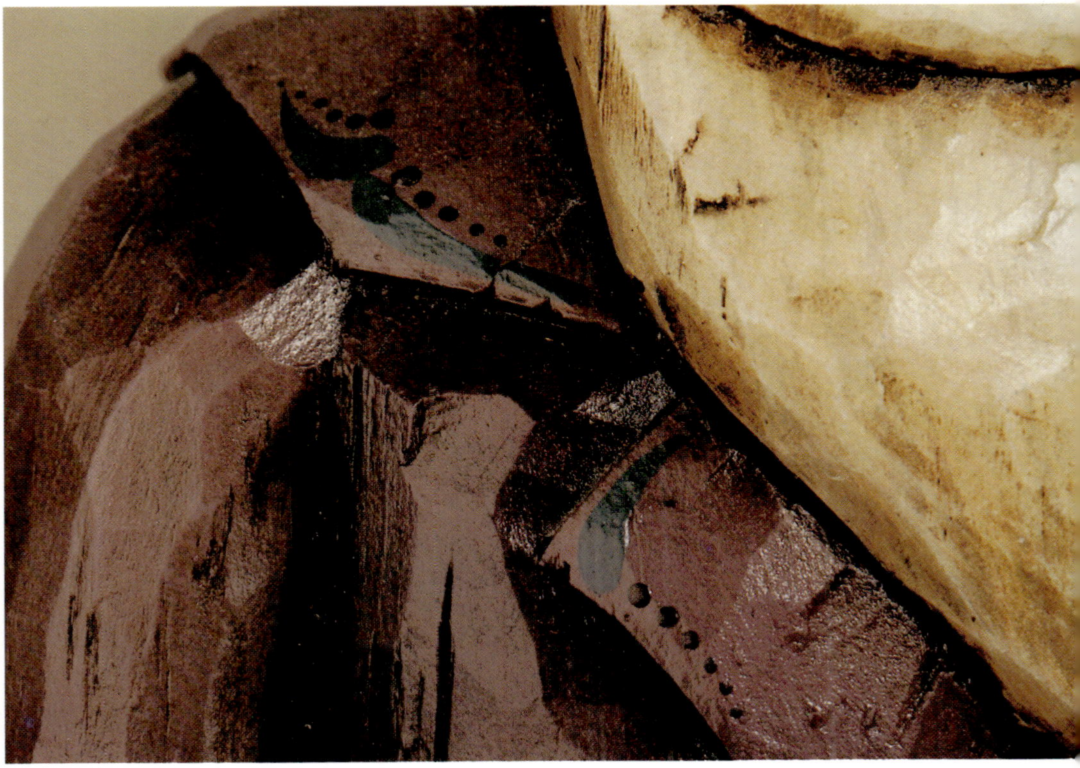

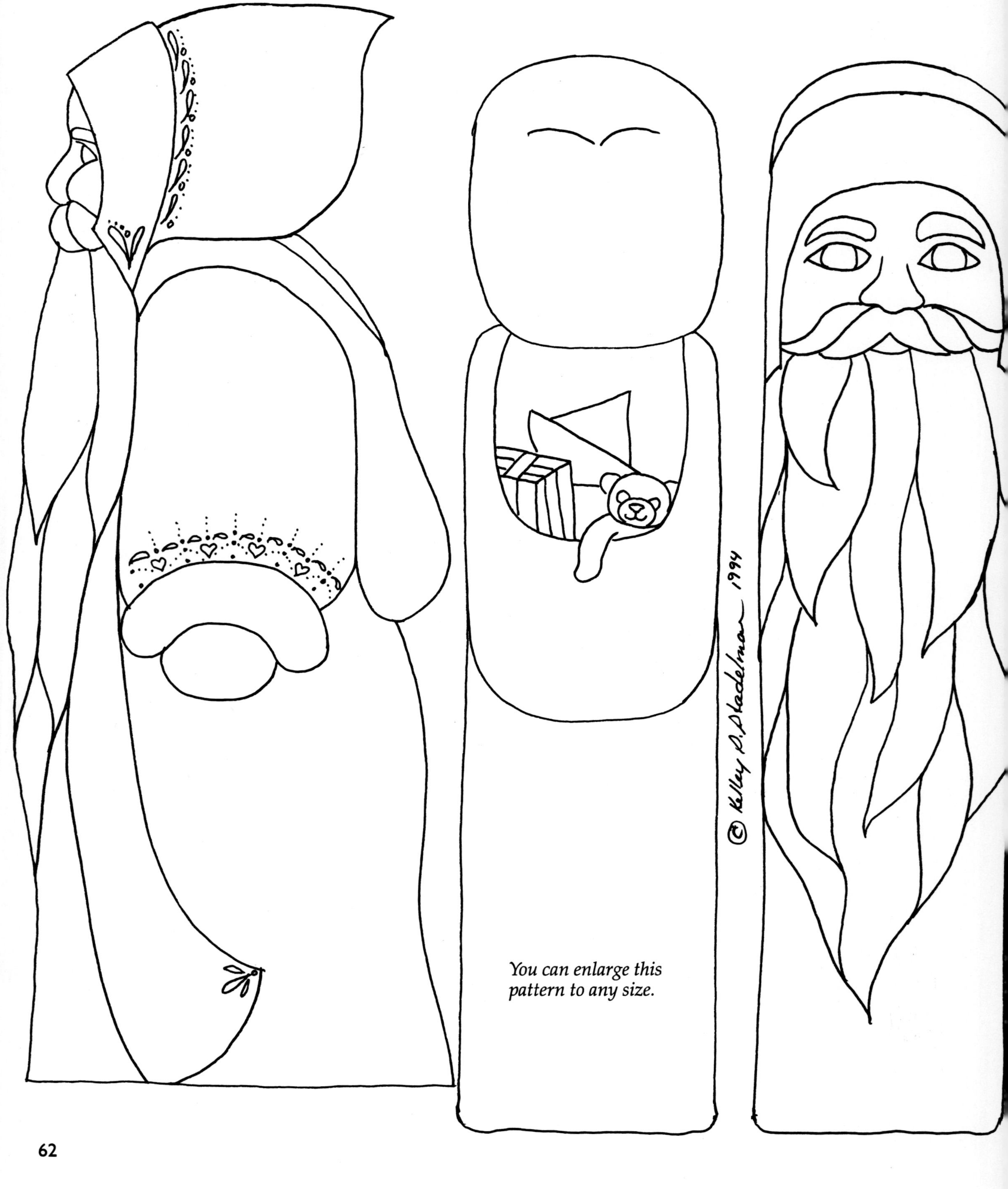

You can enlarge this pattern to any size.

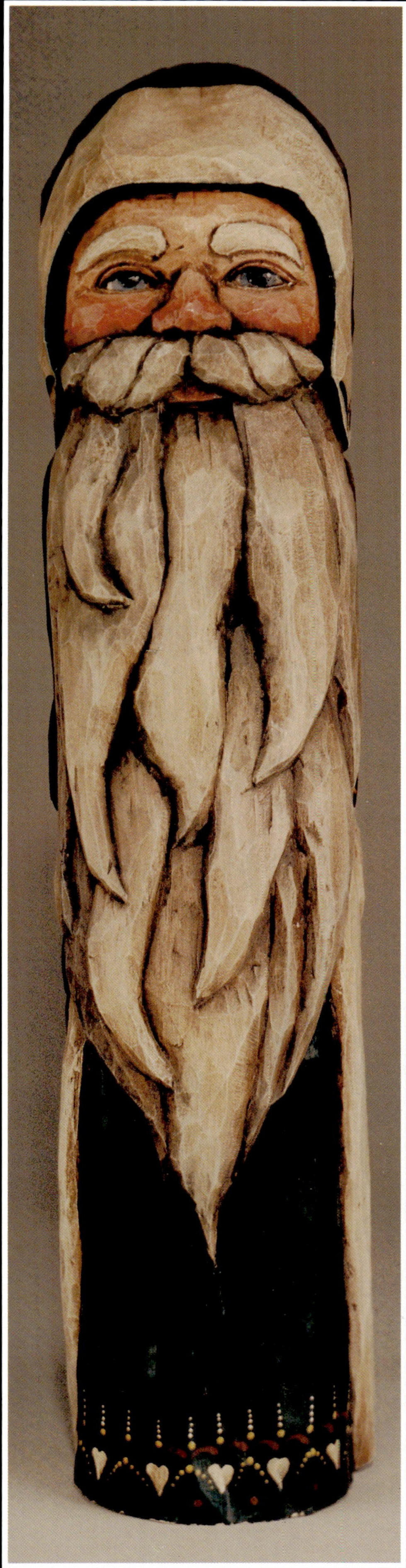

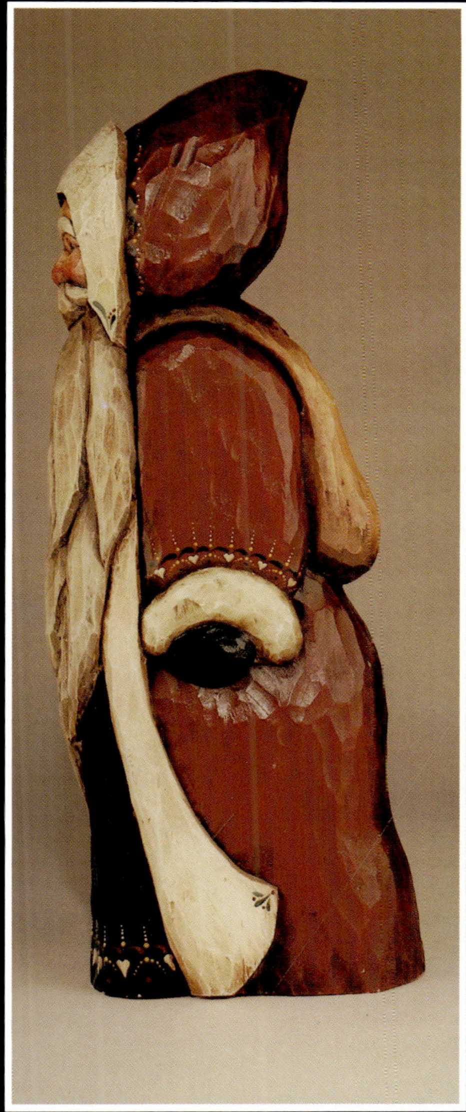

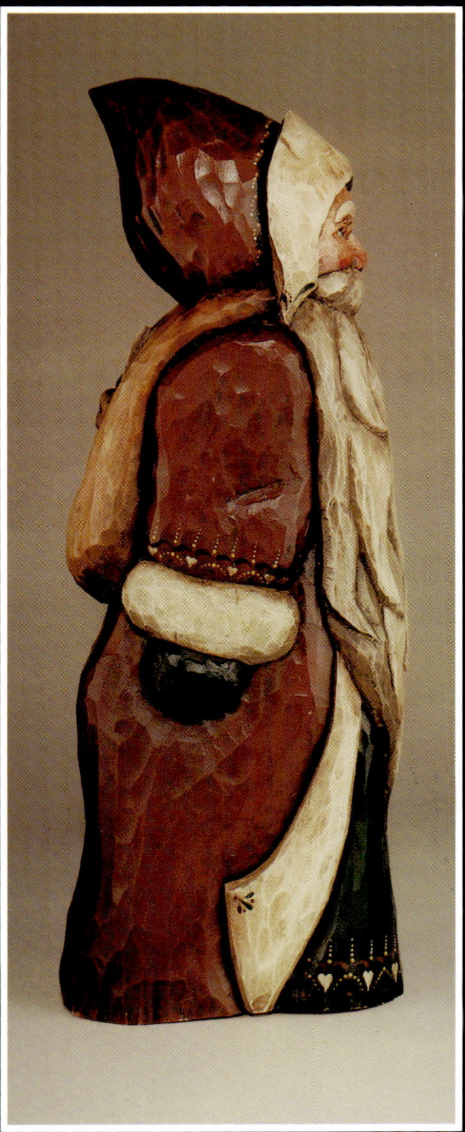

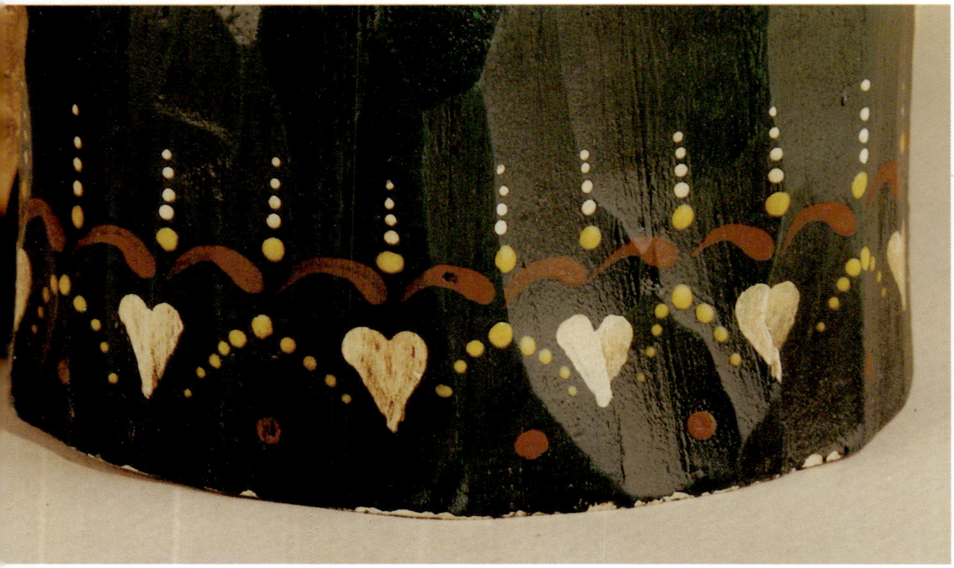

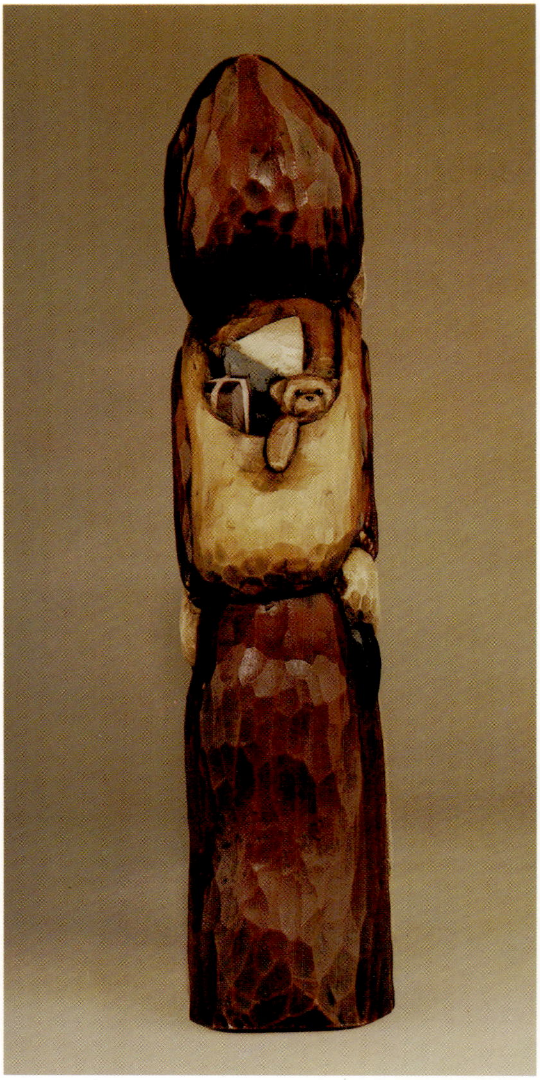

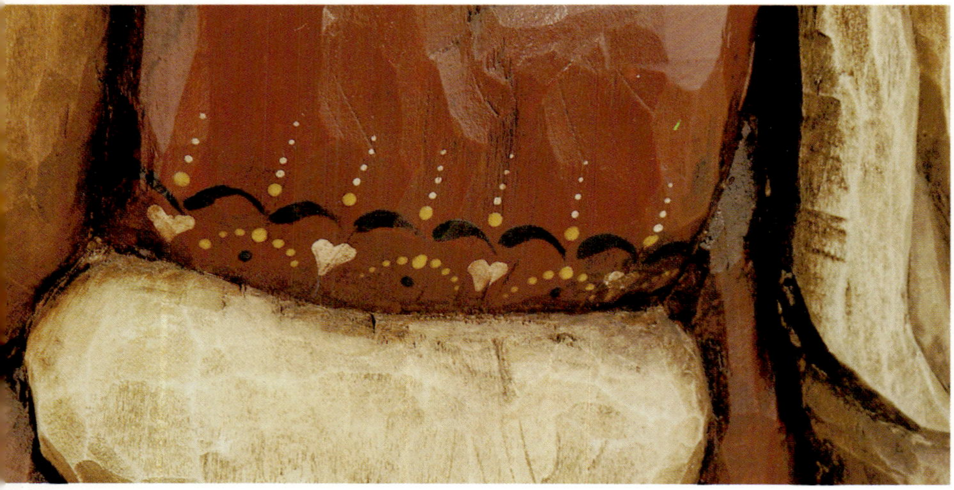

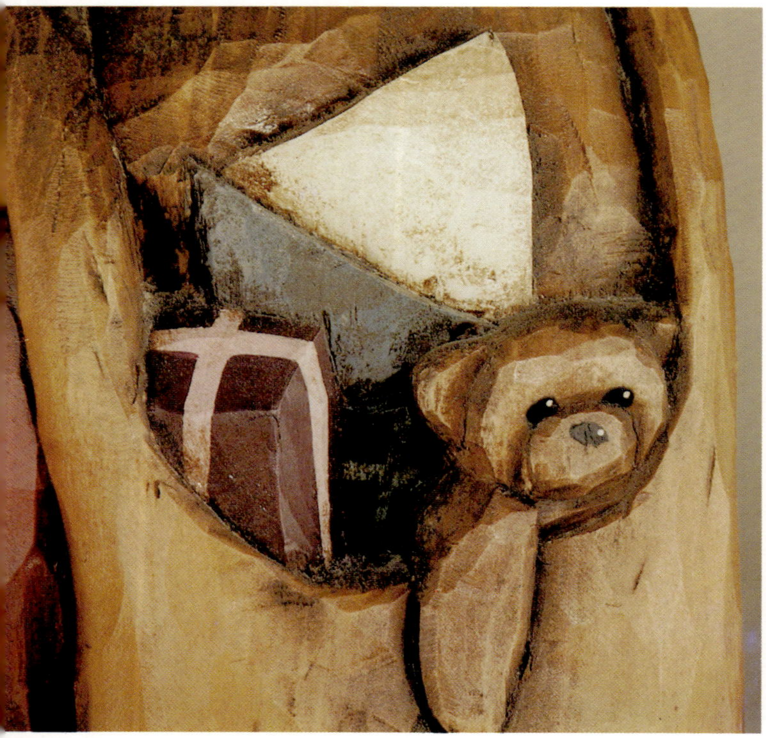

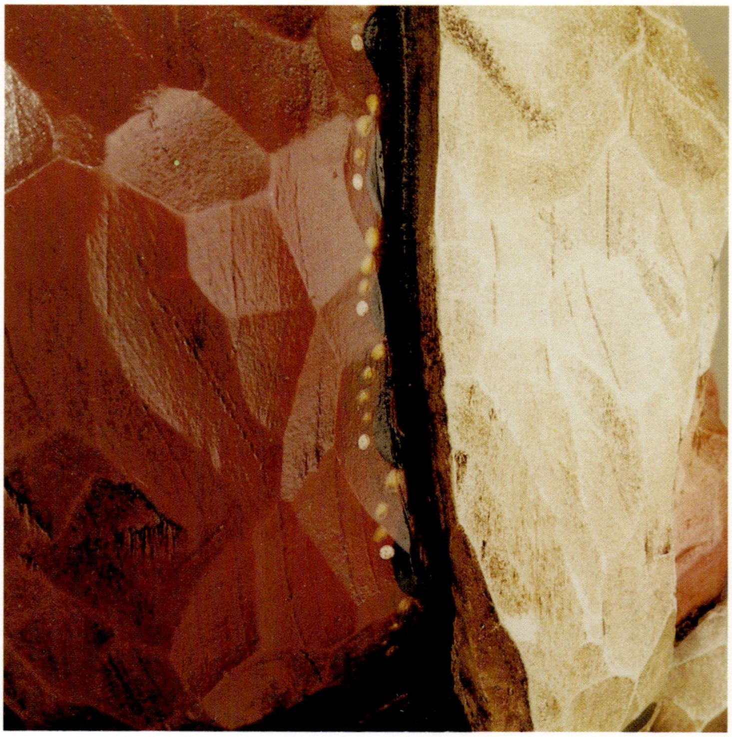